Managing Self-Harm

Self-harm often arises at moments of despair or intensity, and its reasons are not necessarily available to the conscious mind. *Managing Self-Harm* explores the meaning and impact of self-harm, and the sense in which it is a language of the body. It is designed to help clinicians, people who self-harm and their families and carers to understand its causes, meaning and treatment.

Each chapter integrates theory with clinical illustration, enabling the direct experiences of those who self-harm to be heard and reflecting the populations that are most likely to self-harm. The contributors are drawn from a wide range of backgrounds, including clinical psychology, psychotherapy, group analysis and psychiatric nursing.

Areas of discussion include:

- self-harm and young people in foster care and residential settings
- self-harm in women's secure services
- self-harm in people diagnosed with personality disorder

This book does not offer a prescription for self-harm cessation but rather describes therapeutic approaches to working with self-harm, and outlines the complex, subtle and meaningful interactions between those who engage in self-harm and those who seek to understand it. With a specialist interest in women's self-harm, *Managing Self-Harm* will be essential reading for all mental health professionals, including clinical psychologists, psychotherapists, psychiatrists, psychiatric nurses, counsellors and social workers.

Anna Motz is a Consultant Clinical and Forensic Psychologist with the Thames Valley Forensic Mental Health Service. She has particular interest in psychoanalytic approaches to understanding and treating violence and self-harm. She is the Past President of the International Association for Forensic Psychotherapy and the author of *The Psychology of Female Violence: Crimes Against the Body* (Second Edition, 2008).

Managing Self-Harm

Psychological perspectives

Edited by Anna Motz

LONDON AND NEW YORK

First published 2009 by Routledge
27 Church Road, Hove, East Sussex BN3 2FA

Simultaneously published in the USA and Canada
by Routledge
711 Third Avenue, New York, NY 10017

Routledge is an imprint of the Taylor & Francis Group, an Informa business

Typeset in Times by Garfield Morgan, Swansea, West Glamorgan
Cover design by Andy Ward

British Library Cataloguing in Publication Data
A catalogue record for this book is available from the British Library

Library of Congress Cataloging-in-Publication Data
Managing self harm : psychological perspectives / edited by Anna Motz.
p. cm.
ISBN 978-1-58391-704-6 (hardback) – ISBN: 978-1-58391-705-3 (pbk.)
1. Self-mutilation. I. Motz, Anna, 1964–
RC552.S4M36 2009
616.85'82–dc22

2008052887

ISBN: 978-1-58391-704-6 (hbk)
ISBN: 978-1-58391-705-3 (pbk)

To Hannah and Joshua Warburton.

Contents

Contributors

John Adlam is Principal Adult Psychotherapist with Henderson Hospital Services and Principal Adult Group Psychotherapist with St George's Adult Eating Disorders Service at Springfield Hospital, Tooting, London. He is also an Associate of SAM Training and Consultancy Ltd. He is a Visiting Lecturer in Forensic Psychotherapy at St George's, University of London; a member of the Tavistock Society of Psychotherapists; and Vice-President of the International Association for Forensic Psychotherapy.

Lynn Greenwood is a Psychotherapist with a particular interest in adolescents and adults who exhibit behaviours that are destructive to either themselves or others. She works in the Day Unit of St George's Hospital in Tooting, London, as an Associate Psychotherapist of the Clinic for Dissociative Studies and in private practice. She also works in specialist units within private hospitals and has experience of working with inmates of a London prison. Her first play draws on these experiences and was staged in London fringe theatres in 2006 and 2007. Lynn teaches and writes about psychotherapy issues.

Elizabeth Grocutt is a Clinical Psychologist at Oxfordshire and Buckinghamshire Mental Health Care NHS Trust. She works in a women's enhanced low secure unit. She has a special interest in the clinical application of attachment theory to women in secure services and working with women who self-harm.

Heather Jones is a musician and artist. She is also a regular contributor to *The Illustrated Ape*.

Pamela Kleinot is a Psychoanalytic Psychotherapist working with individuals and groups at St Bartholomew's Hospital, London. She trained with the Arbours Association and the Institute of Group Analysis as well as doing a diploma in forensic psychotherapy at the Portman Clinic.

Rebecca Lawday is a Chartered Forensic Psychologist, employed by Nottinghamshire Healthcare NHS Trust. Her role as lead psychologist for Women's Services at Arnold Lodge, a medium secure service, is one in which she provides psychological services to both medium secure and enhanced medium secure women's wards. She has previously provided psychological services to a pilot regional service in the East Midlands, working with men with a diagnosis of personality disorder; she has worked with community patients in Lincolnshire, in both the Adult Specialty and the Child and Adolescent Mental Health Services (CAMHS); and prior to qualifying she completed her forensic training at HMP Whitemoor as part of the development of personality disorder services in the Dispersal prison estate.

Mike Maher works as a freelance Organizational Consultant, Trainer and Psychotherapist. His areas of interest include groups, adolescence, therapeutic communities and other areas of complexity and challenge. He is a Group Analyst and is pursuing further training in systems-centred therapy in the United States.

Anna Motz is a Consultant Clinical and Forensic Psychologist with Thames Valley Forensic Mental Health Services and has worked in forensic services for 18 years. She is the Past President of the International Association for Forensic Psychotherapy and author of *The Psychology of Female Violence: Crimes Against the Body* (second edition, 2008, Routledge). She has a particular interest in the ways in which women express aggression and perversion in relation to children and to their own bodies. She is currently undertaking training in psychoanalytic psychotherapy at the Tavistock Clinic, London.

Vivien Norris is currently Consultant Clinical Psychologist to Barnardo's Multi-Agency Intensive Support Service, a therapeutic fostering service based in Llandrindod Wells, Wales. She has worked for 20 years with children and families in a variety of contexts including residential therapeutic community settings and within CAMHS teams and has undertaken specific trauma-related research.

Christopher Scanlon is Consultant Psychotherapist in the Department of Psychotherapy at St Thomas' Hospital, South London & Maudsley NHS Trust (SLaM); freelance Organizational Consultant with particular expertise in working with services for adults with complex psychosocial problems; Senior Visiting Research Fellow in the Centre for Psychosocial Studies at the University of West England; Visiting Lecturer in Forensic Psychotherapy at St George's, University of London and at the Tavistock & Portman NHS Trust; and Faculty member at the Institute of Group Analysis, London, and the Turvey Institute for Group Psychotherapy. He is also trustee of the Zito Trust – a major mental health charity – campaigning for improved services for mentally disordered offenders and their victims.

Acknowledgements

I would most like to thank the many people who have told me the stories of their self-harming and trusted me to respect these. The voices of many people can be heard throughout the various chapters but I am particularly grateful to Heather Jones and the woman whom I have called Crystal, to protect her anonymity.

I owe special thanks to my husband, Nigel, for reading four of the chapters and making many helpful suggestions. The enthusiasm and patience of the editorial team at Routledge/Taylor Francis, in particular Joanne Forshaw, Sarah Gibson, Dawn Harris and Rowena Mayhew are much appreciated. I am grateful for the comments contained in the anonymous reader's report, which helped shape the final version of this book. I am also thankful to the contributors to this book for their dedication to the task and the care with which they addressed their themes, particularly to Pam Kleinot for her close reading of two chapters.

I am most appreciative of the support of my colleagues in the International Society for Forensic Psychotherapy and the ongoing friendship and inspiration of Estela Welldon. I owe thanks to my colleagues on the M1 Interdisciplinary Training in Adult Psychotherapy at the Tavistock Clinic, particularly to Tim Kent for his comments, William Crouch for his interest and research in the area of self-harm and especially to Caroline Garland and Julian Lousada for their psychoanalytic understanding and insights. I am also grateful to Tobias Zundel for sharing his interest and research in self-harm in young people and to John Woodhouse for his thoughtful comments on Chapter 4.

My colleagues in the Psychology Department at the Thames Valley Forensic Mental Health Service have been enthusiastic about my engagement in this project, and I am particularly grateful to

Elizabeth Clifford, Elizabeth Grocutt, Carol Hiller, Patsy Holly, Charles King, Mat Lister and Brian Thomas-Peter for their support.

Anna Motz
April 2009

Introduction

Anna Motz

This book is designed to help clinicians, people who self-harm and their families to understand its causes, meaning and treatment. The notion of managing self-harm is central to this text. The idea of managing self-harm is inextricably tied into understanding it. The book does not offer a prescription for stopping self-harm, or specific behavioural guidelines but rather describes therapeutic approaches to working with self-harm, and outlines the complex, subtle and meaningful interaction between those who engage in self-harm and those who seek to understand it. What needs to be managed is not only the behaviour and distress of those who self-harm, but also what can be the overwhelming and potentially unhelpful responses of therapists and other workers, who may find the intensity of their own feelings in relation to self-harm too much to bear. When these countertransference feelings can be thought about and contained, they become a tool to understanding what it is that self-harm communicates. At this point, meaningful engagement and therapeutic work can begin.

There are many voices in this book, and each chapter integrates theory with clinical illustration, enabling the direct experiences of those who self-harm to be heard. Throughout the book, the contributors provide clinical material to bring theory alive. The book is designed to describe, illustrate and make intelligible the function, meaning and complexity of self-harm, in the populations most at risk. The selection of contributors reflects the populations in which self-harm occurs most frequently – adolescents, young people in care and women in secure mental health and custodial settings. Many of these people will not feature in the official statistics unless they make actual suicide attempts or are treated in emergency rooms, and disclose that the cause of their injury is self-inflicted.

Self-harm is often characterised by secrecy and so may not actually reach the public domain as the prevalence of self-harm websites demonstrates.[1]

There are other groups of people who self-harm, for a variety of reasons. The book does not contain any discussion of those who choose to self-harm for political purposes through, for example, hunger strike or those who do so purely for sexual or religious reasons.

This volume devotes itself to understanding self-harm in adolescents and adults; the greater prevalence of female self-harm is reflected in the fact that four of the chapters deal specifically with women. The term 'self-harm' in the specific sense is generally confined to burning, cutting, strangulation, head-banging and insertion into the body of sharp or painful objects. Although burning and/or cutting oneself may appear to be highly unusual and bizarre activities, they are not, in fact, uncommon in certain populations, for example among adolescent girls who have been sexually abused. These acts of violence, while directed against the self, also have indirect victims, such as parents and medical professionals who witness these acts of self-mutilation and the scars that are produced. The failure to protect the young women from self-harming can induce strong guilt feelings in these carers when they are faced with these indelible images of distress. Managing these responses is an essential part of the management of self-harm, in that the two are deeply interrelated.

My aim is for the book to be accessible not only to those who work with people who self-harm, but also to people who have inflicted or still do inflict violence on themselves, so that they may find some understanding. Voices of self-harmers themselves are integrated into the book in many of the chapters, in the form of both direct quotations in Norris and Maher's chapter on self-harm in young people in foster and residential care (Chapter 4) and Grocutt, Kleinot and Lawday's chapters on self-harm in women in secure units (Chapters 6, 8, and 9), and written words in the chapter on 'The paradox of self-harm' (Motz and Jones, Chapter 2). Throughout the book, clinical details have been disguised and

1 Available published figures vary from between four per cent in the general adult population to 82 per cent in adolescent psychiatric inpatients (Ougrin, Ng and Zundel, 2009).

anonymised to protect client confidentiality; wherever possible, permission has been granted for clinical decisions to be described.

The contributors are drawn from a variety of backgrounds and, all aside from Heather Jones, are mental health professionals, based in widely different settings. The book presents a range of psychological perspectives on self-harm, its development, manifestation and treatment. While a largely psychodynamic perspective is represented by Motz (Chapter 1), Scanlon and Adlam (Chapter 3 and Kleinot (Chapter 6) other theoretical models presented here include an attachment perspective, described by Greenwood in her chapter on self-harm and eating disorders in terms of their relation to loss (Chapter 7) and by Grocutt in her chapter on the development of self-harm and early attachment disorders (Chapter 5), and in her later chapter on self-harm cessation by women in secure mental health facilities (Chapter 9). Additionally, Norris and Maher present an integrative model to formulate the particular meanings of self-harm for young people in care; they outline systemic and psychodynamic perspectives (Chapter 4). Lawday presents a model of care for self-harming women in secure services that relies primarily on a dialectical behavioural approach, but also draws on findings from attachment research and the experiences and views of service users (Chapter 8).

The contributors are wholly united in their attempt to explore the meaning, function and goal of self-harm, and to understand the individual who relates to them through self-inflicted violence, rather than simply viewing self-harm as dangerous behaviour that must be eradicated at all costs. This does not mean that they ignore its potential destructiveness or lethality but that the focus is on its function, meaning and communicative power. Within this volume, all contributors make a clear distinction between suicidal behaviour and self-harm, whereas other texts written from a psychodynamic perspective highlight the murderous intentionality of suicidal states of mind in acts of self-harm.

Clearly, self-harm can be associated with mental illness, personality disorders, substance and alcohol abuse, and learning disability. Adshead (1997) suggests that an understanding of self-harm should co-exist with a psychiatric evaluation. A central question is whether self-harm will lead to suicide, or whether it can be considered a meaningful form of behaviour that does not have self-annihilation as its aim. The two phenomena of self-harm and suicide are often classified together.

The suicides of 20 young people since 2006 in the Welsh town of Bridgend have focused attention on this serious problem. Despite initial reporting of a 'suicide cult' and a high level of concern about whether the suicides were triggered by social networking sites, a more measured response addressing both self-harm and suicide has emerged, with research and a plan for intervention: the Welsh Assembly Government (2008) has recently announced the launch of a five-year action plan to reduce suicide and self-harm in Wales. This is a thoughtful document that attempts to identify the real social and psychological issues that may trigger such hopelessness in young people, stressing the crucial need to enhance awareness of mental health issues such as depression and the need for early interventions. The draft plan calls for intensive training and support across various agencies dealing with young people, including schools and general practitioner (GP) surgeries.[2] The consultation document is called *'Talk to me'*, highlighting the understanding of suicide and self-harm as a communication.

The draft action plan places emphasis on the role of psychosocial interventions, improving the response of specialist services including Youth Offending and Child and Adolescent Mental Health Services. The action plan also stresses the crucial role of voluntary sector help, which can be invaluable in enabling troubled young people to find a place where they can be heard, and recognises the need for such help to be available day and night.[3] In the document, self-harm is defined as 'an intentional self-poisoning or self-injury, irrespective of the nature of motivation or degree of suicidal intent' whereas the premise in this book is that self-harm refers to those acts of self-injury in which the conscious intention was not to

2 In order to provide the necessary skills in sectors such as health and education for staff to identify signs of mental distress, a training programme – Mental Health First Aid – will be rolled out across Wales. Assistance for those who may be experiencing mental distress will also be available through a Welsh Assembly Government-funded all-Wales, 24-hour, seven-days-a-week telephone and text messaging service. The Community Advice and Listening Line (CALL) will provide an easy way for the people to access emotional support and information on mental health and related matters in a confidential environment via a simple text message or call. The Samaritans also offer 24-hour telephone support for those in distress or despair that could lead to suicide.

3 The new post of National Samaritan Co-ordinator for Wales funded by the Welsh Assembly Government will work closely with other organisations to develop services further for people who need someone to talk to.

die. The existence of unconscious wishes, which can include both suicidal and murderous intentions, means that this distinction is, at times, difficult to sustain.

The Welsh Assembly Government document acknowledges that self-harm is particularly prevalent in young people and that it is 'an indication of underlying social, relationship, emotional and psychological problems. Sometimes it is a way of expressing and coping with the emotional pain they are experiencing' (Welsh Assembly Government, 2008: 7). Ougrin, Ng and Zundel (2009) also emphasise the role of immediate psychosocial intervention in ameliorating distress, outlining how a "therapeutic assessment" following self-harm and suicide attempts can reduce risks for adolescents.

Greenwood's chapter in this book (Chapter 7) echoes this call for pathways for communication to be made available to people at risk of self-harm, raising questions for clinicians about how resources are to be deployed, and what help is to be made available at key transition points in therapy. She highlights the vulnerability of women with eating disorders at these points in their treatment, when they move from an inpatient to an outpatient setting. Such transitions can reactivate experiences of loss and abandonment in an unbearable way; Greenwood suggests that therapists should be available for communications outside of the consulting room. She has modified the traditional model of analytic psychotherapy into a more integrative model, and poses the following challenge to clinicians:

> We cannot be available 24 hours a day, seven days a week but can technology help address some of the problems? For example, some clients may reach a point where they can call, feel reassured by a recording of a familiar and trusted voice and leave a message that requires no response. My colleagues at the Clinic for Dissociative Studies have described to me their clients' use of text or email and similarly, even when I do call back, the client may not pick up but I can leave a message that provides some support until the next scheduled session – or, admittedly, sometimes the next voicemail. Sometimes clients want a response from us (and I include professionals in the NHS, the private sector and private practice). Can our schedules be flexible enough to allow a ten-minute phone call?
>
> (Greenwood, this volume: 155)

The notion of self-harm as communication, requiring an urgent response, raises the central question of how we as clinicians and carers can respond effectively to that request.

STRUCTURE OF THE BOOK

The book is divided into three parts: understanding self-harm; the wider context: systemic issues and self-harm; and women and self-harm.

Part 1: Understanding self-harm

1 Self-harm as a sign of hope (Motz)
2 The paradox of self-harm (Motz and Jones)

In Chapter 1, 'Self-harm as a sign of hope' I suggest that self-harm is fundamentally an attempt to stay alive. It expresses a communication to others and serves a powerful function for oneself, and must be distinguished clearly from suicidal behaviour, although it is clear that, at times, there is a real risk that death could occur. I argue that the main motivation and reason for self-harm is self-preservative rather than destructive.

The title of the chapter refers directly to Winnicott's (1956) notion of the antisocial tendency as a sign of hope, in that the act of aggression, apparently destructive and hopeless, in fact reflects the antisocial person's hopefulness in an environment that can recognise and meet their needs. In this sense too, self-harm can express the hope that there will be a response from others so that a need can be met, and that an environment exists that can withstand assault.

Self-harm serves a multiplicity of functions for the individual, who can achieve a great sense of release from unbearable states of mind and direct violence towards themselves rather than another, enabling what could be considered a 'safe' expression of rage. The functions of self-harm need to be clearly delineated and explored for each individual, and the particular situation in which they find themselves. In Chapter 2 I present a personal perspective on self-harm by Heather Jones, interwoven with my text. Her descriptions offer an eloquent, and hopeful, insight into self-harm, and how other forms of creativity can ultimately help replace the impulses to harm oneself.

Part 2: The wider context: systemic issues and self-harm

3 'Why do you treat me this way?': reciprocal violence and the mythology of deliberate self-harm (Scanlon and Adlam)
4 The trap: self-harm and young people in foster care and residential settings (Norris and Maher)
5 Self-harm and attachment (Grocutt)

Scanlon and Adlam's chapter on self-harm and reciprocal violence (Chapter 3) looks beyond individual acts of self-harm to wider society and the sense in which those who self-harm are dismembered, and themselves the victims of societal acts of violence. The authors argue against what they consider to be the fundamentally misguided description of self-harm as 'deliberate' and consider this to be an example of an 'intentional fallacy'. The chapter is predicated on the premise that self-harm expresses most clearly, the violence that we, therapists, mental health professionals and other integrated members of society, do to those who self-harm. The chapter offers a direct challenge to traditional conceptions of self-harm as intrapsychic events with a deliberate meaning and invites the reader to review their implicit understanding of self-harm. The chapter serves as a critique of existing models of self-harm and offers a radical understanding that puts social forces in shaping and creating individual behaviour at its core. It introduces a section on social systems and the interrelation between self-harm and those who encounter and, they would argue, create it.

In Chapter 4, Norris and Maher present a powerful picture of the real difficulties for staff and young people in foster and residential care, for whom self-harm is a potent mode of self-expression, but also part of a cycle of behaviour that leads to rejection. Dealing with some of the most vulnerable children and young people in society – those in foster and residential care – is a challenging and highly complex area. These young people often self-harm in ways that put their placements in foster, residential or adoptive care at risk, and the response to this can also be destructive, leaving carers feeling helpless, angry and confused. The urgent need to understand this behaviour and to find ways out of 'the trap' of self-harm and its impact on carers is highlighted in this lively, clear and moving chapter. The authors outline a model for understanding self-harm and moving out of the 'stuck-ness'. They state:

> Our aim in this chapter is to look beyond risk and consider the perplexing question of 'What is going on?' for the young people and for those around them when they self-harm . . . and we draw on both psychodynamic and systemic ways of exploring the meanings contained in this behaviour. Our focus in this chapter shifts from the individual to interpersonal and group processes.

These authors draw on a range of theoretical ideas, including attachment theory.

In Chapter 5, Grocutt describes the links between early attachment disturbances and self-harm. She outlines the development of self-harm in the context of attachment theory, also exploring some of the themes presented in the previous chapter dealing with self-harm in the looked-after children system. Grocutt uses both clinical material and theory to demonstrate how self-harm can be understood as an expression of attachment disturbances in childhood, which continue to affect people over their lifespan; the model also situates self-harm in adulthood within the context of ongoing attachment difficulties. Grocutt identifies the ways in which nursing systems and other aspects of caregiving within therapeutic settings can reinforce self-harming behaviour and re-enact earlier disturbances in relationships.

Part 3: Women and self-harm

6 Speaking with the body (Kleinot)
7 Absences, transitions and endings: threats to successful treatment (Greenwood)
8 Self-harm in women's secure services: reflections and strategies for treatment design (Lawday)
9 Self-harm cessation in secure settings (Grocutt)

As I have shown elsewhere (Motz, 2008), the typical target of aggression for women is their own body, or those who they can consider to be extensions of themselves – their children. Women typically locate their sense of identity and their power in their own bodies, which have become their private spheres of influence, to be used as weapons or canvasses on which to depict their painful experiences. In self-harm, this is clearly and graphically articulated, particularly for those women who are confined in secure mental health settings.

Deliberate self-harm is a powerful bodily enactment of psychic pain, which women demonstrate much more frequently than men. In the UK, one in seven women prisoners will self-harm and self-mutilate, while the comparable figure for male prisoners is one in thirty-three (Lloyd, 1995: 178).

The gender difference in self-harming rates is striking. Attacking themselves is not only one of the legitimate channels allowed women to express their anger; it can be considered a form of protest against the idealised and sentimental view of femininity. Self-harm may be seen as an attempt to use the body to point to an underlying, psychic damage, and, as such, is eloquent. It reflects the way that women communicate their experiences and assert control over their private spheres of influence – their own bodies. It can also be understood symbolically as an attack on the body of the mother, as symbolised by the woman's own body (Welldon, 1988). Women typically locate their sense of identity in their bodies; this reflects the tremendous cultural emphasis placed on women's bodies in general, and their reproductive capacities in particular. Self-harm can often involve the insertion of objects into the body, whether orally or vaginally; this has, in my view, powerful symbolic functions and allusions to other, earlier, violations, penetrations and disfiguring trauma.

The rates of self-harm in women are therefore significantly higher than in men, and these rates are even higher when women are placed in confined settings, where their usual controls are absent, and they may feel increasingly helpless and furious, and self-harm becomes the acceptable currency of communication. It has both actual and symbolic functions, that is, to bring the distress to the attention of others who can respond, even if this response only takes place at a physical level, but also to communicate in symbolic form an earlier, apparently invisible trauma.

This book devotes three chapters to exploration of the unique experience of self-harming women in secure settings, from different angles, and one on the association between eating disorders and self-harm, particularly multi-impulsive bulimia and self-harm. In the first of these, 'Speaking with the body' (Chapter 6), psychotherapist and group analyst, Pamela Kleinot, describes her experiences of working in a women's prison. She presents the reader with a rich and highly relevant theoretical understanding of the development of self-harm, with reference to early trauma and severe disruptions in the ordinary experiences of maternal containment and reverie. This sophisticated theory is brought to life with four clinical illustrations of her psychotherapeutic work with women within the prison, over an extended period of time. While her work offers some glimpses of hope and the possibility of change, it also points to the depths of deprivation and disturbance in this population, and to the intrinsic difficulties of working therapeutically within a custodial institution.

Eating disorders are another form of damaging the self, with the same psychic structure as cutting, burning, mutilating and scarring the body, and have self-preservation rather than self-destruction as their aim. They serve a crucial communicative purpose and establish strict boundaries in relation to what can be taken in and what must be expelled violently from the body. The perverse aspects of eating disorders, and the potential for death in what can also be a quest for purity and peace in life, link them inextricably with other forms of self-harm. As the following quotation from a pro-anorexia website illustrates, starvation can be an attempt to obliterate the unacceptable aspects of being alive, while preserving something beautiful and essential, albeit through destruction:

> This is forever. I will do whatever it takes. I want to be thin more than anything, even food.
>
> Starvation is fulfilling. Colours become brighter, sounds sharper, odours so much more savoury and penetrating that inhalation fills every fibre and pore of the body. The greatest enjoyment of food is actually found when never a morsel passes the lips.
>
> One day I will be thin enough. Just the bones, no disfiguring flesh. Just the pure, clean shape of me, bones. That is what we all are, what we're made up of and everything else is just storage, deposit, waste. Strip it away, use it up.

The association between self-harm and eating disorders is well documented, in the psychological literature, in psychoanalytic accounts and in the first-person accounts of women who have self-harmed. In Chapter 7, Lynn Greenwood offers an understanding of eating disorders and their intrinsic connections to self-harm, providing an extended case illustration based on her work in an eating disorders unit. Greenwood (p. 145) describes the intricate connection between eating disorders and other forms of self-destructive behaviour:

> In this chapter, I am consciously choosing to use the terms 'self-damaging' or 'self-destructive' behaviour instead of 'deliberate self-harm'. The latter generally describes attacks against the body: cutting, burning, blood-letting, head-banging, or the insertion of sharp objects. Self-damaging behaviour is a far broader term, encompassing deliberate physical harm and other destructive acts . . .

The third chapter dealing with the particular issues of self-harm in women, its understanding and containment is Chapter 8, written by forensic psychologist, Rebecca Lawday. She focuses on service development and design, rather than individual clinical situations. In this chapter, Lawday presents a comprehensive working model for a women's enhanced medium secure unit at Arnold Lodge in which particular expressions of female distress, such as self-harm, are anticipated and sensitively addressed. Throughout Lawday's rich and informative chapter, the words of one of the clients, Wendy Iffil, remind the reader that this is a service whose development has been directly affected by the views of the service users themselves. Wendy says: 'I feel that women's needs are complex and that they often end up in mental health services as a direct consequence of traumatic life experiences . . .' and poignantly describes the absence of the ordinary experience of touch for women in these environments, perhaps indicating that one of the functions of self-harm is to provide an alternative to other, loving or intimate ways of making contact, touching another person. She writes: 'Women miss out on non-sexual and sexual physical contact. For example, where do you get a cuddle from? Women are restricted from having sexual relationships but nothing is offered as an alternative'. This chapter also situates the challenge of self-harm in the context of service development, offering some best practice guidelines, in accordance with recent Department of Health documentation outlining the need for women-only therapeutic settings, within and outside of secure mental health provision.

Continuing the theme of women's use of self-harm in secure mental health situations, clinical psychologist, Elizabeth Grocutt, describes the process of self-harm cessation in Chapter 9. This chapter is based on her doctoral research in which she explored how seven women who were inpatients in secure mental health units achieved this. She elucidates the various factors that helped the women to stop their addictive behaviour, focusing on the themes that they provided in their descriptions of how and why they stopped self-harming. The individual pathways that these women went down are revealed through an analysis of their interviews, and subdivided into three main themes: the importance of accessing support from valued relationships; regaining control over their lives; and identifying personal incentives to influence and sustain cessation.

Conclusion: 'If you prick us do we not bleed?' The meaning and management of self-harm

In the final chapter, I draw together the ideas and understandings of self-harm that have been explored throughout the main body of this book and offer some final thoughts about how the various strands of the arguments and perspectives fit together.

REFERENCES

Adshead, G. (1997) 'Written on the body: deliberate self-harm and violence', in E.V. Welldon and C. van Velson (eds) *A Practical Guide to Forensic Psychotherapy*, London: Jessica Kingsley Publishers.

Lloyd, A. (1995) *Doubly Deviant, Doubly Damned: Society's Treatment of Violent Women*, London: Penguin.

Motz, A. (2008) The Psychology of Female Violence: Crimes Against the Body (second edition), Hove: Routledge.

Ougrin, D., Ng, A. and Zundel, T. (Eds) (2009) *Self-harm in Young People: A Therapeutic Assessment Manual.* London: Hodder Arnold.

Welldon, E.V. (1988) *Mother, Madonna, Whore: The Idealisation and Denigration of Motherhood*, London: Karnac.

Welsh Assembly Government (2008) *'Talk to Me': A National Action Plan to Reduce Suicide and Self-Harm in Wales 2008–2013* (Consultation Document), Cardiff: Welsh Assembly Government.

Winnicott, D.W. (1956) 'Delinquency as a sign of hope' *Collected Papers: Paediatrics Through Psychoanalysis*, London: Karnac Books/Institute of Psychoanalysis (1992).

Part 1

Understanding self-harm

Chapter 1

Self-harm as a sign of hope

Anna Motz

INTRODUCTION

In contrast to the view that it is a pathological expression of underlying distress, without meaning, reason or hope, I argue that self-harm is a powerful, silent language. It communicates states of mind to others, inscribing a narrative on the body itself. Self-harm embodies unbearable feelings and memories of trauma; it expresses the hope of being understood and cared for.

In this chapter, I present my model for understanding self-harm as an expression of hope in an environment that can respond to this communication and bear its meaning, acting as a call to a longed-for other to see, hear and respond to distress. This model of self-harm does not ignore the fact that it is a serious and potentially life-threatening activity.[1] In this chapter I focus on self-harm as distinct from suicidal behaviour, because, with the former, the intention is not death, but self-preservation. Despite its horror, violence and the genuine despair it expresses, there are other aspects of self-harm that contain within them the hope of meaningful relationships with others, and with oneself. The most commonly seen forms of self-harm are cutting, burning and head-banging while other types of self-injury may be less visible – for example, picking at wounds or tearing or biting at the skin.

Members of the public and psychotherapists alike view self-harm as an attempt to connect with others, commonly considered 'a cry

1 It is on a continuum with suicidal behaviour and has the potential to lead to death, whether accidental or deliberate. There is an association between self-harm and suicide such that episodes of self-harm increase the risk of completed suicide in the following year.

for help', rather than a suicidal expression of isolation, desperation and anger. Throughout this chapter I will present arguments for the understanding of self-harm as a choice to preserve life. I suggest that its central purpose is to escape unbearable pain and establish a private, internal relationship with the self that can nonetheless relate to another person in a profound way. It is both retreat and approach, and is essentially paradoxical, using injury to create healing and withdrawal into the self as an attempt to make contact with others. Despite its conflicts, it is ultimately meaningful.[2]

I consider self-harm to be consciously chosen and, in this sense, deliberate, although there may also be unconscious motivations and meanings of which the individual is unaware. It is behaviour that is without conscious suicidal intent but which harms parts of the individual's own body, with the potential to destroy or damage body tissue; common acts of self-harm include cutting, burning, head-banging and inserting objects into the body. I accept Favazza's (1996: xviii) definition of self-injury as 'the deliberate destruction or alteration of one's body tissue without conscious suicidal intent'. Some authors within this volume argue that self-harm is not deliberately chosen, but rather a forced choice, an involuntary evacuation of a violent state of mind (Scanlon and Adlam, this volume) but I disagree. In my view, the conscious as well as unconscious meaning self-harm has for the individual is central. To deny this is to disregard its communicative function and its role as an expression of hope, not simply despair.

In this chapter, I focus on self-harm as intentional, sometimes an expression of murderousness, at other times an attempt to create order and meaning in the face of confusion and turmoil, and to demarcate an important boundary between self and other, between internal and external and to give shape, colour and texture to overwhelming feelings. Blood is an important symbol in self-harm and connotes purification, liquid containment, warmth, fluidity, sensation and the exposure of what lies within, hidden under the skin, to the outside world. Not all forms of self-harm involve blood-letting, but all have their own private and public symbolism

2 Favazza distinguishes between culturally sanctioned acts of self-mutilation, and those that constitute self-harm, making the important statement that 'self-mutilation is distinct from suicide. Major reviews have upheld this distinction. . . . A basic understanding is that a person who truly attempts suicide seeks to end all feelings whereas a person who self-mutilates seeks to feel better' (Favazza, 1996: 262).

that needs to be understood and responded to. The objects used in the injury, the parts of the body that are hurt and the ways in which the wounds are tended to, and by whom, have unconscious meaning as well as overt meaning, accessible to the self-harmer. Fantasies of self-harm, whether acted on or not, also play a significant role and can offer solace, imagined revenge, and release.

BORDER CONTROL: SELF-HARM AND THE CREATION OF BOUNDARIES

Self-cutting is the most common form of self-harm, and appears to serve a variety of functions, including that of creating an immediate sense of order, sensation and release in what was a state of pure distress and anxiety. The slicing of the skin can be precisely and delicately performed as an attempt to delineate and demarcate boundaries on the surface of the skin. This also symbolises the creation of an internal boundary between difficult psychic states and the creation of a sense of order. Caroline Kettlewell's memoir describes the fascination with seeing how the inside comes out, how the self is constituted internally and the release that this provides, both psychically and physically, as she first uses a razor to cut herself:

> In the razor's wake, the skin melted away, parted to show briefly the milky white subcutaneous layers before a thin beaded line of rich crimson blood seeped through the inch-long divide. Then the blood welled up and began to distort the pure, stark edges of my delicately wrought wound.
>
> The chaos in my head spun itself into a silk of silence. I had distilled myself to the immediacy of hand, blade, blood, flesh.
>
> (Kettlewell, 2000: 27)

It is clear from the above account, frequently echoed by self-harmers, that it serves a powerful function, which enables a kind of purity, focus and order to return to a restless mind. The body survives the assault.

SELF-HARM AS A SIGN OF HOPE

Donald Winnicott's (1956: 314) description of the hope in the antisocial act applies equally to self-harm: 'In the hopeful moment

. . . the environment must be tested and re-tested in its capacity to stand the aggression, to prevent or repair the destruction, to tolerate the nuisance, to recognize the positive element in the antisocial tendency'. In self-harm, the holding environment is the body itself. Self-harm offers the possibility of testing the body to see whether it is an object that can be relied on to withstand and survive assault. It also acts as a test of the mind and its strengths, to defeat the fear of pain and its consequences. I consider the main function of self-harm to be self-preservative rather than death-driven action although, of course, the possibility of death is often present.[3]

As well as being an attack on an individual's own body, self-harm can also attack the minds of others (Campbell and Hale, 1991) who may desperately attempt to stop or prevent it, fearing that suicide or other destruction is the ultimate outcome. Managing self-harm requires the capacity to live with it, as carer, friend or therapist, in order to enable the self-harmer to find other ways to communicate unbearable states of mind.

My central hypothesis is that self-harm is a communication to oneself and others that serves several functions for the individual by offering them a variety of ways of relating to themselves and enacting certain essential roles. In this sense, self-harm reflects a split and divided self, and its enactment offers a sequential series of rewards and compensations. There are a series of splits, both psychic and physical, underlying self-harm; these splits require integration before a self-harmer can give up what has been an effective strategy for survival.

SELF-HARM AS DIALECTIC

The notion of the divided self is central to my conception of self-harm. It relies on a primitive defence mechanism – splitting – as

3 Glasser's (1979) notion of the difference between sado-masochistic and self-preservative violence is relevant here. In sado-masochistic aggression, of the kind found in core complex phenomena, the object is kept alive to be tortured. In self-preservative aggression, the object is considered a threat to survival and must be annihilated. Self-harm can express both types of aggression; at times the intention is to eliminate the badness, through a kind of self-murder, to be allowed to live. At other times it has a more perverse, sado-masochistic quality in that the body becomes the object tortured by the part of the self that identifies with an aggressor. The body in pain is the victim, which is, in turn, tended to.

described by Klein (1946) in her account of how a preverbal infant develops a means of protecting good internal objects from the perceived threat of bad ones. The mother is not viewed as a unitary creature capable of both feeding and depriving the baby, but as either Good Breast or Bad Breast.[4] In crisis, facing psychic threat, an adult individual reverts to using this defence mechanism and divides the world into good and bad. In self-harm, this type of dichotomy is expressed when the toxic contents of the mind are violently discharged onto the body. One part of the self can become calm, purified and released, while another is violated and intruded upon. The movement does not end here though: the body that has been injured, and thus the victim of a savage attack, is then tended to and cared for. The attacking self then becomes the caring, nursing self.[5] The movement from thesis to antithesis and finally to synthesis can be identified in self-harm in that the ultimate aim for the self-harmer is to develop an integrated sense of herself, and to recognise that she is the containing receptacle in which both good and bad impulses inhere. She is both savage aggressor and wounded victim. She is also finally the nurse who can facilitate recovery and act as witness to the violence and its aftermath. The individual moments of contradictory impulses seem altogether disconnected, which I suggest is the function of dissociative mechanisms, preventing the sense of a continuous, remembering self that performs the various actions. Instead, the person who self-harms experiences themselves as wholly aggressor, or pure victim. These discordant states of mind appear to have no sense of continuity.

It follows from this model that one of the aims of the therapy is for the therapist to act as container of both toxic and good feelings, to enable the self-harmer to integrate both sets of feelings into themselves without needing to take violent action to discharge

4 In Klein's (1946) view, the infant evolves from merging with the mother to becoming a separate and integrated self by moving through two positions: first, the paranoid-schizoid position, characterised by splitting (i.e. the satisfying part of the mother and the frustrating part are seen as two distinct entities, the 'good mother' or 'good breast' versus the 'bad mother' or 'bad breast'); and second, the depressive position, which entails an integrative experience of both the mother and the infant himself/herself as a whole person, both good and bad at the same time.

5 This fits the notion of a dialectic movement as first described by Hegel (1979) in *Phenomenology of Spirit* and later adopted by Marx in an understanding of political and economic developments in history.

angry, anxious or shameful states of mind. This mirrors the development of the depressive position in Kleinian terms, in that there is the gradual evolution of a capacity to tolerate ambivalence rather than to function in a state of rigid splitting in which the external world is terrifying – what she calls the paranoid-schizoid position. The self-harmer acts as Other to herself, and what is urgently required is for a re-integration to end this self-alienation; otherwise it becomes increasingly frightening, creating a sense of profound isolation and loss of contact with reality.[6]

When someone penetrates their skin, defaces it, marks it or bruises it, there is a violent intrusion from the external world onto the point of contact with the internal world and the harmed person is left damaged, disfigured and filled with impinging sensations. To do this to one's own body is essentially to become Other to oneself, to enact a split and an attack that could come from an alien outsider. Penetrating the skin thus reflects a divided self and can be a violent replication of the earliest relationship between self and Other. After the penetration and intrusion, the person who has been perpetrator to themselves can now become nurse, tending to the injured body. Nursing the self-inflicted wounds can also be seen as a re-enactment of the early infantile experience of being tended to and cared for by another, usually, though not always, by the mother. This is the other side of the divided self, the caring, nurturing and attentive aspect. It can also be a vital communication to oneself as well as to others; it is a request for a healthy, nurturing part of the self to attend to the injured aspect with care, respect and understanding. Nursing the wounds often plays an important part in the ritual of self-harm.

We can therefore see that there are a series of roles, taken on and played out sequentially, all of which serve important psychic functions for the self-harmer. At the moment of self-harming, the individual is in a highly unpleasant state of emotional arousal – anger, anxiety or acute distress – and needs to discharge this unbearable state through violent action. They become their own tormenter and subject the body to an assault, releasing the unmanageable states of

6 I suggest that this type of state, so typical of women diagnosed with borderline personality disorder, can be exacerbated by therapists who attempt to reify the individual states of mind as distinct personalities, as can be found in some work with 'multiple personality disorders', because this only perpetuates the sense of splitting and fragmentation.

mind through a conversion of mental to physical pain. Scanlon and Adlam (this volume) understand this as the expulsion of a violent state of mind. In this moment of self-harm, they treat the body with cruelty or indifference, seeing it as a poison container, perhaps also replicating a relationship they had with a violent or abusive parent, who met their own needs through a similar kind of cruelty towards them, in childhood. After this violence ends, a wound is left, whose blood needs to be stopped; there may be other physical consequences in the form of bruising, scabbing or pain. Sometimes, inserted objects remain obstructive in the body, preventing the ordinary function of the digestive system or causing internal cutting. The situation is not one that can simply be left. Another persona is now summoned up, a healing, nurturing and altogether more benign source of comfort. This is another aspect of the self, the witnessing and nursing self. At times, this Nurse part of the self can accompany the self-harmer to an actual concrete hospital, and there will be a public disclosure of what has happened; at other times, this Nurse self works in secret, tending to the wounds.[7]

The body is used as the stage onto which these dramatic aspects of a divided self can express themselves, both as aggressor and nurse, in the service of the final aim of re-integration and creation of a coherent sense of self. The skin as boundary acts as a kind of psychic container, but for those who do not have an interior sense of integration, the dis-integration is played out on the body and its surfaces.

Underlying self-harm there is a divided sense of self. Self-harm can form part of an 'elimination fantasy', based on a primitive defence of splitting, in that the 'bad' aspects of the self are cut out, allowing the 'good' to flourish. It can also be a vital communication to oneself as well as others in that it is a request for a healthy, nurturing part of the self to attend to the injured aspect with care, respect and understanding.

THE LANGUAGE OF SELF-HARM

Self-harm can be understood as a way of saying through gestures and acts of violence, that which cannot be put into words. Through

7 Motz and Jones provide a personal account of the Nurse in Chapter 2.

self-harm the body speaks. I will begin the exploration of the language of the body with a description of the meaning and function of the skin, and being held, in infancy since the skin and its mutilation is a central feature of the act of self-harm. Bodily symbols and gestures develop from these crucial early experiences; they pre-date language but articulate the most fundamental human needs. When these experiences have been traumatic, the infant can be affected in a way that leaves them 'stuck' in a preverbal stage of distress, without the use of words to describe their painful experiences. In adulthood, times of crisis can re-awaken these early feelings, whose intensity is then managed through violent action rather than language or reflection.[8]

From earliest infancy, skin and its sensations are central to the emotional experience of the baby, who is held against their mother's breast, nursed, caressed, tickled and bathed. For some babies the experience of being dressed and undressed is itself an attacking, disintegrating event, and for almost all, comfort is derived from skin-to-skin contact with mother, and the experience of being put down, away from her, is distressing, causing them to cry. The psychological evidence for the significance of skin-to-skin contact in early bonding is robust,[9] and the analytic literature asserts the primacy of early experience in providing the foundations for the construction of an integrated self.[10]

For babies who have not had the reliable presence of the maternal holding environment, the physical sensation of being held, fed, bathed, soothed and having their needs met, this has a dramatic impact on their sense of internal integration. It is evident that from infancy, integration starts from the outside in – physical containment enables psychic containment and the development of

8 The role of early attachment experiences in the development of an integrated sense of self and the link with self-harm is explored further in Chapter 5.

9 'Regardless of their theoretical position, many scientists and pediatricians are convinced that touch and close bodily contact are necessary conditions for the infant's normal and healthy development (Ainsworth *et al.*, 1978; Bowlby, 1958; Brazelton, 1977; Hassenstein, 1973; Ribble, 1944; Spitz, 1945; Stirnimann, 1940/1973)' (cited by Grossman *et al.*, 1981: 159).

10 'In its most primitive form the parts of the personality are felt to have no binding force amongst themselves and must therefore be held together in a way that is experienced by them passively, by the skin functioning as a boundary. The stage of primal splitting . . . can now be seen to rest on this earlier process of containment of self and object by their respective skins' (Bick, 1968: 484).

a coherent sense of self, and ultimately the construction of a perception of internal and external, a notion of one's own mind. The body ego, as Freud (1923) termed it, is the first ego, and disruptions in its care have a significant impact on the development of the psychic structures, the ego or the sense of self in mediation with the external world.

Skin is the boundary, the protective shield, that separates self and other but also the point of contact with another, and the line between inside and outside, the surface onto which sensation is felt; it is a boundary, site of perception and point of impact. Separation can be understood as the loss of the shared skin and contact with another can be experienced as a form of penetration, in which the skin's barrier is threatened. Skin gives us the possibility of touch, with its desires, some forbidden, others permitted.

The connections between disorders of the skin and early attachment experiences are central to understanding both the development and meaning of self-harm. Dinora Pines' (1993) fascinating work on unconscious uses of the female body, explores the impact of trauma on the skin and on other facets of the body. Bick (1968) too provides rich illustrations of how the path of early experience can be traced on the skin, and its disorders. The link with early infancy, and its embodied memories, is central. This work is developed further in the studies of Ulnik (2007) on skin disorders, viewed from a psychoanalytic perspective, based on the idea that the skin has important links with unconscious processes and is originally experienced as a common, or shared skin, linking infant with mother: Ulnik (2007: 14) describes how memories can be re-awakened through contact with the skin:

> Feelings of excitement, ideas and old memories, but also new associations can be revived or awoken by a mere physical contact with the skin. . . . The simple stimulus of a tickle, a pinch, a feeling of warmth on the skin, the feeling of getting close to someone, are re-translated and re-transcribed . . . and are interpreted as estrangement, cruelty, getting close, cuddling, aggression or detachment of the skin. This could be explained by the link between touching and the cruelty drive, by experiencing the feeling of contact as a loss of the protective barrier against stimuli and also by experiencing separation as the loss of a skin shared by the significant other, which wraps the bodies of both.

Trauma and self-harm

The role of trauma in creating a disturbed sense of oneself, and giving rise to psychic defences against pain, has been well documented in both analytic and empirical literature, including work by Yates and colleagues (Yates, 2004; Yates *et al.*, 2008) in the United States, which identifies developmental pathways to self-injury. In this illuminating work, based on prospective studies of adolescents who were abused in childhood, either sexually or physically, the role of self-injury as a regulatory mechanism for coping with the consequences of early childhood trauma is clear in that the trauma creates disturbed and impoverished ways of managing emotion and affect – the self-injury enables some kind of coping to take place.

For people caught up in the compulsive behaviour characteristic of self-harm, libidinal energy has become intertwined with death instincts, the pull towards destructiveness. The desire for self-harm has the force of an addiction, which is beautifully articulated in Betty Joseph's (1982) paper, 'Addiction to near Death'.

> My impression is that these patients as infants, because of their pathology, have not just turned away from frustrations or jealousies or envies into a withdrawn state, nor have they been able to rage and yell at their objects. I think they have withdrawn into a secret world of violence, where part of the self has been turned against the other part, parts of the body being identified with parts of the offending object . . .
>
> (Joseph, 1982: 455)

In this paper she describes the pull of the death instincts, the masochistic constellation of these forces and the powerful compulsive aspect of this in patients intent on creating despair and hopelessness in their therapist through projective mechanisms. To achieve this is, however, to triumph in a death-dealing way, because the person who could help, and act as a healthy and hopeful part of the mind, gets caught up in destructiveness, rather than the possibility of recovery.

The task of the therapist is to remain in touch with the part of the patient that wants to preserve life and to retain their own capacity to think about the experiences they are being shown and made to feel without losing themselves in the hopelessness; they need to withstand assaults on this life-affirming aspect and allow the patient to re-integrate it into themselves. Joseph powerfully argues that the person caught up in this kind of hopelessness and self-destructiveness experiences unconscious excitement as they immerse themselves in the pull towards despair and near death. This takes place within the subjective experience of intense depression and can manifest itself through self-mutilation, biting, eating, tearing the skin and other acts of violence against the self. The turmoil and destruction are, nonetheless, addictive, and offer a kind of pleasure. The notion of nearly dying, but not quite, also conveys the sense of risk and experimentation that can be found in those who enact dangerous levels of violence on their own body.

Welldon's (1992) seminal work on the development and manifestation of female perversion further illuminates the function and meaning of self-harm. For self-harmers, the aggressive impulse is turned inwards onto their own bodies. This may have a sexual component, creating a release from tension similar to that achieved through orgasm. For Welldon, the origin of this self-harm is the woman's early object relations, that is, her experience of being mothered:

> During adolescence, if she hates her mother's sexual body and is unable to identify with her and her body, the adolescent girl will use her hand to attack her own body in a compulsive way by, for example, cutting her arms or wrists . . . In doing such harm to their bodies they are expressing tremendous dissatisfaction, not only with themselves but also with their mothers, who provided them with the bodies they are now fighting.
>
> (Welldon, 1992: 40)

The following material illustrates the models presented above. It describes Crystal, a 32-year-old woman on a locked secure ward, whose treatment revealed a kind of 'addiction to near death' in her self-injuring and in the depression that at times threatened to overwhelm her and me, her therapist. Her attacks on her own body also had some perverse elements, namely their addictive quality and the sense of enlivenment they generated. She demonstrated some hopefulness in the therapy and went on to make some substantial changes in her self-mutilation and dramatically improved her quality of life. Some aspects of the case study have been changed to preserve Crystal's anonymity.

CLINICAL ILLUSTRATION: CRYSTAL, A WOMAN MANAGING EXTREME SELF-INJURY

Crystal was a large, imposing woman, with striking, bright eyes and a radiant smile, often hidden by her tendency to hang her head down and avoid eye contact. She was an inpatient in a mixed-sex secure ward, following her admission to an open unit where she was considered 'unmanageable' because of her frequent assaults on her own body, including inserting and swallowing sharp objects. She was an eloquent, intelligent woman who engaged in various forms of self-injury; she said that this was to express her distress and relieve her of painful memories.

I worked with Crystal for a year of once-a-week psychotherapy until she was transferred to a female-only ward. Like so many women in secure conditions, she had been brought into the forensic services because of violence towards herself. She had occasionally been violent towards nursing staff, who felt that she was not suitable for the open ward. In the past she had made threats to kill her stepfather, who had abused her sexually for many years during her childhood while living in the family home. She had not known her biological father, who had died before she was born.

Almost as soon as Crystal had been admitted onto the ward, she evoked strong reactions from other patients and staff; some felt concerned, protective and curious, while others became angry and disturbed, feeling that she should be stopped from behaving violently towards herself or moved to another ward. Her large, unkempt presence conveyed the impression of something wild or even inhuman and this created fear and a sense of helplessness in many who watched as she banged her head against the wall repeatedly. She frequently cut her arms and would often ask for help with dressing the wounds. Crystal secreted weapons, in the form of broken fragments of DVD cases, and pieces of stone from the hospital grounds, and would use these objects in her self-harm, through cutting, or vaginal insertion of broken shards of glass or plastic; she also scalded herself with hot liquids and burnt her arms with cigarettes.

The symbolic significance of cutting and burning her arms struck me as profound. She craved arms that could hold her, caress her, but had only known arms that held her down, to rape and beat her. She often kept her arms folded up, protecting herself against unwanted contact and displaying the deep scarification on them. She embraced nurses to whom she was close in a kind of 'bear hug' and her arms enveloped them. A mother's comforting arms and gentle touch had been painfully absent from her early life; her mother, like her stepfather, had treated her violently. Inserting painful objects into herself also had clear symbolic significance, as she seemed to attack her own insides, particularly her sexual organs; in a sense, this repeated the violent sexual assaults of her past.

Crystal paced the hallways frequently, sometimes appearing quite dissociated,[11] in a world of her own, muttering as if in conversation with invisible enemies, or friends, sometimes laughing to herself, at other times cursing. Her language at other times could be lucid, colourful and expressive, as revealed in conversation and in her writing, but she avoided talking about her early life experiences.

Crystal's psychiatric diagnosis had changed from psychopathic personality disorder to borderline personality disorder, from schizophrenic to schizo-affective disorder. Her current consultant psychiatrist was considering returning to her original diagnosis as suffering from psychopathic personality disorder in the light of her recent disclosure that she wanted to murder children, and her apparent lack of remorse following severe assaults on nursing staff and patients on the open ward.

The complexity of her presentation and the sense in which she defied categorisation was clear. She inhabited the borders of psychiatric categories, as she did the borders of past and present, as memory constantly intruded on her waking mind. In this sense, she was indeed a woman with a borderline disorder, seemingly borne of her past experience of humiliation, emotional, physical and sexual abuse, terror and betrayal.

The severity of Crystal's self-harm was mirrored in the severity of her history of childhood sexual, emotional and physical abuse. She had been the victim of incest and sexual abuse by multiple perpetrators from ages 9–17. Her stepfather, a religious man and public figure, had been sexually predatory in private and had passed her around his friends to abuse. She had been the eldest of four children and was a pretty, intelligent child, who had learned that she must not try to disclose the abuse because she would only

11 Dissociation is a psychic defence often found in individuals who have experienced severe trauma, as a protective mechanism to prevent emotional overload. See de Zulueta (2006).

be accused of lying and punished by her apparently depressed mother, as had happened on the two occasions when she tried to tell her what was going on. She believed that her mother had also been the victim of incest from various statements her mother had made, and from her refusal to allow Crystal to see her own father, Crystal's grandfather.

As the abuse had progressed to full intercourse and gang rape, Crystal could not contain her distress and wet the bed frequently, resulting in further beatings and verbal chastisement by her mother. Sometimes her mother would run her scalding hot baths in an apparent attempt to cleanse her of the urine, but at a symbolic level to rid her of the impurities of sexual violation, as though she had somehow encouraged or invited this. Her mother knew about the abuse without acknowledging what she knew, and this left Crystal in a place of deep pain and isolation, desperate for some witness to her traumatisation. Her mother could not bear to act as witness, or protector, and Crystal had, instead, to be punished and cleansed through the burning baths, which were painful on her skin. Social services had been involved briefly with the family because of the mother's own terror of the domestic violence to which she had also been subject and Crystal recollected a peaceful time where she had been in foster care for several months, before abruptly being brought back home where the abuse had started all over again.

When Crystal was 11, after a night spent in the hands of her stepfather and his friends, she had found a razor in the bathroom and made small incisions on her feet and on the inner sides of her thighs. Crystal described this as marking to herself what had happened, and also providing a sense of relief that she explained was a physical release from psychic torment. She had felt altogether helpless at home and harming herself in this way was, she explained, a way of reminding herself that her body was in fact hers, not her stepfather's or the other abusers; she wanted to mark and scar it as she chose. She saw her self-harm as a kind of branding and an outlet for anger and guilt, saying that it also helped her to 'feel real' at times when she felt quite dissociated. She also wanted to protect others from the rage she felt towards her abusers, as she wanted to prevent her younger sister from being abused as she was. She felt that she needed to sacrifice herself for her sister. In this sense, the self-harm was closely associated with a desire to protect others; it enabled her to express fury at herself, rather than at others, and to endure the trauma of abuse so that her sister would be spared.

Therapeutic contact

When I first began therapeutic work with Crystal she appeared eager, and quickly engaged with me, saying that she was desperate to make sense of what had happened to her and to stop hurting herself. I felt overwhelmed as she poured out memories of the extreme abuse to which she had been subject, drew pictures of herself in symbolic form, with images of monsters, blood, snakes and fire, and presented me with well-crafted but violent poetry. My awareness of her intense hopefulness was painful as I wondered how to help her manage and contain the raw power and perversion of her experiences, still tormenting her in memory and enacted on her skin. She seemed to put me in the role of the thoughtful and protective maternal presence that should have stopped the abuse she had endured, and in the role of the rescuer who could somehow find the magic words that would make its horror bearable.

The early sessions were filled with descriptions of the past, in terms of vivid and detailed accounts of sexual violation by men and neglect and beatings by her mother, and also with exposure of her recent self-harm. I felt moved, protective of her and, at times, enraged by the treatment she had endured, but this was challenged when I saw how she re-victimised herself. Occasionally too, I felt physically sick when she seemed to flash her scars at me, as if inviting some kind of dramatic response, which I resisted making.

I felt that my bodily countertransference of disgust and my fascination reflected her feelings as a victim of childhood sexual abuse, as did my profound sense of helplessness. Her rage was directed not just at the incestuous stepfather who repeatedly raped her, passing her around like a doll, but also at her distant, rather brutal, mother, who was unable to listen to Crystal's disclosures of incest and abuse. In turn, she targeted her fury at her own female body, emerging herself fully in the task of self-torture and then a kind of nursing, a parody of ordinary maternal care as she tenderly bathed and dressed her wounds. Crystal's sado-masochistic relationship with her own body also expressed female violence that bound her intimately to herself, to the exclusion of others.[12] She directed her rage against her own body, representing both the

12 This is described in my earlier work on maternal abuse and female perversion (Motz, 2001).

sexually and physically abused body of her child-self and also the adult body of her mother. She also attacked her reproductive organs through her internal injuries. The sudden exhibitionist quality of 'flashing' her scars also communicated the perverse aspect of her self-injury that, at times, seemed to give her an erotic satisfaction. This is not unusual in self-harm and is connected with the sense of immersion in the self, and the eroticisation of hatred of one's own body.[13] My desire to flee or, alternatively, to stare at her naked wounds, seemed to connect with her sado-masochism, her fascination with her wounds, and their symbolisation of her sexual abuse. Her internal injuries also re-created an experience of intrusion, violation and pain, occurring in secret but sometimes requiring external agents to tend to, in an exposing intervention. 'The public expression of her private pain' (Adshead, 1997: 111) was all too evident.

By flashing her scars at me it seemed that Crystal was both entreating me to become the perverse maternal object and also making me a helpless witness to her self-destruction, and its evidence in her vivid, raw scarring. As she invited me to view her self-mutilation more, exposing both her scars and wounds, my mind seemed to be assaulted more powerfully and my body became hyper-responsive to her communication. I responded with intense visceral feelings to these intrusive and violent projections. There was some danger that I would be caught up in some kind of perverse enactment as my thinking was attacked and my own body brought into play. I reflected on this possibility in supervision and this enabled me to resist the desire to retreat, or to become collusive in Crystal's secret acts of self-harm.

The meaning of the scars, the sites of the injuries and the balance between secrecy and public exposure were significant and she began to put her thoughts and feelings into words and to process them in visual narratives rather than simply in lone images of power and terror in her drawings. I, in turn, felt less under siege and the sessions became calmer and more thoughtful. I also became increasingly aware of strong feelings of warmth, interest and empathy towards Crystal, as I saw how she struggled to manage her

13 Stoller (1975: 4) describes perversion as 'the erotic form of hatred' and explores the sense in which sexualised aggression in adulthood is an attempt to master earlier trauma.

memories and fears, and how her creativity enabled her to make some kind of sense and order out of inchoate feeling. These positive countertransference feelings provided a balance to the fear she also evoked, not least, for her own survival, and served as anchors for me, so that I could stay still and calm in her presence.

As therapy progressed, Crystal began to explore the extent of her own murderousness, as well as self-destructive feelings. The link between her homicidal and suicidal feelings was clear, although she still did not wish to die, and used her self-harm to help her to live. She described a recurring dream of killing a child, and intrusive memories about a particular episode of her own abuse that had involved women as well as men. Her horror at her own murderousness, her strong identification with her own abusers and desire to harm others as she herself had been harmed, took centre stage in the sessions. The fact of her dual status as perpetrator as well as victim became painfully clear and destabilised her. Crystal's self-harm escalated significantly at this time; she began to use ligatures and to make hanging attempts, timed to coincide with times when nurses would check on her as part of the ward's observational regime.

Crystal's descriptions in the sessions of her physical urges to damage herself and others, and the immediacy of her memories of abuse, were raw and disturbing. During one of these sessions I felt out of control of my own body; I had a powerful urge to interrupt the session to evacuate, to leave the room to expel the awful feelings. I found it increasingly difficult to think about what she was saying; my mind was focused on my physical discomfort. When I thought more about this almost unmanageable feeling of wanting to escape, to rush to the toilet, to breathe again, I realised that Crystal's violent and excited states of mind were projected into me, enabling me to know firsthand what she was experiencing. I understood that it was this state of uncontained violent, fearful excitement that led to her self-harming, and the dissociation that accompanied it. I found it impossible to breathe and think, just as she did when she tied ligatures using the sheets on her bed.

The domestic nature of the weaponry appeared to me to have great symbolic value, not only indicating the creativity and ingenuity of her capacity to construct weapons out of ordinary objects but also in terms of perverting the function of what she was given by the hospital. For someone who has been sexually abused in brutal and violent ways for years, sheets no longer have a benign and comforting meaning and indeed may be reminders of previous suffering and helplessness. Using sheets to self-harm may, for example, be an unconscious attack on the system of care that fails to protect her. Likewise, overdosing on prescribed medication can be seen as an assault on the help provided by the medical and nursing staff, a clear statement that the attempts at comfort are useless, and can be used to poison rather than treat the patient. Being in the room with Crystal, where her memories lived, revealing themselves on her scarred, unhealed body, was unbearable for us both, at times, but we were able to hold on to the hope that the violence would eventually subside.

Crystal's use of her writing, drawing, dreams and memories in our sessions, and my capacity to bear and articulate the lived experience of parental cruelty and perversion, seemed to provide her with a degree of containment but ultimately did not take away her need to self-harm. At times, this urge was intensified after therapy sessions in which particularly difficult experiences and memories came back to her, and eventually she became mute and curled up in the sessions, turning away from me in a foetal position and losing contact altogether. I understood her deathliness in the therapy to reflect a kind of 'cutting out' that reflected her 'cutting up'. When feelings became overwhelming, she felt that she had no choice but to go inwards, cutting out thought, memory and the presence of another. She told me that at such times she could only think in images, and flashes, not in words.

Following the physical turmoil of earlier sessions, this middle period in the therapy became a kind of retreat, as Crystal largely withdrew into herself. After several weeks of remaining largely mute and remote, her voice, and a more connected quality, returned. She told me that she no longer wanted to explore what had happened in the past, as she had felt compelled to do in earlier sessions, but wanted to focus on 'the here and now', and learn how to relate to her present surroundings as they were, not as shadows of the past. As I had never directed her in any way this presented no difficulties for me, and showed me that her capacity to confine memory to a psychic space and begin to demarcate a boundary between past and present seemed to have developed. We continued to meet weekly and her self-harm also continued, but its frequency and intensity abated. She was eager to enter a female-only unit, where she wanted to feel 'safe' enough to return to exploring her early life experiences, although she expressed reluctance to end therapy. Shortly before she left she began to have sexual feelings towards male staff, which both disturbed and excited her. She herself understood this to be a kind of hope, that her libidinal feelings could once again emerge, directed towards other people rather than distorted and used masochistically, through self-harm.

Through working with Crystal, albeit for a shorter time than originally envisaged, I learned about the power of dissociation, the confusion between suicidal and murderous impulses, the pain of giving up self-injury, as well as the horror of being made to bear witness to it. In her penultimate session Crystal described her wish to have been killed in childhood, not to have remained alive to be tortured, saying: 'I wish I had been a murdered child'. She accepted my interpretation that through her self-injury she had repeated this pattern of keeping herself alive to be hurt, becoming the perpetrator of her own abuse. It seemed too that she had shown a degree of hope in showing me her wounds, her scars, such that I might understand her trauma and self-harm and, through recognising their significance and meaning, allow her to defeat the compulsive need to re-enact the trauma on herself. I suggested that ending therapy might evoke thoughts of death, and loss. She became tearful and told me that she wanted to write to me, and that she had felt not judged, but understood by me. Unlike her mother who could not bear to listen to her disclosure of incest, I could hear and believe her and respond with some understanding. She did, in fact, write to me, and had engaged well with the group therapy programme on the women-only ward to which she moved, saying that her self-harm continued, but with less intensity. Although ultimately I could not prevent Crystal from inscribing her history on her body, I could, at least, read it with her.

Crystal gave consent for this description of our work to be published, and told me that she had been able to give up the impulses to self-harm, except for 'once in a blue moon', after almost two years in the women-only unit. In this setting she felt supported in expressing feelings of anger, frustration and sadness in the daily community meetings, whereas on the mixed ward she felt she was re-living traumatic experiences on a daily basis. She had been able to find alternative ways of expressing her feelings and managing distressing memories in the women-only unit, where she was able to engage in non-verbal therapies, including art, music and drama therapy. Crystal required not just one voice to speak with, but a wide repertoire of expressive modes, and was, with the help of female therapists and patients, able to build on the hope and creativity she had always shown, even at the depths of her self-harming.

SIGNING WITH A SCAR

Self-harm can be seen as more than just a form of communication but also as a means of self-creation and closer to affective states than words are. Straker (2006) considers self-cutting an act of self-identification. She terms this cutting 'signing with a scar' and views it as a form of affective communication, arguing that it is a mode of expression that is not just an inadequate form of language for the inarticulate. To view self-harm as simply the inability to verbalise fails to account for the high levels of literacy and eloquence of many self-harmers about themselves and their emotions and essentially misses the main function of self-harm: 'over and above the function of self-soothing, self cutting is the attempt to put into place the elements involved in the building of a self-structure. These include mirroring, the establishment of a boundary, the building of an autobiographical narrative, and the impregnation of verbal signifiers with signifiers of the flesh' (Straker, 2006: 93).

The limits of words are rarely confronted in accounts of self-harm, as the silence surrounding it can be deep and shameful, and the hope is that language will bridge the gap between alienation and acceptance. The belief is that if words can be found, the urge for various forms of self-mutilation will abate. Straker asserts that self-harm is not a lesser language but can actually be a more meaningful one for the person who is attempting to know and understand themselves through it. This challenges the underlying assumption that once it can be spoken about, the compulsion to self-harm will dissipate. If the 'language' of self-harm is more than just a message to others, as Straker describes, it is more difficult to give up. Self-harm does more than just signal to others, it meets deep needs for identity, beyond the communicative function.

My emphasis on self-harm as a form of language that creates as well as expresses, accords with this conception, adding weight to the notion of the flesh-made word. Indeed, the religious connotations of this idea have great relevance, as there is often a profound transformational act intended by self-harm, with echoes of scarification and stigmata, signifying the presence of another, unseen aspect to the self that is made explicit through scars.

The significance of scarification is culture-specific, but there are certain patterns that emerge cross-culturally. Favazza (1996), in his discussion of culture and psychiatry, describes how, in the Tiv tribe in West Africa, scarification serves as an initiation rite marking the passage from girl to woman, and boy to man. He shows how the scars themselves signal allegiance to a particular family and heritage, serving to signify fertility and locate people in time and place. He writes: 'Thus, the scars serve to anchor time and space and to ensure the continuity of life' (Favazza, 1996: 155). This has clear parallels with self-harm in the UK and the United States in several respects: it begins in adolescence, it is often learned through social interactions with others who engage in it, and it has unconscious links with identity as adult sexual beings. Favazza uses the cultural examples he provides to explore the significance of the scar itself and concludes that 'it seems likely that the scars resulting from self-mutilation may themselves have symbolic meaning relating to notions of rebirth, the continuity of the life process and the stability of relationships' (1996: 156). Meaning is clearly ascribed not only to the wound but also to its visceral evidence in a scar, whose presence may reflect a psychic, as well as bodily, healing. The scar as emblem, as the signifier of what has gone before, is essential.

This idea is substantiated by the empirical work of Grocutt (Chapter 9, this volume) looking at how and why women in secure settings stop self-harming. She describes how showing the scar was a feature of her clinical interviews:

> During the interviews many women revealed the physical scars and burns from their self-inflicted violence. This form of exposure could be interpreted as a need to communicate the level of extreme distress and chaos they had experienced, or to initiate a response or reaction. Alternatively, revealing their scars established a context for their cessation narrative and may have served as symbolic of the 'old self' and what they had since achieved.
>
> (Grocutt, this volume: 185)

SIGNING AS METAPHOR

Clinical illustration: Signing and self-harm

Although in this chapter I have mainly concentrated on self-harm in women, men too self-harm. The following clinical material relates to a man who used violence, in self-harm, as a powerful means of self-expression. The reasons for his self-harm apply to women in similar situations and have a more general resonance. Again, I have disguised aspects of the case to preserve anonymity.

A striking example of the impossibility of being heard in one's own voice comes from the experiences of a man, Thomas, who was profoundly deaf, and who had spent much of his early life in a residential school for deaf children, where, unsurprisingly, he felt wholly isolated and abandoned by his hearing family. He was not taught how to use sign language, as at the time it was thought best to teach deaf children to lip read and to make the sounds of speech.

In the home for deaf children, Thomas had been known only by a number, without a name, revealing how he was seen as without identity, dignity or true subjectivity. He was one in a series of abandoned deaf children, who could be abused without fear of disclosure. His later savage attacks on himself – his arms and genitals – seemed to be re-enactments of what had been done to him, and signifiers of the flesh – self-inscribed aspects of his history and its impact on his identity. When hearing from him, through an interpreter/signer, about being called by a number, and his use of self-harm, the image it evoked for me was of the numbers tattooed on the wrists of concentration camp inmates during the Holocaust; for many, these became an indelible mark of horror, and survival.

The cruelty to which he and thousands of other deaf children were subject is hard to imagine as, for many children who could not speak and had no other language with which to articulate their pain, to experience physical discipline or even sexual manipulation was simply a way of life. These children had been sent away by their families of origin to be cared for in residential schools where they could be taught to speak, without hearing. Parents were told that such education was in the best interests of their child and had little sense that there could be a way of integrating a deaf child into their own household. It was rare that parents could use sign language and indeed the idea was that deaf children should, instead, be taught to lip read as if hearing and to make speaking sounds, without hearing the sounds that they made or the quality of their mimicry. The aim was to appear to others as though they could hear, regardless of the actual state of their deafness, and the tremendous isolation and vulnerability this created.

At this residential school, Thomas endured repeated experiences of physical abuse and punishment, ways of being controlled and restrained that restricted and pained him, in an attempt both to control unruly behaviour and to instruct him in the art of speaking – saying words whose sound and meaning he did not know. Additionally, his only form of physical affection and concern came from a teacher, who incorporated sexual abuse of him in bathing and dressing routines. This powerful association of sexual behaviour between adults and children with affection and attention was to shape this man's life, presenting him with enormous difficulties throughout adult life, coupled with a pervasive sense of isolation and desperation. Years later his presentation at psychiatric services was conceptualised as reflecting a personality disorder, and he was admitted to mainstream psychiatric wards where some of his early experiences were unconsciously re-enacted by staff, in a catastrophic manner.

Thomas's isolation and fear in adulthood, and its echoes of his early life, symbolised to me the unbearable experiences many have lived through, the horror and shame of which simply cannot be put into words. His memories were visual – flashes of horror – and his distress visceral – literally written on his body through self-harm, in which he pierced his flesh. His wounds appeared like maps of pain and chaos. It was almost impossible for those around him to offer him the proper help and understanding that he sought. He looked 'normal' and his deafness was invisible to others, who treated him as though he could, and should, hear, failing to respond to his communications that he, in fact, could not. He was the proverbial good child who should be 'seen but not heard' in a way that left him vulnerable to abuse.

His voice sounded frightening and unusual when he spoke. Other forms of expression, like using sign language, were not accessible in the mainstream ward; this was reminiscent of his early abuse in a children's home where he had not had other ways of letting people know what was happening to him, too young to write, unable to speak and without carers who could 'read' him. He had to show his feelings on his skin, through dramatic and alarming acts of self-harm, which elicited the care of those who nursed him. These attacks on himself also contained rage at those who could not respond to his needs without seeing it writ large, in angry wounds that made no sense at first glance. He turned his rage onto himself, perhaps protecting others from the force of his murderousness.

The fact of his deafness, without the capacity to sign, and his emotional, physical and sexual abuse in residential care as a child had sealed his sense of isolation and exile, and intensified his desperate and unfulfilled desires to disclose both past and present abuse. Those who were there to care for and protect him had either neglected or abused him, at a time when he could not write, sign or talk.

Thomas stands metaphorically for all those men and women whose pain and trauma cannot be told, or heard, and dramatically demonstrates the creation of another form of language through violence and self-injury. He was still inscribing his experiences on his body when I saw him, even though he now had the possibility of other forms of communication. His self-injury encoded earlier trauma and was an important part of his sense of himself. The description given by Miller and Bashkin (1974: 647) in relation to a client they describe also fitted this man who 'preserved in the flesh, in a dramatic and conspicuous manner, the history of events he could not integrate into the fabric of his personality'.

For many self-harmers, the language of the body is a source of free expression as well as a compulsion. The element of choice in self-harm is one of the central paradoxes in understanding its meaning. On the one hand, images of self-harm can feel like alien voices and thoughts that dominate and control the waking mind of women and men in response to stress and rage. On the other, it can be a potent symbol of ownership and control of the body, whose occurrence itself is an act of protest. It is a re-assertion of control and ownership of a body that may have been used and violated by others. For others it is seen as a form of antidepressant, an effective, if addictive means of release from unbearable states of mind, which has its own internal and external meanings.

CONCLUSION: MANAGING SELF-HARM

Countertransference responses to self-harm are meaningful sources of information, providing therapists and other workers with essential data about the intentions and states of minds of their clients. The dilemma for the practitioner is to accept the self-harm as important while enabling their client to give it up, if and when they choose to (are able to) and become free of its hold on them. For therapists to be able to manage responses to the violence and intense distress that self-harm can create, on the body and in the minds of those who encounter it, it is essential to have supervision and teaching, as well as reflective space, to try to process the meanings and feelings it evokes: 'The task of mental health workers is to be receptive to hearing about experiences that can feel beyond words, without becoming unthinkingly caught up in the clients' projections, and taking part in destructive re-enactments . . . Patients are trying to live with overwhelming emotional pain and project this into staff through various communications such as self injury, very direct sexualised communications, physical assaults and vicious personalised attacks . . . the unconscious hope is that the nursing staff can do something positive with the communication' (Aiyegbusi, 2004: 114).

Until the communications and significations of self-harm can be recognised and understood, and where possible replaced with equally potent modes of expression and self-structure, it will retain its hold. The many needs it serves will continue to be met until other ways of soothing, creating, relieving and articulating the self can be found. The task of the therapist is to retain hope, at times when the self-harmer feels it is lost, and show them that despite their assaults on themselves and others, they can withstand this death dealing drive and re-integrate aggressive and loving feelings in a safe and manageable way. The hope can eventually be returned to the self-harmer and the addiction to these near-death experiences (Joseph, 1982) can loosen its grip. But for the therapist, who mirrors the despair as well as the hope of self-harm, it is essential to retain a sense of the meaning, order and private symbolisation that is being presented to them to unravel, respect and de-code.

Attacking the body to see what it can withstand and retain in embodied memories can be an attempt to know oneself. The capacity of those who work with people who self-harm to withstand its hostility, and their own distress, offers hope for the possibility of containment, and understanding. Through true relational contact, and the experience of a 'mental nurse', that is, another person whose mind can survive assault and remain intact and thoughtful, the self-harmer can eventually relinquish their own attacks on themselves and the pleasure of their own self-nursing. Murderous and suicidal thoughts can be kept in the mind, rather than enacted. It can become possible for emotional communication to be achieved and for the overwhelming pull to self-harm to diminish. Intimacy with others becomes increasingly possible without the overwhelming immersion in the self and its wounds; the self-enclosure, secrecy and ritual that self-harm creates can eventually be transformed into contact with another, a reaching out rather than a reaching in. The sense of becoming a whole person who can contain discordant parts and fragments will also be invaluable in the development of a capacity to manage self-harm. We have a duty to recognise and meet the hope expressed through marks on the body with the belief that we can contain and nurture the personal struggle to find a less self-destructive way of being and relating.

REFERENCES

Adshead, G. (1997) 'Written on the body: deliberate self-harm and violence', in E.V. Welldon and C. van Velson (eds) *A Practical Guide to Forensic Psychotherapy*, London: Jessica Kingsley Publishers.

Aieyegbusi, A. (2004) 'Thinking under fire: the challenge for forensic mental health nurses working with women in secure care', in N. Jeffcote and T. Watson (eds) *Working Therapeutically with Women in Secure Settings*, London: Jessica Kingsley Publishers.

Bick, E. (1968) 'The experience of skin in early object relations', in M. Harris Williams (ed.) (1987) *Collected Papers of Martha Harris and Esther Bick*, Perthshire: Clunie Press.

Campbell, D. and Hale, R. (1991) 'Suicidal acts', in J. Holmes (ed.) *Textbook of Psychotherapy in Psychiatric Practice*, London: Churchill Livingstone.

de Zulueta, F. (2006) *From Pain to Violence: The Traumatic Roots of Destructiveness* (second edition), New York: Wiley.

Favazza, A. (1996) *Bodies Under Siege: Self-Mutilation and Body Modification in Psychiatry and Culture* (second revised edition), Maryland, MD: John Hopkins University Press.

Freud, S. (1923) *The Ego and the Id*, SE XIX.

Glasser, M. (1979) 'Some aspects of the role of aggression in the perversions', in I. Rosen (ed.) *Sexual Deviation*, Oxford: Oxford University Press.

Grossmann, K., Thane, K. and Grossmann, K.E. (1981) 'Maternal tactual contact of the newborn after various postpartum conditions of mother–infant contact', *Developmental Psychology*, 17: 158–169.

Hegel, G.F. (1979) *Phenomenology of Spirit*, Oxford: Oxford University Press.

Joseph, B. (1982) 'Addiction to near death', *International Journal of Psycho-Analysis*, 63: 449–456.

Kettlewell, C. (2000) *Skin Game: A Memoir*, New York: St Martin's Griffin.

Klein, M. (1946) 'Notes on some schizoid mechanisms', in M. Klein (ed.) (1980) *Envy and Gratitude and Other Works 1946–1963*, London: Hogarth Press.

Miller, F. and Bashkin, E.A. (1974) 'Depersonalisation and self mutilation', *Psychoanalytic Quarterly*, 43: 638–649.

Motz, A. (2001) *The Psychology of Female Violence: Crimes Against the Body* (first edition), Hove: Routledge.

Motz, A. (2008) *The Psychology of Female Violence: Crimes Against the Body* (second edition), Hove: Brunner-Routledge.

Pines, D. (1993) *A Woman's Unconscious Use of Her Body*, London: Virago.

Stoller, R.J. (1975) *Perversion: The Erotic Form of Hatred*, New York: Pantheon Books.

Straker, G. (2006) 'Signing with a scar: understanding self-harm', *Psychoanalytic Dialogues*, 16: 93–112.

Ulnik, J. (2007) *Skin in Psychoanalysis*, London: Karnac Books.

Welldon, E.V. (1992) *Mother, Madonna, Whore: The Idealisation and Denigration of Motherhood*, New York: Guilford Press.

Winnicott, D.W. (1956) 'Delinquency as a sign of hope', *Collected Papers: Paediatrics Through Psychoanalysis*, London: Karnac Books/The Institute of Psychoanalysis (1992).

Yates, T.M. (2004) 'The developmental psychopathology of self-injurious behaviour: compensatory regulation in posttraumatic adaptation', *Clinical Psychology Review*, 24: 35–74.

Yates, T.M., Carlson, E.A. and Egeland, B. (2008) 'A prospective study of child maltreatment and self-injurious behaviour in a community sample', *Development and Psychopathology*, 20: 651–672.

Chapter 2

The paradox of self-harm

Anna Motz and Heather Jones

SELF-HARM AND SELF-SOOTHING

It appears paradoxical to create a wound to heal one, yet this is the drive so clearly found in self-harm, in which various, apparently conflicting, roles get played out on the surface of the body. This apparent paradox reveals the fight between life and death instincts found in the act of self-harming; here violence against the self is used to preserve life.

The way in which self-harm is used to create self-soothing as well as a demarcated sense of self can be best described in the words, ideas and feelings of an individual who has immersed themselves in the act, in order to convey the urgency of the behaviour, its complexity and its paradoxical nature. I use the words of Heather Jones throughout this chapter, interwoven with my text. She is a musician and artist who writes about her own self-harm, and its transformation in her work and in her choice of a snowflake tattoo on her wrist, as a reminder of how she has physically inscribed her pain onto her body. Heather's descriptions vividly illustrate the multiplicity of meanings and forms of self-harm as she discusses not only her self-cutting, slicing and self-soothing but also her drug addiction and involvement in abusive relationships as ways of hurting herself, some consciously chosen, others less so.

Heather describes many aspects of her experiences, and includes drug use, burning, self-cutting and piercing in her definition of self-harm, seeing all of these as manifestations of the same phenomenon of deliberate injury. She contrasts this with the other ways of harming oneself, by proxy as it were, through violent relationships or high levels of risk-taking.

RELEASE ME: SELF-HARM AND PERCEPTUAL ARMOUR

Heather describes self-harm as a shield against emotional pain.

> I think there is something quite real and clear about deliberately inflicting an injury on yourself, which is different than other incidences that result in harm to yourself. I think somewhere in the unconscious acts that result in damage to oneself there have to be many different effects to the senses, which I will try to explain as best I can, but in the deliberate and consciously chosen acts of injuring, whether that's by slicing, cutting, burning or that kind of drug taking, there is first an immediate sense of release. 'Release me' is the plea to your self, then a wave of something like release does seem to come as the response. I'm sure the pain response in the brain that is naturally occurring is something like an opiate effect, so taking any kind of opiates like heroin, especially if you're injecting, might not be dissimilar to the chemicals the brain makes when you inflict an injury on yourself – it's pretty immediate either way.
>
> What follows is like a blanketing effect, or like pain 'washing over and through you' then numbing, dampening and deadening and definitely like armour if armour is what you need – a perceptual armour. If it is a perceived pain you're in, and that could be emotional or psychological and not due to any actual threat or abuse from someone else, if you are alone, to find a perceived release from that pain it seems like a fairly accurate thing to do, considering the brain does respond to injury to the body, and drugs do have medicinal value . . . there are so many young people intuitively or instinctively doing this as a way to find a release from pain, whether actual or perceived.

THE NURSE

As Heather shows, the opportunity to be the Nurse to oneself is a powerful pull:

> The Nurse is borne of searching out a kind of healing.
>
> I began piercing myself, ears, nose, face when I was 14 – some of them I would take out right after, it was more about

> seeing how things felt and mind over matter, will over pain. I was always experimenting with pushing needles into strange places like my knees and hands to see, almost like acupuncture – I don't think this is as much to do with self-harm as it is perhaps an instinct to adorn, as we know has origins as far back as earliest man, but it is a strange compulsion to get started on at a young age where I come from, and it had some sort of effect, because I recall the same feeling of a sense of doing something very private and intimate with myself – most of it being entirely secretive – and then checking the wounds, nursing them even was a kind of care for myself that followed. I think somewhere in that sequence is the idea that seems to hold a clue to understanding something about the way it seems to unfold always with me, still to this day.
>
> I've become aware of how The Nurse perhaps can instrument self-harm. But rather than recoiling from my nature to respond to another human being in crisis, I would rather find ways to understand all this and manage the economy of give and take with myself better. To be a better nurse to myself as a daily practice, without it being about tending to a self inflicted wound or administering drugs to myself. I call this part of me 'The Nurse' because she administers a kind of nurture and love, albeit sometimes twisted, there is a kind of process at work that strives to be healing ultimately, even if it starts with perhaps doing damage to myself, it is borne of searching out a kind of healing.

This drive to heal through hurting is clearly described, both by Heather above, and in Straker's (2006) conception of self-harm as an attempt to create a self-structure; a sense of a meaningful relationship with oneself in place of a chaotic or fragmented one. The self-wounding should, as Heather notes, ultimately be replaced with self-nursing without a physical wound, or an act of self-injury through drug injection, but may require the act of violence as a starting point. In a symbolic sense, this is a kind of self-mothering that happens through a distortion of ordinary care-taking, evoking an injured child whose wounds need to be tended to. It seems clear that this need is greatest for those who have been deprived of this psychic and physical containment in early life, or have experienced other forms of neglect, or intrusive, disrupted and abusive care.

SELF-HARM AS A DEFENCE AGAINST INTIMACY

There is also a sense of terror in close relationships that have not provided holding in early life; self-harm serves to defend against the threat of loss, offering concrete action in the place of painful thoughts. Heather, who was herself adopted, describes how frightening it is to love someone; she imagines her own abandonment even from the moment of connecting with another person:

> I think some people are more predisposed than others to the effects of Oxytocin. I was interrupted like that at birth because I was adopted. I didn't have a natural bonding in infancy, and then I was shuffled around for a bit. I was four or five months old when I came to the parents that raised me, so I didn't have bonding. And that, I think maybe is why I feel the effects of Oxytocin really acutely, and so when I experience it like when my son was born and when I have fallen in love it really gets a hold of me in this really bizarre way. Maybe I get obsessive compulsive around it. Also I find it a real interruption in my senses and in my physical wellbeing even. I feel automatically I associate that feeling of bonding with what follows, which is loss. So, I think almost before I even feel a sense of bonding and love for a person I immediately jump to the end conclusion, which is pain and separation and loss.

TALISMAN

Self-harm has tremendous symbolic importance and binds the woman to her own body, sometimes to the exclusion of others. It can be viewed as both a defence against intimacy with another and an act of communication with the self. It can create something like a self-referential world, a private language, in which physical marks have unique signification and meaning. In this sense, the act of creation, of writing and marking, is evident too on the body. Heather describes this function as a Talisman.

> But the cuts and the scars and track marks become like a Talisman that you wear hidden – to anyone who gets close enough to see it's a symbolic marker, to what side of life you're walking on – 'how deep is your damage?'.

> I tried to think of other ways I could create a Talisman to remember to deal with the compulsion to slice or poke myself without doing it. A couple years ago while I had been pretty drug free for a long period of time, I felt stressed, and I kept having this sense that I wanted to slice my arms open. I knew I didn't want to inject drugs, and I knew I didn't want to start cutting myself, but my elbows felt invisible, like they were burning, a very strange energy built up in my frustrated elbows and blocked hands – I don't know – it was such a strong compulsion that instead of doing it I decided to draw a gash on each arm, with the Frankenstein-like suture lines crossing the gash. I thought it looked like a demonic grin, it felt like something demonic wanted out, so I wrote on one arm, 'take the heat out' and on the other, 'his fertile grin'. I repeated this for several days until it was almost my birthday and my friend suggested we get a tattoo together. In all those years I had never gotten a tattoo. When everyone and their mother was getting covered in ink, it seemed not a very personal thing to do with your body, but I thought it was time and so I got a Snowflake in white ink tattooed on the inside of my left wrist – as a Talisman to remind myself, 'take the heat out'.

The scar itself has great significance, and serves as a memento, war-wound, witness, and also as a site of entry into the inside of the body. It can become a site of archaeological excavation, in a sense, as well as a visual marker:

> It can be a Talisman to yourself, because you come back to it after the event in which it was created, after the deed is done, you've got this fresh wound, or these scars, you know, you might check it every now and then. You might, as you're getting dressed, get a glimpse of it, and that might bring you back to that moment where you now can reflect on what you did with the ability to think a little more clearly and with maybe a more rational mind at least.

SELF-HARM RE-INTEGRATES THE DIVIDED SELF

Self-injury is a means of both self-alienation and self-unification. In this apparent paradox of the split and re-unified self, the perpetrator/victim recognises themself as the author of their own actions:

> I needed to kill something in me, this awful feeling like worms tunnelling along my nerves. So when I discovered the razor blade, cutting, if you'll believe me, was my gesture of hope. All the chaos, all the sound and fury, the confusion and uncertainty and despair – all of it evaporated in an instant and I was for that minute, grounded, coherent, whole. Here is the irreducible self. I drew the line in the sand, marked my body as mine, its flesh and its blood under my command.
>
> (Kettlewell, 2000: 37)

Once again the blood itself is embraced and its release is seen to signify that the body is under the control of the mind, 'the blood marked my body as mine'.

SELF-HARM AND PERVERSION

The link between self-harm and sexual abuse has been well-documented in the literature and is evident in the population of women and men who are diagnosed with borderline personality disorder. The function of self-harm for those whose bodies have been used sexually by adults for their own gratification can include the release of tension and anxiety described earlier, but also reveal something of the part of the self that can act as perpetrator towards the helpless, victim aspect. Anna Freud's (1936 [1942]) notion of identification with the aggressor is helpful here, in that the will of the self-harmer is like the abuser, who can inflict pain, violation, marks and bruises on the body of the child, now in adult or adolescent form. In this way, the mind of the self-harmer can be free, split off from the brutality or violence that the body suffered.

Self-harm creates a powerful release from tension and offers a short-lived sense of euphoria; for some, an even orgasmic sense of relief and relaxation, adding to its addictive quality. This is, however, only achieved temporarily as the mind itself can quickly become occupied with intense images of self-harm, rehearsals of it, and destructive feelings, which another part of the mind would like to annihilate. The split is created not just between mind and body, but also between aspects of the mind itself. And, like other addictive behaviours, once acted on, the sense of release and euphoria quickly fades, and the desire to act again is intensified as feelings of guilt, depression, shame and emptiness return. It is this circular aspect of self-harm that gives it the quality of a perversion, addictive and compulsive. In another sense though, self-inflicted violence brands the body and can act as a means of warding off unwanted contact, keeping sexual advances at bay.

ATTACK ON BEAUTY

Heather describes how drug addiction and self-harm in the form of cutting and picking at the skin reflect the same impulses to ravage and destroy the self, and to shatter the outside impression that all is well. For people who have experienced trauma in childhood, their outward appearance can feel like a mask and self-injury a form of truth-telling. It can also be a defence against the threat of sexual overture and abuse, and in this sense is a protective act against being desired. Self-mutilation of the face, for example, is a highly public and often shocking sight, which seems to function as a way of warding off contact. It can also be understood as an attack on idealisations of the skin, of the outward appearance, that belies the inner horror.

> Shooting cocaine and speed inevitably gives way to this other kind of self-ravaging – picking the face – a lot more like a billboard of self-loathing when your face is all picked open into a mess of blemishes. I would become a horror – it always becomes a horror no matter how well you hide it.
>
> I have a friend who is probably the richest and most privileged person I know and sadly she seems to be bent on hardcore crack and smack addiction, but the strangest thing is, this is a woman who could afford any cosmetic treatment, facials, products, skin care, dermatologists etc., and when she gets in the mirror she comes out with sections of her skin picked and squeezed away till raw and bleeding – for no visible reason – and the only thing I can relate it to is that it's a pure expression of her self-hatred, for as much as she can conceal it with drugs and party talk and carefree behaviour, I know that she doesn't like that person looking back at her in the mirror very much the way she unwittingly ends up mutilating her face

just as soon as she starts scrutinising herself up close the way she does . . . being beautiful is sometimes a burden, because you get this unwanted attention, people don't see you for who you are inside, and you draw people in with a magnetism that maybe you aren't aware you have, where you then have to stand boundaries or else you get abused . . . sometimes it's about de-beautifying yourself.

SELF-HARM AND UNCONSCIOUS PAIN

As Heather and others frequently describe, self-harm arises at moments of despair, or intensity, and its reasons are not necessarily available to the conscious mind. It can also take the more complex form of attraction to someone else, a violent or emotionally abusive partner, who can enact their destructiveness for them. Women who self-harm often describe their unconscious attraction to destructive relationships; this is a kind of self-harm by proxy.

> [O]ne's own mind, is also so labyrinthine and smoke-screened for what the brain keeps hidden from our conscious minds, that what ails us or compels us can only be revealed through the intuitive process of making creative work, which for me is either writing, poetry, sometimes visual work, but mostly song writing, recording and performing music. That's how I have learned to survive – and understand. And when I allow myself the distractions from these practices for any length of time I start to whither and want to die.
>
> The Nurse appears in love as well – loving someone who is worse off than you, more damaged, someone who has had little or no real love in his life. The Nurse always rises to the challenge, even at great cost to myself. I always love the underdog. There is nothing more beautiful than a wounded sensitive soul. I can empathise – and perhaps feel a little closer to my own humanity, therefore suspending the usual disbelief or suspicion we have in others. I have had at times the delusional belief that if someone has known trauma and pain then he will know how I treasure love in the face of all this trauma and pain out there and in here. But in actuality some other kind of dynamic seems to always play out – something like a sado-masochistic exchange.

CREATIVITY AND SELF-HARM

Heather has used her creativity to manage what she calls her impulse to savage herself both through the tattoo she described earlier and through her art:

> Slicing – When I was young – after losing my virginity to someone who orchestrated the conquest in a less than special way – that was the first time I had ever cut myself – I carved a 'J' – his initial – in my forearm, then after that I started playing with blades and sewing needles and straight pins and all that. It very quickly took the form of adornment as it was the early eighties when Punk Rock was a new thing in Southern California with the safety pin through the cheek and multiple piercing aesthetic and so on – I learned one from the Mexicans in the neighbourhood by my school, or at least I think I did, perhaps it was a dream, or an urban myth – whichever, this image stuck with me from childhood, of the Cholla girls from the 'barrio' of Midway City who dressed and did their make-up a certain way with dark lipstick liner and heavy black coal eyes. I seem to remember they would also cut rhinestones into the skin on the line of their drawn-on eyebrows.
>
> That image whether real or imagined stayed with me till I was a teenager when I began experimenting with embedding gemstones into my hands – and more recently that image made its way into a song of mine, called *Midway City*, which has a verse that alludes to that imagery. So, by writing about things that linger in my memory that are attached to impulses to savage on myself in some way, I think it puts it into its proper context – that haunting image and the compulsion that followed it is exorcised by existing in a song that I sing.

Heather also describes this process in relation to her tattoo, in the shape of a snowflake:

> Then I wrote about all of that and put it in a song I called at first *Need* – then later when I recorded it the title became *Snowflake* –
>
> When a snowflake falls on my skin
> It takes the sting out of the tail of that demon
> When tonguing the teeth of his fertile grin

> I've not had that compulsion to slice or cut my arms or anywhere else for that matter ever since.

Heather describes how self-harm links to other forms of self-abuse, including drug addiction and eating disorders:

> Drug abuse, however, did rear its ugly head again finally – after about seven years of abstaining more or less from hard drugs, going through periods of serious health kicks that included the whole works: detox diets, Bikram Yoga, two to three litres of water a day, giving up alcohol and cigarettes for a period even . . . I even went as far as to have a course of colonic irrigation one year – which all made me realise something about myself: I do 'health' the same way I do harm. I now believe that I'm moderately anorexic, something I know that is a drive at a base level to be so extreme with my body. Eating very little along with a lot of physical activity can be like walking a tight rope with myself – trying to maintain the energy I need, conserving energy for when I need it, trying however I can to stabilise my mood, sometimes feeling too raw to be able to engage socially with people, all of these things became apparent.

Heather's statement that she 'does health' the way she 'does harm' expresses the fundamental difficulty she has in attending to herself, meeting her needs and providing for herself the kind of ordinary good-enough mothering of which she was deprived in infancy. This leaves her in a constant state of tension, attempting to care for herself without harming herself, and presents her with an ongoing dilemma – of facing her own self-destructiveness without disowning it in a false, unsustainable way. It is a part of her, and links her to her history, but threatens, at times, to consume her, and so she has had to find a way to use it positively. Her creative expression in writing and music appears to offer her the possibility of both carving an identity and releasing her feelings without destroying herself in the process.

The idea of purification, of taking away the toxic feelings through colonic irrigation, self-harm, violent attacks on herself or abstinence from alcohol and drugs, is central to the motivation for self-harming and it may be that this drive for perfection, for a pure state of being, is the universal fantasy underlying self-harm. The dissolution of the fantasy of purification and the capacity to bear the fact of destructive forces that co-exist with loving and nurturing ones is a central task for those who self-harm.

REFERENCES

Freud, A. (1936 [1942]) *The Ego and the Mechanisms of Defence*, London: Hogarth Press.

Kettlewell, C. (2000) *Skin Game: A Memoir*, New York: St Martin's Griffin.

Straker, G. (2006) 'Signing with a scar: understanding self-harm', *Psychoanalytic Dialogues*, 16: 93–112.

Part 2

The wider context

Systemic issues and self-harm

Chapter 3

'Why do you treat me this way?'

Reciprocal violence and the mythology of 'deliberate self-harm'

Christopher Scanlon and John Adlam

> Between the acting of a dreadful thing
> And the first motion all the interim is
> Like a phantasma or a hideous dream . . .
> The Genius and the mortal instruments
> Are then in Council, and the state of man
> Like to a little kingdom suffers then
> The nature of an insurrection.
> (Shakespeare, *Julius Caesar*, Act 2, Scene 1)

INTRODUCTION

> [W]hatsoever a man soweth, that shall he also reap.
> (St. Paul, *Epistle to the Galatians*, 6: 7)

Traumatised people who attack, poison or mutilate their own bodies do so as a defence against a set of impulses that might otherwise result in them attacking the bodies of others and also to preserve themselves from internalised threats to their own minds, which, unopposed, they fear would cause the 'insurrection' that would drive them mad. The phenomenon that is *self-harm* is made all the more complex by widespread and pervasive attitudes within modern mental health, social care, education and criminal justice systems to the effect that people who do harm or neglect themselves do so *deliberately*. Consequently, societal and professional attitudes, rooted in paradigms of *rationality*, are too often judgemental and derogatory – and therefore also harm-full. The quasi-rational strategies, policies, procedures and clinical models that are then put in place to respond to the problem of 'deliberate self-harm' frequently become thoughtless and, at times, actively punishing. Patients who 'deliberately' attack their own bodies are therefore experienced as 'deliberately' manipulative, 'deliberately' attention seeking and 'deliberately' refusing to be well and to conform to societal ideas about what 'being well' entails. These attitudes serve only to humiliate the person with the mutilated body and to further reduce their self-esteem; and so exacerbate the 'presenting problem'. At this point, the parallel violence between the individual and the system of care has become reciprocal and the question about who, or what, started it becomes moot as each party becomes locked into a vicious cycle rooted in a mutual attribution of malign *intent*. Sufferer and carer alike find themselves locked in reciprocal and identical complaints: 'why do you treat me this way?'.

The National Institute for Clinical Excellence Guideline (2004: 7) defines self-harm as 'self-poisoning or injury, *irrespective of the apparent purpose* of the act' (our italics). Skegg (2005: 1472) comments that 'the adjective "deliberate" is now not favoured by patients in the UK'. Similarly, the Royal College of Psychiatrists (2006: 1) advises service users that the term 'deliberate self-harm' is inaccurate and going out of use, adding that 'the word "deliberate" unhelpfully blamed self-harm as a reaction to painful feelings'. However, the term, with its attribution of intent and free will to the individual, and its unfortunate common usage as the acronym 'DSH', remains widespread and often automatic in clinical practice in the UK. This difference of perspective between the guidance of policy makers and the realities of practitioners and service users has far-reaching implications for the practices, policies and procedures that are put in place to respond to people who actively damage or severely neglect their bodies.

OVERTHROWING THE KINGDOM: THE IRRATIONAL AND THE NON-RATIONAL

In this chapter we offer a further critique of the supposedly deliberate or intentional quality of such actions through a considered review of constructs of self-harm and with particular reference to *personality disorder* – acknowledging that not all self-harm and self-neglect is related to personality disorder and that not all people with personality disorder damage, mutilate and poison their bodies (although in our experience, in one way or another, most do). We argue that such behaviours can be understood as emerging from the subjects' internalised experiences of interpersonal violation and neglect, which, in turn, have given rise to violent states of mind. That is to say, we consider that the subject most often is in a violent state of mind because this state of mind has been *violently pushed into* them. In common with Chapman (1983), we suggest that it is important to distinguish the irrational from the non-rational and so to understand self-harm as non-rational: that is to say, rooted in what Schön (1983) called 'the swampy lowlands' of affective and relational domains of understanding and misunderstanding rather than more cognitive, behavioural, conditional and rational domains.

In this sense, between the impulse to violence and the 'acting of a dreadful thing', the 'little kingdom' which is the rational part of the mind has indeed suffered 'the nature of an insurrection'; but rather than judging such actions as irrational, they are better understood as a product of the individual being overwhelmed by *non-rational* experiences – that is, by experiences of distress. We suggest that the system of care therefore does *violence* to the individual who attacks their own body by attributing a rational intentionality ('they did it deliberately') to them in this way. This attribution repeats a violence already 'done unto' the individual when their distress is associated with a low social worth and construed as 'malingering', laziness or petulance rather than in the somehow more *deserving* categories of 'mental illness' or 'diminished responsibility' (Roth, 1972; Stockwell, 1974; Kelly and May, 1982; Johnson and Webb, 1995). We take particular issue with the acronym 'DSH' because in *its* laziness and petulance, this societal attribution is no less violent than is the suturing of a cut wrist without anaesthetic just because it is *rationalised* under the heading of 'A&E' procedures (Norton and Dolan, 1995; Adshead, 2001). Declerck (2006), in his work on the homeless people of Paris, makes a similar point about *our* insidious societal sadism when he describes how the plight of those people whose precarious attachment to wider societal norms is compounded by our need to punish them by ensuring that health and welfare provision will always remain structurally inadequate. He suggests that we are punishing them because we hate them, and we hate them because they refuse, and in their refusal are experienced as mocking everything that we hold dear (Declerck, 2006: 163).

These problematic societal and professional attitudes to violated bodies are so pervasive because societally we would prefer not to think about why another human being would want to attack themselves. The phenomenon is felt to threaten our ideas about health and well-being in the same way that those who are 'intentionally homeless' threaten our idea of what it is to be and to feel housed (Adlam and Scanlon, 2005; Declerck, 2006). This understandable avoidance is rooted in the fear that we might all become infected by the madness that is both at the roots and in the branches of this bizarre plant. For example, recent newspaper reports in the UK responded to the undisputed increase in young women attending A&E departments following incidents of self-harm by proposing that these women were imitating and emulating certain celebrities who were seen to be self-harming. It was as if it was being suggested that self-harm was so contagious that otherwise healthy and happy young people could 'catch' it from the television – rather than tackle an alternative analysis: that there may an increasingly large number of young women who are struggling to express their disaffection and pained sense of alienation.

As a society, we do not distinguish attacks on one's own body from attacks on another's body, in the sense that we consider both to be offensive: we merely allocate the societal response to different parts of the system of care, which then indulge in varying types of 'treatment', depending on the perceived *degree* of responsibility and 'deliberateness' involved in this offensiveness. As Motz (2001) reminds us in the subtitle to her central text on female violence, these behaviours are 'crimes against the body': if the patient who drinks bleach when the 'kingdom of his mind' is overthrown, were instead to enact his rage against another, a more overt type of punishment would be visited upon him. We prefer to believe that whether or not a person attacks themselves is a question of choice and so the responsibility for whether or not the person exercises that choice is located entirely in their mind and body. That he may thereby be also *unconsciously* expressing his non-rational experience of his suffering becomes difficult to hold in mind. We have discussed elsewhere how these statements also hold true in relation to the violent offender whose attacks are on other people's bodies (Scanlon and Adlam, 2008, 2009).

These supposed preferences defend and reinforce the notion that violence, whether directed against one's own body or against the body of another, is ultimately a rational phenomenon, the behavioural end product of faulty or deviant cognitions, and that if we can put in place proper policies, procedures and treatments, then we can put a stop to it. This is a comforting thought because we do not like to think about our own impulses to attack and our own capacity for violence – not least for a widespread societal retaliatory violence, which, like the Queen of Hearts, literally calls for certain of these offenders' heads to roll. As a society we unconsciously credit ourselves that we 'deliberately' *abstain* from attacking our own bodies and tend therefore to deprecate or dismiss the 'inadequacy' of those of us of 'lesser will', who we experience as 'deliberately' *indulging* themselves in an impulsive selfishness. The system of care joins with the individual who attacks their own body in too readily embracing explanations for these violent behaviours that are predicated upon conscious cognitions. The patient who tells us 'I stabbed myself to make you pay attention to what I'm saying' is in effect (although *not* in intent) reassuring us of our own importance in our clinical role: 'If you attend to me properly you will make me (and therefore yourselves) feel better'. In this way the real suffering is much easier to dismiss or to dissociate than it would be if we were instead confronted with a more accurate and disturbing non-rational explanation: 'I stabbed myself with no thought as to the outcome, in a violent state of mind that I could not manage or understand, which was triggered in the here and now for reasons that I was not aware of and which I found frightening . . .'.

By means of this non-rational and unconscious collusion, both patient and practitioner – the socially excluded individual and the system of care – are thereby delivered from the prospect of confronting the reciprocal violence arising from the hostile dependency that binds them each to the other. Rather, we maintain that this reciprocal violence can only really be understood through a detailed examination of the complex historical, unconscious, non-rational and reciprocal interpersonal, group and psychosocial binding, within which we all live and die. Towards the end of this chapter we will offer a vignette taken from a reflective practice group to illustrate some of these dynamics and to emphasise that it is *our* violence towards, or our collusion with others' violation of, individuals who self-harm that needs to be worked on, if their violence and self-violation is to abate.

'DELIBERATE SELF-HARM': MODELS AND DEFINITIONS

> [T]he explanation of any phenomenon should make as few assumptions as possible, eliminating those that make no difference in the observable predictions of the explanatory hypothesis or theory. 'Occam's Razor' (methodological principle originally attributed to William Ockham, c. 1288–1348)

As we have outlined above, we believe that the term 'deliberate self-harm' is problematic and conceptually incoherent. It may therefore be useful to begin with an overview of how we consider that we – and our patients – came to be burdened with the notion in the first place.

A World Health Organization multi-centre study offers the following definition for deliberate self-harm:

> An act with non-fatal outcome in which an individual deliberately *initiates* a non-habitual behaviour, that without intervention from others will cause self-harm, or deliberately ingests a substance in excess of the prescribed or generally recognized dosage, and which *is aimed at realizing changes that the person desires via the actual or expected physical consequences.*
> (Platt *et al.*, 1992; quoted in Haw *et al.*, 2001: 48; our italics)

There are two conceptual difficulties with this definition. First, the patterns of *repeated* attacks on the body that are, in our observation, most commonly associated with negative reactions from clinicians and from wider society, are disregarded in favour of a focus of attention on the single act, as if it could be understood in isolation. In this way, the act by which the behavioural sequence is *initiated* is thus taken out of its social environment; it is brought into 'the hospital' and so becomes decontextualised. The *deliberate* quality of the behaviour thereby becomes located in the *first* such act, whereas we would argue precisely the opposite: that in so far as the term 'deliberate' is at all accurate (although still not helpful) it applies to *subsequent* acts in the repetitive cycle. Our understanding of this cycle of violence would be that, in the small part of the act that is consciously motivated, the individual is seeking to *recapture the memory* of the relief that he *associates with* the initial act of violence. Some quality of *deliberation* (a slightly different point) is often associated with the rituals that develop to sustain the behaviour; in much the same way as the heroin injector goes in pursuit of ever more elaborate rituals, and ever diminishing returns, in search of the experience he associates with that first 'rush' or desired state of anaesthesia.

The second difficulty with the above definition is that the suggested aim of the 'act with non-fatal outcome' is to influence an object, be it an individual or the wider system of care, to act in a certain way in response; which, we suggest, implausibly implies an almost Machiavellian, 'psychopathic' capacity for manipulative medium-term planning. The attribution to the individual of the expectation of a specific desired consequence again implies that the act is in some way intentional, rather than driven by unconscious cycles of repetition that become habitual and by the sufferer's incapacity *to think*, and in particular to think about the experience of unbearable pain associated with the loneliness of being excluded from active and conscious participation in both their internal world and social world discourses.

Skegg (2005) lists the wide range of terms in use worldwide to describe what she calls 'non-fatal self-inflicted harm': 'attempted suicide', 'parasuicide', 'self-poisoning' or 'self-injury', 'self-mutilation' as well as 'deliberate self-harm'. She notes that the term 'deliberate self-harm' is used in the UK for 'all episodes survived, regardless of intent', which confuses rather than clarifies, because the words 'deliberate' and 'intentional' are in effect synonymous. More consistently, but in our view equally problematically, Klonsky *et al.* (2003: 1501) define deliberate self-harm as 'the intentional injury of one's own body without apparent suicidal intent'; the manifestation of what Pattison and Kahan (1983) have described as a 'deliberate self-harm syndrome'. Through these and other more general definitions, it appears that the term 'deliberate' came into being in order to distinguish *genuine* suicide attempts from a sort of *para-violence* that was not aimed at 'deliberately' killing the body of the self. Motz (2001) notes this distinction and the contrast between those authors whose models are predicated upon an absence of suicidal intent and those who hold that, even in cases of non-fatal self-harm, a very real, but unconscious, self-murder is being attempted (Campbell and Hale, 1991).

Isaacson and Rich (2001: 213) offer an even more general and problematically tautological definition of 'deliberate self-harm' as 'any act by an individual with the intent of harming himself or herself physically and which may result in some harm'. They are also more hesitant about the assumption of conscious intent:

> Deliberate self harm may also constitute a more or less dysfunctional way of achieving wanted changes of life – for example, escape, attention, manipulation of others. The intent in each person is complex and ambivalent. Although some aspects of suicidal behaviour might be interpreted as *rational*, the behaviour is contrary to basic biological principles of survival.
>
> (Isaacson and Rich, 2001: 213; our italics)

We would suggest that attempts to categorise these *acts* on the basis of how they relate to a 'deliberate' or intentional attempt to kill oneself (or internalised others) are also problematic because they do not allow for the possibility that these actions could also be understood as violent acts of *self-preservation*, where the unconscious aim is to stay alive in the best way available at that moment. Gabbard and Wilkinson (1994) make a similar point when they address the potential dangers inherent in the clinician's wish to 'cure' the suicidal patient of their wish to die: for it may be the vitality inherent in this 'suicidality' that keeps them alive. Caught between the Scylla of the unbearable heaviness of being and the Charybdis of doing enough bodily harm to *preserve* one's life, the individual must steer a difficult and treacherous course and there are people who, despite their longing for safe passage, are nonetheless pulled into the whirlpool or pushed onto the rocks that spell out their doom. The question here would be whether there was an intention to die or whether death was the unlooked-for consequence of failed attempts to stay alive. It is very dangerous for the self-harming individual who has 'deliberately' stayed inside the fatal dose of paracetamol – or who, in the deep cutting of his body, repeatedly 'manages' to miss a main artery – to be met with the attribution of 'manipulation', out of which springs the dreadful, exasperated and, unfortunately, not so uncommon, violent challenge: 'If you *really* wanted to kill yourself, you really should do it like *this* . . .'.

Brown *et al.* (2002) explored reasons for self-harm or suicidal behaviours in women diagnosed with borderline personality disorder but noted some limitations of their study in that 'people may not know or remember their intents, or their intentions may not always correspond to the actual variables controlling their behaviour' (2002: 201). They documented a range of self-reported reasons for self-harm or attempted suicide, which fell into broad categories of affect dysfunction, a wish to avoid/escape and interpersonal influence. In an earlier study of self-reported reasons for taking an overdose (Bancroft *et al.*, 1976), a third of respondents reported that they were seeking help, 42 per cent were 'escaping from the situation', 19 per cent said that they were 'trying to influence someone' but 52 per cent of respondents knew only that they were seeking to obtain 'relief from a terrible state of mind'. There is a dangerous and endangering tension between practitioners' views that such acts are *deliberate* and manipulatively *seeking something* and service users' reports that their actions were motivated 'more simply' by the painful desire to escape from an overwhelming experience of distress in relation to which they felt powerless: within which they had a very limited sense of agency and personal autonomy, and so a very real sense of *diminished responsibility*. So long as the system of care is covertly criminalising these actions through the attribution of intentionality, the very understandable wish for relief from these terrible states of mind, even if momentarily attainable, will be short-lived indeed.

Psychoanalytically informed accounts have tended to emphasise the importance of non-rational, unconscious aims and drives in the individual and the publication of related unconscious communications to internal and external 'others'. Adshead (1997: 111) describes deliberate self-harm as a 'symptom of internal distress, which has both a private and a public message'. She explores links to psychotic states of mind associated with borderline personality disorder and notes that dissociation 'may help to explain why *rational* argument, or emphasis on thinking alone, does not help patients to stop' (1997: 111; our italics). Campbell and Hale (1991: 288) describe suicide as 'an act aimed at destroying the self's body *and* tormenting the mind of another'; an act which they see as a reflection of a psychotic or perverse state of mind in which all awareness of the extent of the actual violent quality of the act is unconscious. Welldon (1988, 1996) includes self-harm among the symptomatic indicators of perverse states of mind in women. She suggests that men tend to enact violent and perverse actions against others – including women; whereas for women the object of their violent actions 'is usually against themselves, either against their bodies or against objects which they see as their own creations: their babies' (Welldon, 1988: 8). In her later volume Motz (2008) builds on this hypothesis to explore in detail the psychodynamics of self-harm in women, which she describes as 'a powerful bodily enactment of psychic pain' (2008: 195) and a 'meaningful communication about psychological distress [which] therefore serves a valuable function' (2008: 234). However, none of these authors addresses the problematic nature of the attribution of intentionality and they also tend to use the terms 'self-harm' and 'deliberate self-harm' interchangeably. The consequence of this, we suggest, is to negate the *potential* value of the function of the *non-rational* communication, by attributing a *negative* value to the act itself.

Motz (2001) also makes the important feminist case that some women can regain and reclaim a sense of autonomy in their lives through self-harming behaviours. Referring to a study of women who self-harm in special hospitals (Liebling and Chipchase, 1992), she writes that self-harm 'may be the only means by which some degree of control can be reclaimed by the women, and some ownership of their lives asserted' (Motz, 2001: 233). We accept the force of this position but we would also argue that this putative reclamation of autonomy can only really be understood as a rationalisation *in hindsight*, which, although retrospectively recovering some potential for creativity from the violence, does not explain or account for the violence at the time of the enactment itself. Indeed, we would argue that the attribution of 'deliberateness', even if couched in terms of a creative reclamation of a sense of self-esteem, threatens to undermine any political gains that might be made, since societally such actions are still perceived as 'manipulative' or 'attention seeking' and so these women may continue, albeit inadvertently, to stoke the fire of their own structural oppression.

As regards men who attack their own bodies, neither Welldon nor Motz overlooks the phenomenon of male self-harm and self-neglect. However, it is our experience that their shared idea that it is women who self-harm and men who attack others has to a significant extent taken hold within the system of care, with the unintended consequence that male self-harm has increasingly come to be seen as anomalous and so more hidden; as if it only happens for want of an external object against whom to direct the aggression. The probable trends towards both the under-reporting and the under-estimation of male self-harm, for example in relation to anorexia and bulimia, may therefore be exacerbated. The dichotomous argument also assumes, contrary to usual definitions, that personality-disordered persons, whether men or women, have a secure and lasting sense of their own gendered state and place within the wider social world (Akhtar, 1995). For this reason, in this chapter, we have adopted the otherwise counterintuitive male pronoun except where giving a specific case example.

'INTENTIONALITY DISORDER': VIOLENT AND UNHOUSED STATES OF MIND

> . . . the lives of the people here who, though they have an instinctive craving for human contacts, can't bring themselves to yield to it, because of the mistrust that keeps them apart. For it's common knowledge that you can't trust your neighbour; he may pass the dis-ease [our hyphen] to you without your knowing it . . . .
>
> (Albert Camus, *La Peste*)

Brenman (1985: 279) explicitly explores the notion of treatment as providing a psychological home for the patient, where mutual shared concern involves 'the mother giving a home for the baby inside her mind, and the baby giving a home for the real mother inside his mind'. For Winnicott (1986), *home is where we start from* and the 'secure base' of Bowlby's attachment theory (1969, 1973, 1980) is another way of saying that in ordinary development there is a core experience of 'home', that is, of an experience of oneself as being *housed* in another person's mind and so able to live comfortably in one's own body and hence take up one's place in the wider social world. In modern attachment theory, failures of reflective function and mentalisation – the capacity to know of another's mind, having felt known by it – are held to be directly related to the incidence of violence (de Zulueta, 1993; Adshead, 2002; Bateman and Fonagy, 2004). We propose an explicit formulation of a *violent state of mind*: one in which both *memory* and *desire* have become so unbearable that *thoughts* have become unthinkable (Bollas 1987) and the mind is in the grip of an overwhelming internal pressure to *evict* these elements of experience.

People who attack their bodies, therefore, could be understood as communicating something of their experience of not being, or having been, securely housed in the minds of others. This experience becomes a generalised complaint, a grievance, which is rooted in profound mistrust of the accommodation and hospitality offered (or withheld) by those formal societal structures that we would ordinarily look to in order to help us feel safe. Elsewhere we have discussed these states of mind as an indication of what we have called an *unhoused mind* and have considered the disturbed social relationships, consequent upon the need to publicise and communicate this state of unhousedness, as a form of psychosocial dismemberment, expressed as an incapacity or an unwillingness to join in or take part (Adlam and Scanlon, 2005; Scanlon and Adlam, 2008, 2009). Essentially, we are therefore examining the phenomenon of self-harm as a symptom of *group* or social dis-ease [sic], indicative of what Foulkes (1948: 127) described as the 'interpersonal location of disturbance' or what Bion (1961) might have called a disturbance of 'groupishness'. Our focus is on the disturbed and disturbing reciprocal responses acted out *between* a *self-perceived* societal 'in-group' and a self-harming 'out-group'; and in particular on the violating society's attribution of *intentionality* towards this 'out-group', which is constructed as being 'deliberately' non-conforming.

As a consequence of the incapacity of the violently self-harming out-group to feel safe, either within their own minds or within formal societal structures, it follows that living and working with people who attack their own bodies is often as difficult and demanding for friends and families, mental health, social care, education and community justice practitioner teams and organisations as it is for the attacker himself. This is so because, as suggested above, these attacks, in their various forms, are both an interpersonal communication and a publication of both an inner experience of distress and of dissatisfaction with the attacker's current social world (Adshead, 2002). The grief underpinning this distress cannot be expressed in other, more adaptive and socially acceptable, ways because it is unbearable – and so also unthinkable – but crucially, it is also because it is rooted in a need to communicate, in the here and now, something of the profoundly disturbed and disturbing interpersonal, familial and social relationships that are at the historical roots of their current distress.

Any clinician working within the field will have observed histories of childhood abuse and neglect, and listened to painful and anguished stories of physical and psychic intrusion and abandonment that are both the cause and the effect of a very real sense of impoverishment of body, mind and spirit. The sense of inner emptiness that follows from this transgenerational communication of distress brings in its wake further impoverishment as the abused become abusive, the neglected neglect, the deprived deprive and the violated become violent (de Zulueta, 1993; Sinason, 1996). The spirit is broken and a vicious spiral of violent impoverishment is taken into a heart and mind that then wants to scream about the savagery of gods and men (Alvarez, 1974). The 'cry for help', which is the most common attribution to such presentations and which is also often accepted by the individual themselves, may simply be a 'cry of pain' (Williams and Pollock, 2000): the silent, anguished 'O' of Munch's *The Scream*. This howl of pain might also be understood as an attachment behaviour, *instinctively* seeking proximity to the primary care-giver (Bowlby, 1969), but we would argue that it would be a giant leap, and in terms of Occam's Razor an unnecessary one, to attribute 'intent' to this cry, any more than we would be right to attribute *rational* intent to the proximity-seeking cry of the infant.

Liminal lives: *Schwellenangst* and the problem of 'temporary housing'

In order to continue to live, such individuals always carry with them a sense of longing to rediscover the psychic and interpersonal home that they lost (or never experienced). This wish for a psychological home is nonetheless a terrifying prospect because it is also often equated with a dread of being engulfed, of losing all sense of one's identity (Glasser, 1996). Thus, they fear the 'security', the entrappedness of 'being inside' something, while all the time there is a contradictory and equally strong hope that they could be known (Menzies, 2001), and so inside the mind of others. The German word *Schwellenangst*, literally the anxiety of or on the threshold, captures this state of living precisely. Caught between these two poles of longing and fear, life becomes an endless oscillation between the intrusiveness of pushing things inside and the abandoning distances of outside; the painful loneliness and longing of the outsider; a liminal, threshold, borderline state of being.

Our shared incapacity to bear these painfully oscillating states of mind, to reflect on the experiences of the profound sadness underpinning them, results in the grief itself being lost from the communication. In its place, a profoundly painful grievance emerges and is publicised and communicated to the surrounding world and to all who are accommodated within it in ways that the 'unhoused' are not. This, essentially antisocial, attempt to communicate something of this experience through self-harm is a violent one that is simultaneously directed against the inner and outer *bodies* that can accommodate neither their grief nor their grievance. That is to say, it is directed against the individual's own body, where the pain has come to reside, and is simultaneously an articulation of a complaint to and about the social world from which the individual has become dis-membered. This mutilation or poisoning of their own body is often experienced as bringing relief from this inner torment, born of this sense of dis-memberment and social exclusion through the relocation of this painful state of mind into the precarious and temporary housing of their pained body.

Of course, the sense of relief provided by this temporary housing is short-lived, and as the grievance returns they once again become psychically unhoused and psychosocially dis-membered. All unconscious and non-rational attempts to evict the painfulness and the distress from the mind and relocate it into the body are doomed to fail; and, in their failing, establish instead a vicious and offensive *spiral* of violence and violation that becomes habitual, repetitive, recidivistic and eventually addictive as these failed attempts to find refuge become ever more frantic. For some, the centre of this vicious spiral is suicide (or murder); but for most, it represents a constant and painfully oscillating attempt to find an accommodation for their distress – an unconscious, restless attempt to find a home. In the case of individuals who self-harm, this metaphorical psychosocial dis-memberment is also expressed through a literal dismembering of their own physical body that involves a very real, aggrieved and grievous, bodily harm.

INTENTIONALITY AND HARM MINIMISATION: 'SAFE' SELF-HARM?

It follows from this psychosocial and group dynamic analysis of self-harm that it is not easy for the system of care to know quite how violent it has become in its attempts to offer responses and remedies for the problem. A case in point is offered by the recent treatment initiatives that involve offering 'safe' razor blades to hospitalised self-harming patients, on the principle that harm minimisation is felt to be the greater good (Royal College of Nursing, 2006). In this model the materials for self-harm are provided to the patient by the clinician as part of the ongoing negotiation and implementation of a care plan, in much the same way as clean 'works' are provided to intravenous drug users by substance misuse services. The wisdom of the latter example, both in relation to concern for the drug user himself, *and* in relation to public health concerns about the spread of infection, is perhaps now beyond dispute. The notion of 'safe self-harm' is much more problematic.

In both examples the ancient maxim of Hippocrates, 'first, do no harm', is replaced by a more *modern* approach, which might be stated as 'if possible, and for now, do less harm'. It is interesting, however, to explore the differences between the two scenarios presented. In the case of the problem drug user, the 'intention' behind the policy is to reduce the damage, both to the individual and to society. In the case of providing 'safe' blades for cutting, we would argue that this inevitably involves an increased level of interpersonal violence, which, although cloaked in the rhetoric of harm reduction, invites the clinician into an active collusion with the perpetration of a 'crime against the body' or into the negotiation of an acceptable level of violence, in ways that would not be accommodated if this were a crime against someone else's body. The moral and ethical issues of this dynamic are complex indeed and it is beyond the scope of this chapter to explore them to the full. However, if we peel back the lid from this particular can of worms it may be possible to glimpse what could be a truly alarming conclusion. Could it be that, rather than distributing clean 'works' to drug users to minimise the damage they do to themselves, we do it *primarily* to protect ourselves from the threat of *contagion* that is more concretely manifested in the spread of HIV and hepatitis. The individual who self-harms is not a threat to us in quite the same way. Whereas the 'drug user' threatens 'us' with a contagion of real physical disease, which calls forth from us a physical response, self-harm presents us with the type of psychosocial *dis-ease* that we imagine we can more easily isolate and attribute to an intentionality, which we can then dismiss as individual psychopathology. It is then *safer to retaliate* because we will not catch anything. The 'sanitised' and socially sanctioned *violence* thus meted out under cover of the patient's right ('intentionally') *to choose* can only take place under controlled conditions in a quiet room on a hospital ward. By way of contrast, we have not yet heard anyone calling for safe self-harm for prisoners, where the fantasy might be that there could indeed be a 'deliberate' spreading of a real infection from blood-letting.

THE STRUCTURAL PROBLEM WITH 'DELIBERATE SELF-HARM'

We have emphasised the violence of self-harm and the violent states of mind that produce it, and we have followed our theme of reciprocal violence, exploring ways in which the individual who self-harms has further violence visited upon him, meted out by societal structures who can themselves be seen as experiencing violent states of mind in which unbearable thoughts and feelings have to be evacuated. Gilligan (1996), using an epidemiological analogy, describes violence as like a disease and makes a distinction between *structural* and *behavioural* violence. The latter, the interpersonal violence, the dis-ease of the individual, he sees as always taking place in the context of the former, that is, within the formal structures, strictures and expectations of an infected and sick society from which the *deviant* or the *dispossessed* are excluded. In a similarly powerful political and philosophical critique, Zizek (2008: 1) refers to these dynamics in relation to what he calls 'systemic violence', which he defines in terms of 'the often catastrophic consequences of the smooth functioning of our economic and political systems'. He distinguishes *subjective* violence, equivalent to Gilligan's concept of behavioural violence, from two forms of *objective* violence: the 'systemic' and the 'symbolic', the latter of which is manifest in a corruption of language which is also typically to be found in traumatised organisations as described by Hopper (2003). The term 'deliberate self-harm', we argue, is an example of this symbolic violence; and the problematic response to the subjective violence of self-harm is, in Zizek's terms, the function of our assumption that nothing untoward is happening until a violent act occurs:

> [S]ubjective violence . . . is seen as a perturbation of the 'normal', peaceful state of things. However, objective violence is precisely the violence inherent to this 'normal' state of things. Objective violence is invisible since it sustains the very zero-level standard against which we perceive something as subjectively violent.
>
> (Zizek, 2008: 2)

Jordan (1996) also addresses the problem of social exclusion from a socioeconomic perspective and reaches broadly similar conclusions. He observes that although individuals are at their most vulnerable when they have fewest personal capacities and social resources, they are, nonetheless, able to manage themselves and participate usefully in a society that is prepared to invest in a desire to offer them effective protection and meaningful opportunities to participate. The links in the UK between social exclusion and the increased ill-health and violence that follow have also been observed by Charlesworth *et al.* (2004). In this epidemiological review of poverty-related health problems, they conclude that societies with larger income differentials are likely to have a larger burden of relative deprivation, a more hierarchical social structure and so place a greater burden on those who they describe as 'living' inferiority. In their epidemiological study of adverse childhood experiences in the United States, Fellitti *et al.* (1998) further conclude that psychosocial deprivations and traumatic events also have serious consequences for general levels of health and a reduced life expectancy. Skegg (2005) identifies low socioeconomic status, low levels of education, low income, adverse childhood experiences and poverty as clear risk factors predicting self-harm in adulthood, with self-harm admission rates shown to be higher in areas of relative deprivation and childhood socioeconomic disadvantage.

These various psychosocial, political and philosophical analyses suggest that not only are power differentials, relative deprivation and social exclusion inevitable within our current social structures, but also that we have a need for them in order that 'we' can have a more secure sense of our own well-being in relation to 'them', the dis-eased. If self-harm might be understood as an 'inarticulate speech of the heart', a murmuring symptom of the dis-ease that becomes located between people (Foulkes, 1948), then perhaps part of what cannot be articulated, when the individual is in the grip of a violent state of mind, is the sense of alienation and exclusion linked to psychosocial dis-memberment: his sense of protest and outrage at an excluding but also violent and dangerously self-centred world. This is a world that experiences him as deliberately, intentionally disgusting and provocative, and so judges him to be *intentionally offensive*. As such, he is seen as providing 'us' with the rationale for placing him 'beyond the pale' because, through his actions, he has *intentionally* placed himself beyond the pale! Small wonder, then, that there are so few words for this experience.

The self-harming or self-neglecting individual then provides us with further ammunition for us to visit our violence upon him, in that he offers us, in hindsight, various rationalisations for his behaviour that allow us to convince ourselves that his actions were intentional. This is, of course, partly because he sees us as more powerful than he is and tends often to feel that he may as well give us what he thinks we want to hear. He says to us, for example, that cutting brings relief from his distress, or that he had to act out in order to achieve his conscious goal of being admitted to hospital or to 'get back' at his abusive family. In joining with him in seeing his actions as *rational* and intentional, we collude with him in not wanting to understanding the madness to which his distress has brought him. But this is a double-edged blade that also cuts into our collusion with the madness of this position – although this is more difficult for us to acknowledge. The outcome of this reciprocal madness is that we are in danger of colluding with the patient's idea that 'they' have gained a major victory over 'us', in 'their' battle not to get better.

However, it is for them a victory won at a terrible cost, for we, the 'defeated', move on from the rationality to infer intentionality and promptly, in one way or another, to slam the door back in their faces. If, on the other hand, we could reflect on the madness of this co-constructed 'intentionality disorder', it would then become harder to permit the latent or overt violence that we can find ourselves intending to do unto our clients; to punish them for their 'deliberate' refusal to gratify our professional and personal selves by getting better and needing less from us. In order to do this, of course, we would need to take account of our own non-rational experience, which we fear as we fear madness itself. We might also have to ask why we organise ourselves societally and in groups and families in such a way as to do so much violence to certain sections of our society.

ACCOMMODATING VIOLENT STATES OF MIND: RE-MEMBERING THE DIS-MEMBERED

The experience of being unhoused within one's own mind, body, social group and community necessarily and inevitably gives rise to disturbed and disturbing relationships with the social world and particular others within it. The inner disturbance and dis-memberment that is the source of the emergent grievance needs to be communicated and publicised, because the unbearable grief that underpins it cannot be tolerated and therefore cannot be expressed. This public communication then becomes a violent act (the term 'forensic' derives from the word 'forum' or 'public space') within which the grief is denied, with the result that both subject and object may hear only the grievance. It is a communication of a discourse of intrusion and entrapment and a wish to get out of it. Of course, in ordinary parlance, similar wishes to 'get out of it' are expressed by people who misuse alcohol and drugs or who attempt to starve themselves, perverse individuals who misuse others for their sexual gratification, or people who indulge in risky behaviour, dangerous sports and gambling. Many of these activities share a similar aetiology and like patterns of self-harm are similarly addictive. Our focus here has been on those people who self-harm or self-neglect the integrity of their own bodies, and on the impact of these actions on those who would stand in the way of such actions and have to respond to the publication of the distress that lies at their centre. To illustrate and explore this point we now turn our attention to how appropriately managed supervision and work discussion groups might offer *fora* where some of the reciprocal violence we have been describing might be processed and de-escalated.

Elsewhere, one of us has suggested various techniques and mechanisms through which such various types of reflective groups might be structured and composed (Scanlon, 2002). A central aim of these reflective matrices is to allow the unconscious experience of group members to be made more available through an educational exchange in the group. In this context, the reflective group becomes a 'transitional space' (Winnicott, 1971; Schön, 1983, 1987) that is relatively free from the pressures of the 'real world' of practice and within which the dynamics outlined above can be safely explored and thought about. Scanlon suggests that this reflective space becomes a shared fantasy world of imagination in which group members collectively attempt to imagine what they and their patients have been doing together through a process of free association. Zinkin (1989) offers a word of caution by stating that there is much to be learned in this joint imaginative venture providing, of course, that all remain aware that what they are imagining together is not 'the truth'. Thus, a central task for these groups is to create a reflective space within which the reflective group serves as a hall of mirrors, or a resonant echo chamber, within which the dynamic issues may be amplified and condensed (Foulkes, 1948, 1964). As the supervisees become better able to *reflect-in-action* in the supervision group, so they will be able to use this experience as a bridge to transferring this enhanced reflective functioning back into the here and now of the therapeutic space itself (Schön, 1983, 1987; Scanlon, 2002). The reflective space, therefore, occupies an intermediate space between the as yet unthinkable world of practice and the abstract world of ideas. The members think about their reactions to the clinical material presented and together they attempt to interpret what is revealed in discussion about the psychosocial structure of the organisation in their minds (Armstrong, 2005). We suggest that this provides a highly relevant locus, or forum, for exploration of the problems of societal attribution of intentionality to the patient who attacks his body.

Vignette

In a mixed work discussion group, one member, a nurse working in an inpatient psychiatric unit, brought the following material:

> We were told that a young woman had been admitted into the hospital four months previously, suffering from anxiety and depression. She settled quickly on the ward and appeared to be making good use of her respite – although she had resisted various attempts to discharge her back home. A story began to emerge of the patient's early life experience of parental alcoholism and resultant financial and emotional impoverishment and deprivation. As the weeks of her admission began to move into months, she became increasingly agitated and began to self-harm, initially with superficial cuts, then more deeply. As sharps became harder to obtain, she would go out from the hospital and damage herself in public. On the ward, she began to scald herself with boiling water. The nursing team felt

baffled by the apparent 'irrationality' of these behaviours and started to try to make sense of them by believing that she was 'sabotaging' their 'good' treatment intentions. Her otherwise seemingly inexplicable behaviour was also causing considerable distress to the other patients and to the young woman's mother, who had made a formal complaint, as a result of which she was demanding, and being granted, daily updates from senior nursing staff about her daughter's deteriorating state of mind and body.

In discussing the case, it was apparent that the nurse presenting the material was representing other members of staff in the system of care who were equally baffled by the 'irrational' behaviour of the patient and that he and his colleagues were becoming more angry and resentful towards her about the aggrieved position that they felt they were being placed in. As we discussed this further it quickly became apparent that their resentment, formed in relation to the violence of the patient, was related to a feeling that they were now also being bullied by the patient's mother. This led the group to formulate a hypothesis that the experience of being bullied by the mother might be part of the wider psychosocial problem that was contributing to the patient's self-harm. This opened up a conversation within which we were given to understand that the patient had experienced her mother to be ambitious and demanding and had high expectations that her daughter would be able to achieve what she, the mother, had never felt able to do, and raise herself out of her impoverished circumstances.

These expectations seemed to have little to do with the daughter's own wishes and desires and it was also observed that the patient struggled to assert herself with her mother. The group then further hypothesised that the self-harm could be understood, in part at least, as an expression of the patient's experience of being caught between Scylla and Charybdis, and her wish to escape from this entrapped state of mind and to steer her own course. We also came to understand that, in acquiescing to the mother's demands, the staff, in unwittingly colluding with the mother's continuing intrusion into her daughter's life, had come to find themselves in a position that paralleled the position of the patient. They too felt helpless to resist her mother, because she was successfully able to invoke, and violently to exploit, a version of 'carers' rights and privileges that afforded her a temporary identification as one of the 'haves'. She could then engage in a kind of tyranny, a structural violence of her own, one that trampled upon the right of the patient to be protected, and to recruit the care team into colluding with her. It became apparent that the psychosocial consequences of the nurses' offers of 'help' also contained a concealed threat; that in 'getting the patient better' and sending her 'home', they were also sowing the seeds of her becoming 'dis-eased' again.

This complex formulation was taken up within the group member's workplace and slowly a protective perimeter was established, in which the mother's violating assumption that she had a right to be involved in her daughter's life was challenged by the care team. This, of course, inflamed the mother, who did after all have some rights in the matter, although it could be said that from one point of view she had, through her earlier neglect of her daughter, perhaps already abdicated them. The mother became still more aggrieved and, in her aggrieved state, became more vociferous and violent in her complaints; however, these complaints were increasingly dealt with through administrative rather than clinical channels. Without anything being said to the by now mute patient, the self-harm started to decrease in intensity and frequency. The patient began to talk about her fear of her mother's demands on her and she was eventually able to develop and to preserve her own protective perimeter with her mother. In this imaginative, composite case study it was not reported whether or not the patient's mother was able to access her own grief, rooted in her violent and violating need for her daughter – but, even in imagination, let us record our hopes that, for the greater good of all, she might have been able to do so.

In this vignette the bewilderment and resentment stirred in relation to the self-harm was rooted in an attribution of conscious intentionality. Even if there are elements that are 'deliberate', such as the rituals preceding and subsequent to the act that we have discussed above, we would contend that the behaviour of the self-harming individual can only be fully understood by locating it in a reciprocal relationship within which we as 'other' are unable or unwilling to hear the 'silent scream'. The problematic dynamics played out in the here and now of the clinical encounter in our vignette can best be understood as a reflection and a paralleling of the wider psychosocial violence and violation which we argue is at the root of the patient's individual presentations. In these ways we hope to have shown how the problem of self-harm is a social and group problem that demands what Bion (1961) might have called a *binocular* response, in which the complicated figure/ground *gestalt* of individual and group psychopathology can be kept in balance.

SOME CONCLUDING REMARKS

In this chapter we have argued that the disturbances associated with self-harm and self-neglect in both men and women can best be understood within a conceptual frame of reciprocal violence in which the violent act is a publication of personal distress that can only be properly understood as a psychosocial phenomenon. We have suggested that ideas of psychic 'unhousedness' and psychosocial 'dis-memberment' might be useful ways of conceptualising the experiences of people who, as a result of traumatic intrusion or abandonment, have been forced to evict themselves from the rational parts of their own minds into the temporary housing of their own mutilated or poisoned bodies. We have suggested that the capacity of the system of care and those working within it to come together in groups or in communities of practice (Schön, 1983, 1987; Scanlon, 2002) to understand their part in these unfolding psychosocial discourses is an essential component of a considered response to our shared disturbance of groupishness.

Although it has not been the particular focus of this chapter, we would also like to suggest that group- or *milieu*-based therapies (Campling and Haigh, 1999) would, for the reasons outlined above, be the treatment of choice for many. By seeking to locate the disturbance within the individual, we are separating them out and keeping them apart, *non-rationally* imposing a kind of quarantine rather than *thinking about* these complex and reciprocal dynamics. We may find ourselves in collusion with either active or more passive-aggressive positions of societal sadism, from within which we give razor blades to 'them' because we really do not care enough to *think with* 'them' about their relationship with 'us'. However, in order to establish appropriate therapeutic milieux and to consolidate their place within the system of care, we need first to address the widespread, non-rational societal mythology that self-harm is contagious and that the dis-ease of 'intentionality disorder' must be quarantined and kept at bay by mental health professionals covertly recruited by society into the role of border guards, with exclusion, rather than social inclusion, the unstated objective.

In so far as we struggle as a society to include people who self-harm in our thinking and in our structures, the risk is that we do violence to them and, by extension, to ourselves: for who are such individuals if not the unwanted children of the intrusive/abandoning society and systems of care that we have together 'chosen' (?) to establish.

REFERENCES

Adlam, J. and Scanlon, C. (2005) 'Personality disorder and homelessness: membership and "unhoused minds" in forensic settings', *Group Analysis*, 38: 452–466 (Special Issue – Group Analysis in Forensic Settings).

Adshead, G. (1997) 'Written on the body: deliberate self-harm and violence', in E.V. Welldon and C. van Velsen (eds) *A Practical Guide to Forensic Psychotherapy*, London: Jessica Kingsley Publishers.

Adshead, G. (2001) 'Murmurs of discontent: treatment and treatability of personality disorder', *Advances in Psychiatric Treatment*, 7: 407–414.

Adshead, G. (2002) 'Three degrees of security: attachment and forensic institutions', *Criminal Behaviour and Mental Health*, 12: S31–S45.

Akhtar, S. (1995) *Quest For Answers: A Primer of Understanding and Treating Severe Personality Disorder*, London: Jason Aronson.

Alvarez, A. (1974) *The Savage God: A Study of Suicide*, Harmondsworth: Penguin.

Armstrong, D. (2005) *Organisation in the Mind: Psychoanalysis, Group Relations and Organisational Consultancy*, London: Karnac.

Bancroft, J., Skrimshire, A. and Simkin, S. (1976) 'The reasons people give for taking overdoses', *British Journal of Psychiatry*, 128: 538–548.

Bateman, A. and Fonagy, P. (2004) *Psychotherapy for Borderline Personality Disorder: Mentalization-based Treatment*, Oxford: Oxford University Press.

Bion, W.R. (1961) *Experiences in Groups*, London: Routledge.

Bollas, C. (1987) *The Shadow of the Object: Psychoanalysis of the Unthought Known*, London: Free Association Books.

Bowlby, J. (1969, 1973, 1980) *Attachment and Loss, Vols 1–3*, London: Hogarth.

Brenman, E. (1985) 'Cruelty and narrow mindedness', *International Journal of Psycho-Analysis*, 66: 273–282.

Brown, M., Comtois, K. and Linehan, M. (2002) 'Reasons for suicide attempts and nonsuicidal self-injury in women with borderline personality disorder', *Journal of Abnormal Psychology*, 111: 198–202.

Campbell, D. and Hale, R. (1991) 'Suicidal acts', in J. Holmes (ed.)

Textbook of Psychotherapy in Psychiatric Practice, London: Churchill Livingstone.

Campling, P. and Haigh, R. (1999) *Therapeutic Communities: Past, Present and Future*, London: Jessica Kingsley Publishers.

Chapman, G.E. (1983) 'Ritual and rational action in hospitals', *Journal of Advanced Nursing*, 8: 13–20.

Charlesworth, S., Gilfillan, P. and Wilkinson, R. (2004) 'Living inferiority', *British Medical Bulletin*, 69: 49–60.

de Zulueta, F. (1993) *From Pain to Violence: The Traumatic Roots of Destructiveness*, London: Whurr.

Declerck, P. (2006) 'On the necessary suffering of the homeless', in R. Scholar (ed.) *Divided Cities: The Oxford Amnesty Lectures 2003*, Oxford: Oxford University Press.

Felitti, V.J., Anda, R.F., Nordenberg, D., Williamson, D.F., Spitz, A.M., Edwards, V., Koss, M.P. and Marks, J.S. (1998) 'Relationship of childhood abuse and household dysfunction to many of the leading causes of death in adults: the adverse childhood experiences (ACE) study', *American Journal of Preventive Medicine*, 14: 245–258.

Foulkes, S.H. (1948) *Introduction to Group-Analytic Psychotherapy: Studies in the Social Integration of Individuals and Groups*, London: Heinemann.

Foulkes, S.H. (1964) *Therapeutic Group Analysis*, London: Allen & Unwin.

Gabbard, G.O. and Wilkinson, S.M. (1994) *Management of Counter-Transference with Borderline Patients*, Washington, DC: American Psychiatric Press.

Gilligan, J. (1996) *Violence: Reflections on our Deadliest Epidemic*, London: Jessica Kingsley Publishers.

Glasser, M. (1996) 'Aggression and sadism in the perversions', in I. Rosen (ed.) *Sexual Deviation* (third edition), Oxford: Oxford University Press.

Haw, C., Hawton, K., Houston, K. and Townsend, E. (2001) 'Psychiatric and personality disorders in deliberate self-harm patients', *British Journal of Psychiatry*, 178: 48–54.

Hopper, E. (2003) *Traumatic Experience in the Unconscious Life of Groups: The Fourth Basic Assumption: Incohesion: Aggregation/Massification or (ba)I:A/M*, London: Jessica Kingsley Publishers.

Isaacson, G. and Rich, C. (2001) 'Management of patients who deliberately harm themselves', *British Medical Journal*, 322: 213–215.

Johnson, M. and Webb, C. (1995) 'Rediscovering unpopular patients: the concept of social judgement', *Journal of Advanced Nursing*, 21: 466–475.

Jordan, B. (1996) *A Theory of Poverty and Social Exclusion*, Cambridge: Polity Press.

Kelly, M.P. and May, D. (1982) 'Good and bad patients: a review of the literature and a theoretical critique', *Journal of Advanced Nursing*, 7: 147–156.

Klonsky, E., Oltmanns, T. and Turkheimer, E. (2003) 'Deliberate self-harm in a non-clinical population: prevalence and psychological correlates', *American Journal of Psychiatry*, 160: 1501–1508.

Liebling, H. and Chipchase, H. (1992) 'A pilot study on the problem of self-injurious behaviour in women in Ashworth Hospital', *Division of Criminological and Legal Psychology Newsletter*, October: 19–23.

Menzies, D. (2001) 'The emergence of hope through the experience of being known: finding one's true self in the group', *British Journal of Psychotherapy*, 18: 227–237.

Motz, A. (2001) *The Psychology of Female Violence: Crimes Against the Body* (first edition), Hove: Routledge.

Motz, A. (2008) *The Psychology of Female Violence: Crimes Against the Body* (second edition), Hove: Routledge.

National Institute for Clinical Excellence (2004) *Self-Harm: The Short-Term Physical and Psychological Management and Secondary Prevention of Self-Harm in Primary and Secondary Care*, London: NICE, www.nice.org.uk/nicemedia/pdf/CG016NICEguideline.pdf (accessed 20 December 2008).

Norton, K. and Dolan, B. (1995) 'Acting out and the institutional response', *Journal of Forensic Psychiatry*, 6: 317–332.

Pattison, M. and Kahan, J. (1983) 'The deliberate self-harm syndrome', *American Journal of Psychiatry*, 140: 867–872.

Platt, S., Bille-Brahe, U., Kerkhof, A., Schmidtke, A., Bjerke, T., Crepet, P., De Leo, D., Haring, C., Lonnqvist, J. and Michel, K. (1992) 'Parasuicide in Europe: the WHO/EURO multicentre study on parasuicide. I. Introduction and preliminary analysis for 1989', *Acta Psychiatrica Scandinavica*, 85: 97–104.

Roth, J. (1972) 'Some contingencies of the moral evaluation and control of clientele: the case of the hospital emergency service', *American Journal of Sociology*, 77: 839–855.

Royal College of Nursing (2006) *Safe Self Harm – Is It Possible?*, www.rcn.org.uk/newsevents/congress/2006/agenda/6 (now archived in RCN Lirbary).

Royal College of Psychiatrists (2006) *Self-Harm*, www.rcpsych.ac.uk/pdf/self-harm%20lft.pdf (accessed 18 February 2008).

Scanlon, C. (2002) 'Group supervision of individual cases in the training of psychodynamic practitioners: towards a group-analytic model?', *British Journal of Psychotherapy*, 19: 219–235.

Scanlon, C. and Adlam, J. (2008) 'Homelessness and disorder: the challenge of the antisocial and the societal response', in C. Kaye and M. Howlett (eds) *Mental Health Services Today and Tomorrow. Part 1: Experiences of Providing and Receiving Care*, Oxford: Radcliffe.

Scanlon, C. and Adlam, J. (2009) 'Nursing dangerousness, dangerous nursing and the spaces in between: learning to live with uncertainties', in

A. Aiyegbusi and J. Clarke (eds) *Caring for Offenders: An Introduction to the Psychodynamics of Forensic Mental Health Nursing*, London: Jessica Kingsley Publishers.
Schön, D.A. (1983) *The Reflective Practitioner*, New York: Basic Books.
Schön, D.A. (1987) *Educating the Reflective Practitioner*, New York: Basic Books.
Sinason, V. (1996) 'From abused to abuser', in C. Cordess and M. Cox (eds) *Forensic Psychotherapy: Crime, Psychodynamics and the Offender Patient*, London: Jessica Kingsley Publishers.
Skegg, K. (2005) 'Self-harm', *Lancet*, 366: 1471–1483.
Stockwell, E. (1974) *The Unpopular Patient*, London: Royal College of Nursing.
Welldon, E.V. (1988) *Mother, Madonna, Whore: The Idealisation and Denigration of Motherhood*, London: Karnac.
Welldon, E.V. (1996) 'Contrasting male and female perversions', in C. Cordess and M. Cox (eds) *Forensic Psychotherapy: Crime, Psychodynamics and the Offender Patient*, London: Jessica Kingsley Publishers.
Williams, J. and Pollock, L. (2000) 'The psychology of suicidal behaviour', in K. Hawton and K. van Heeringen (eds) *The International Handbook of Suicide and Attempted Suicide*, Chichester: John Wiley and Sons.
Winnicott, D.W. (1971) 'Transitional objects and transitional phenomena', in *Playing and Reality*, London: Pelican.
Winnicott, D.W. (1986) *Home Is Where We Start From: Essays by a Psychoanalyst*, Harmondsworth: Penguin.
Zinkin, L.M. (1989) *Clinical Supervision: Issues and Techniques*, London: British Association of Psychotherapists.
Zizek, S. (2008) *Violence*, London: Profile.

Chapter 4

The trap

Self-harm and young people in foster care and residential settings

Vivien Norris and Michael Maher

INTRODUCTION

In this chapter we will look at self-harming behaviour involving children and young people in care – in foster care and residential provision. Self-harm in its broadest sense is highly prevalent in this group of children and young people, ranging across a wide spectrum of behaviours such as absconding, aggression, misuse of drugs and alcohol, eating difficulties and self-cutting. Although some of these behaviours are also prevalent in the general population, they occur with more intensity and regularity in children in care. These behaviours are underpinned and driven by broader difficulties in relating, emotion regulation (the ability to contain one's own emotions), impulse control, reflective function (the ability to reflect on the impact of one's own and others' behaviour), thinking and self-esteem (e.g. Siegel, 1999). There are many reasons as to why this may be the case, among which the most fundamental lie with the disrupted early attachments and often continued disruption in these young people's lives, which compromise opportunities for forming sustained relationships.[1]

Assessment of risk and safety management plans obviously form an important part of work with young people exhibiting risky behaviour. The predominant culture within the looked-after system is organised around risk, with the aim being to keep young people safe. This, however, may translate into risk-averse practice, which often comes at the cost of attention to potential therapeutic or

1 See Richardson and Lelliott (2003) for an overview of the mental health of looked-after children.

developmental gains for the young person and their relationships. So we see frequent placement changes, or moves in and out of residential settings, when behaviour escalates. While it is clearly crucial to assess and manage risk associated with specific behaviours as well as we are able, we need to consider the costs of ending relationships and the repeated message to young people that they 'cannot be managed'. Most commonly it will be foster carers who are saying 'I cannot manage this any more' and the central challenge then is how to equip and support them sufficiently so that they are able to survive and sustain meaningful relationships with the young people in their care.

Our aim in this chapter is to look beyond risk and consider the perplexing question of 'What is going on?' for the young people and for those around them when they self-harm. We will focus primarily on self-harm where it is not overtly suicidal in intent and will not be considering the specific needs of young people with disabilities who may present with repetitive self-harm.

In thinking about self-harm, we draw on a range of theoretical ideas, including attachment theory and trauma and its impact, and we draw on both psychodynamic and systemic ways of exploring the meanings contained in this behaviour. Our focus in this chapter shifts from the individual to interpersonal and group processes.

ATTACHMENT AND TRAUMA

Although development and maturation continues throughout life, early life experiences are fundamental in the formation of a template (internal working model) for subsequent interactions. There is increasingly powerful research evidence linking the earliest relationships with changes in brain development (bringing together attachment theory and neurological development). For many young people within the looked-after system, the typical historical context is that they will have experienced at least one and often many breakdowns in care and they are likely to have experienced and/or witnessed abuse. Some of their experiences are extreme. Repeated traumatic and damaging experiences have to be managed in some way by an infant or child. Where sense cannot be made of the experiences, they may be laid down in developmental difficulties. The clinical evidence is that the impact on the children's sense of themselves and how they experience and respond to others is profound (Fonagy *et al.*, 2002). As a result of how they develop coping strategies and construct roles (ways of organising the self) to manage their intolerable early environments, they may have little notion that others are able to interpret, understand and reflect their experiences, the fundamental building blocks of a stable sense of self. In addition to early trauma, they will have missed out on good-enough care.

For subsequent carers of these traumatised children and young people, a common experience is of a powerful pull towards a repetition of patterns that may appear destructive to both the young person and those around them. Patterns of re-enactment may in some situations vividly represent previous experience.

Case vignette

Casey was a competent young woman with a history of childhood abuse and infrequent but serious self-harm. At the time of this episode she was living in a therapeutic community. Most of the time she maintained helpful and warm contact with her peers and carers. Episodically and without an obvious cause, Casey would enlist a 'friend' to accompany her to buy alcohol. On one such occasion the two young women went on a 'shopping trip' and, having procured alcohol, Casey consumed a large amount and left her friend to go for a solitary walk. After some time the 'friend' found a staff member and in a state of panic described her fear that Casey was drunk and would be drowned in the river. When Casey was found she was very drunk and had cut her arms severely, requiring hospital treatment. Casey became very abusive, refusing treatment, and the ensuing struggle finally resulted in Casey being physically held by a male while she was given sutures. Casey screamed 'get off' throughout. Once Casey had had time to recover she apologised to the adults involved and was unable to say anything more about what had occurred.

Anyone involved in an episode such as that described above is inevitably left with a sense of bewilderment, and an urgent wish to answer the question 'what was all that about?'. In order to explore these processes further, and suggest answers to this critical question, we will concentrate on self-cutting specifically. Quotations in italics come directly from research carried out with young people and carers (Norris, 1997).

SELF-CUTTING

When young people are asked about their self-cutting, the explanations they give are predominantly intrapersonal. They frequently feel misunderstood, particularly when other interpersonal factors are suggested as contributory factors. There may be a wide range of reasons for cutting, which may change and also be difficult to articulate. Most commonly it is seen as a short-term way of coping with unbearable feelings and as a coping strategy from what may be a limited repertoire: *'I don't know how else to deal with my problems. I either cut, take aerosols or run'*. Cutting may provide a focus for unbearable internal pain and confusion, creating concrete proof of how wounded and damaged they feel and allowing some control: *'So I can have physical pain rather than just what's inside'*. It may provide relief and distraction and have a short-term calming effect but this is often followed by feelings of shame and self-disgust, particularly about the wound: *'They see the scars and see you like an alien, and to some extent you are'*. For some young people, cutting arises from a profound sense of worthlessness and self-hatred, or a fear of hurting others.

A cyclical pattern is often apparent whereby the self-cutting provides relief from unbearable feelings; this is followed by feelings of shame or disgust; and then some further trigger (be it an event or a thought) again overwhelms the young person. Some authors have described this as an addictive cycle. Although self-cutting is predominantly about finding a way to keep on living, there is always the chance of an 'accident', the result of which could be much more serious. The existence of this dangerousness may be an important factor in the cutting behaviour.

When considering a specific behaviour such as self-cutting, which is overtly harmful, the most striking feature when the behaviour comes to light is the dramatic impact it has on others. For instance, responses from A&E departments are often denigratory, and carers commonly express high levels of anxiety and anger about the behaviour. It is not known how much self-harm continues without the awareness of others, and this issue may be contentious. Our experience within residential and family settings is that the messages from young people are often highly ambivalent in this respect. For instance, they may go to their room and cut themselves while playing loud music, or wear long sleeves to cover cuts in a demonstrative fashion: *'You do want them to know but you don't want them to know'*. We would argue that whether or not an act of self-harm is clearly communicated, the child or young person's thought about whether anyone cares is often central. This links to the earliest relationships whereby an infant develops a sense of itself via the complex interactions with an 'other', and the idea of an 'other', whether nurturing or persecutory, develops in mind.

The issue of why self-harming behaviour has such a dramatic impact on those around the young person has particular resonance when considering the care of children. In addition to the societal taboos about particular behavioural expressions, the role of being a 'carer' appears to be fundamental. Most parents would see a primary role as keeping their child safe from harm, and injury to children commonly evokes complex primitive feelings (anxiety, anger and the wish to offer succour).

In the looked-after child context, the 'duty of care' to keep the child from (further) harm is formalised, and the primary carers are paid to provide this care. However, the carers' security in their role may be compromised by the organisational context, which, although designed to provide support to carers and young people, is frequently constrained by a multitude of factors, and there is often uncertainty about how long these primary carers will remain in that role. When asked about the impact of cutting on carers, different responses emerge. Carers who have not experienced the behaviour before may feel highly anxious and frightened by the behaviour, often linked to a fear of death: *'I feel such a high level of concern that I can't think. I'm overwhelmed by my feelings'*. Some carers describe nurturing responses, with a powerful urge to protect the young person from further harm: *'I just want to wrap her in cotton wool and take away her pain'*. Over time, and as repeated incidents occur, a sense of confusion and impotence may emerge, with carers describing feeling 'cut off' and at times feeling angry with, and persecuted by, the young person: *'We don't have normal reactions at all . . . They come to you, you wrap them in bandages and it's like serving dinners . . . It's a coping mechanism . . . You can't afford to feel anything'*.

In trying to make sense of self-harming behaviours, we have found it important to move beyond the individual and consider different levels of explanation. Figure 4.1 illustrates the potentially self-maintaining cycles that may develop around self-harming behaviour (Norris, 1997).

In what follows we use the concept of a role as an organisation of the self in response to demands of the environment. A child who has experienced trauma is likely to have developed defensive roles to deal with this experience, and these roles are commonly present in relationships with substitute carers.

First consider the intrapersonal cycle illustrated on the left of Figure 4.1. Start with the 'Damaged self', the self-experience we take as pre-existent, a child's sense of themselves as *'damaged goods'*, the self-perception they have developed to manage the difficult and confusing demands of the environment in their fractured lives. From this position, the child inevitably becomes in touch with feelings generated by loss. Intense separation anxiety and strong – but only partially successful – attempts to avoid grieving are characteristic of traumatised children in these contexts. When the avoidant 'flight' responses fail – as they must – the anxiety and unbearable feelings, which derive from the experience of loss, threaten to overwhelm the child. We would argue that the feelings are inevitable in the scenario of the child being wanted by the person offering care, as this in itself causes further pain and confusion to the child, making them more likely to remember their loss of others who they wanted to care for them. Hence, hope and care itself is both wanted and experienced as deeply painful. Self-harm can act as an affect regulation device in such circumstances, whereby the child achieves some control over and distance from these threatening feelings: *'It's hurting somewhere else, but it doesn't hurt your soul'*. This leads to relief, which does not last long, as the self-disgust which follows the 'giving in' to the addictive impulse adds another layer to the experience of self as damaged and a victim.

Moving beyond an intrapersonal cycle, all such behaviours take place in a context, and the context will determine whether the role and its attendant behaviours are supported and continue, or whether it does not have the context in which it can thrive. To see how the context often unwittingly supports the self-harming, let us start with the 'self as carer', a self-perception common to foster carers and residential workers and which derives from both their own attachment histories and their work role. When faced with a child who is bent on self-damage, this naturally produces very difficult feelings in one tasked with 'looking after' them. Powerful

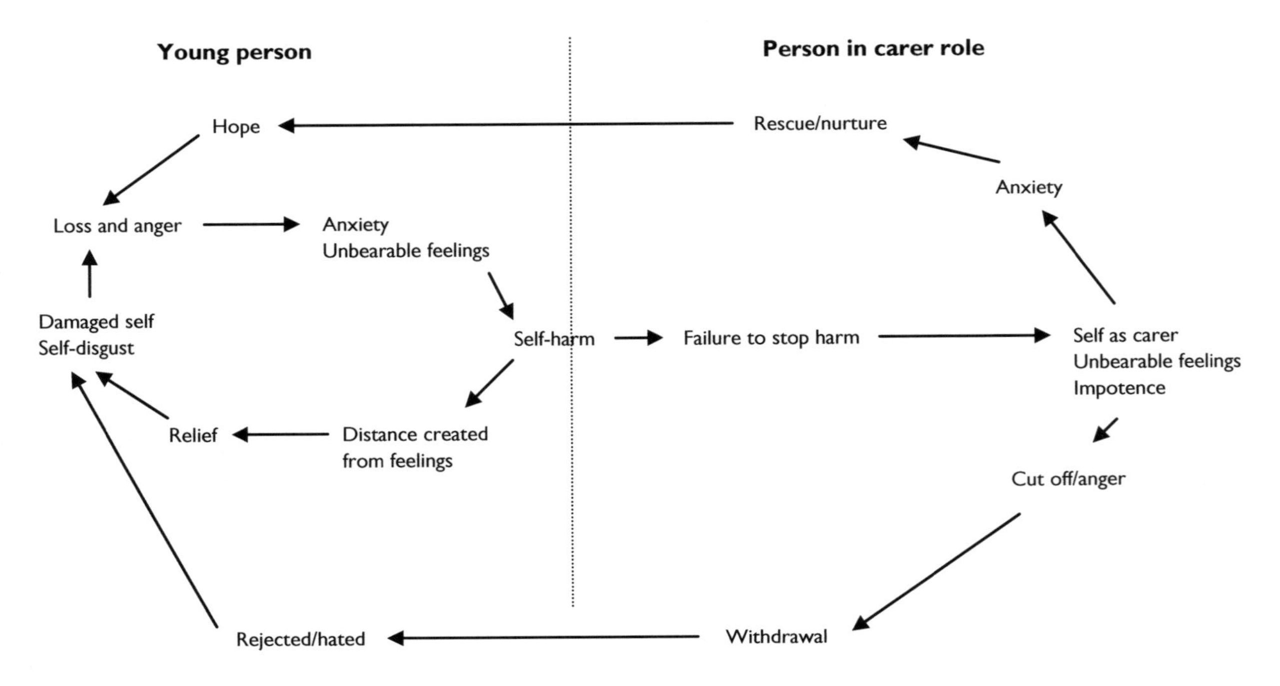

Figure 4.1 Intra- and interpersonal cycles that may develop in self-harming behaviour

among the feelings this often generates is the reaction to impotence, and how this threatens the sense of the carer's role, and the need they feel to be helpful and for the caring to be appreciated. In such a context, neither party can give the other what they want. The carer cannot relieve the child of their painful feelings; the child cannot gratify the helper by seeming helped: *'I've tried a lot of approaches over the years to get to where I am now. Nothing has made a lot of difference'*.

Faced with this dilemma, carers often react in one of two ways. Some will redouble their efforts to caretake, to find a way of relieving the child of their feelings without their having to resort to self-harm. Driven by anxiety (sometimes reinforced by the agency's defining success as 'stopping' the child from self-harming) they undertake epic attempts to rescue the child from their self-destructive paths. We have known some extraordinary promises made to children under these circumstances, along the lines of: 'You can trust me. I will not let you down. I am different from all those others that have gone before. When the crisis arrives – when the urge to cut becomes uncontrollable – call me and I will be there and we will find a way together to manage without you cutting yourself'. Such promises, such specialness and the misguided goal to stop the self-harm, inevitably have to fail. When they do fail, the hope that has been engendered in the child by such heroic efforts comes crashing down; another experience of loss and let-down from a trusted adult is added to the catalogue of experiences that feed into the continuance of the experience of self as damaged.

Others will react to the perpetrator aspect of the behaviour, rather than the victim aspect (as above). They react to the difficulty of the 'no-win' situation they as carers are put into by cutting off their feelings or by expressing anger through terseness, coldness and unavailability. All these withdrawal reactions are experienced by the child as rejection – the adult is not accessible to be engaged with. This feeds into the cycle via the experience of being unlovable, worthy of rejection and abuse, which again leads to the continuance of the self-harming behaviour, and the buttressing of the cycle.

These patterns can be understood from a number of theoretical standpoints. From a psychodynamic perspective, they might be described in terms of projective identification. Drawing on a systemic model, both the reactions can be seen as carers being induced into reciprocal roles in reaction to the defensive roles that contain the self-harming behaviour. We will come back to the importance of getting out of such role-locks later in the chapter.

While many day-to-day responses to self-harm would not fall at the extreme end of these poles, the pull towards polarisation, particularly in group settings, is very powerful. When discussing experiences with staff groups, it is common to find specific staff members who hold 'special relationships' with young people whereas colleagues may hold an entirely oppositional view: *'And then I wonder "what is she [carer] getting out of it?"'*.

Managing a bearable distance in the relationship between a young person and carer may be a constant theme and at times the experience of intimacy with a young person may shift to an unbearable intensity, which leads one or other participant to withdraw abruptly. The capacity to repair fractured relationships and the ongoing quality of relating between the adult and young person may be brought into focus via the self-harming behaviour.

Self-harming behaviour occurs in the context of overwhelming experiences, which are hard to bear for all concerned. The potency of self-harming acts may lie in their ability to convey irreconcilable ideas in a way that matches the intensity and complexity of the young person's experience. The young person is desperate both for care and to find a way to manage distress and yet via the behaviour becomes both the perpetrator and victim of the act and the subsequent pain. The parallel process is apparent in carers' frequent experience of being invited into either victim or perpetrator role in their response, feeling helpless and persecuted by the behaviour or their (suppressed) angry and denigratory reaction.

WHY SELF-HARM?

At different times and across different cultures, people suffering from severe psychological distress express that distress in ways that are socially available. Self-harm is a language of distress currently favoured by young people. Why should this be the case? What is there particularly about this act that has made it so popular?

In offering a way of thinking about this question, we draw on the work of Ian Hacking (1995). In his work on transient mental illnesses, how certain conditions arise and thrive at different times and in different social contexts, he points to a way of engaging with this elusive question. Using this approach, we see that adolescents who cut themselves then become classified as 'self-harmers', or 'cutters'. People classified in certain ways – in this case defined by their behaviour, and with the attitudes that accompany the behaviour – can conform or grow into the ways that they are described, but they also evolve into their own ways, so that the classifications and descriptions have to be continually revised. The concept of the meaning of self-harming behaviour may itself be so made and moulded by clinicians' attempts at knowledge and intervention, and by self-harmers' development of their own group identities, and wider social reaction to these attempts, that there is no stable object (self-harming behaviour) to have solid knowledge about. Hacking calls this 'the looping effects of human kinds' (Hacking, 1995: 21).

An example of this is in how the activity of self-injury has 'come out' over recent years. There is now an International Self-Harm Awareness Day, and those who self-harm are encouraged to wear orange bracelets to indicate their affiliation to this behaviour. If this move gathers support and becomes widespread then it will have an effect on the traditionally private, secret nature of the activity, and has the potential to impact on the sense of shame, which is an important factor in the maintenance of the shamed, self-disgusted side of the cycle. This could have positive effects. On the other hand, a potentially worrying development can be observed in some contexts (e.g. child psychiatric settings) where the self-harming becomes so common as to be considered 'everyday' and carers become immune to strong feelings evoked by it, so some young people concerned may drift towards potentially more lethal behaviour. The evocation of anxiety in the carer may be an important feature.

The above shifts notwithstanding, self-harm shows no sign of going into decline. It has the medical and social space in which it can thrive, and it does this in part because of its essential mysteriousness; the problems it presents relating to how to understand and how best to respond without falling into a trap are themselves the source of the power it holds for those who harm themselves and for those who seek to understand, explain and help. When there are so many possible causes, when so many factors are or may be at work or compete to be the dominant thesis of the aetiology of the behaviour, the result is that the act becomes shrouded in disagreement and elusiveness and this elusiveness may be part of the power of the act. It remains outside our understanding and therefore symbolically outside our control. It confounds us, and confronts us with difficult feelings generated by confusion and impotence.

Indeed, this may be how it is for those who self-harm too – who feel in its compulsive grip for reasons that they too find hard to fathom. A part of the mind wants to stop and another part feels it cannot and worries about itself.

IMPLICATIONS

The central problem lies in the unbearableness of the young person's experience both for them and for those close to them. The young person's early experience is likely to have been intolerable and they are left with deep ambivalence about being cared for: *'You feel they [adults] shouldn't like you or care about you . . . in a hate world it would be easier'*. Their sense of self is likely to be fragile and unintegrated and the way emotions are expressed are likely to be confusing.

Although self-harming behaviour may present a management problem, it is important not to confuse it with the underlying problem, which has much more to do with the way the young person relates and makes sense of the world. Where complex difficulties are commonly labelled and medicalised, it is very easy to confuse the 'symptom' for the problem, and group childcare settings in particular may organise themselves around tackling and stopping the behaviour as the central focus. However, the presenting behaviour itself deserves respect, as it is there for a reason, and may have helped the individual to survive thus far.

With respect to intervention, our experience is that the most effective ways of managing self-harm in these settings is to work with the adults who are most central in the young person's life. If they are more able to 'bear witness' to underlying distress, to keep trying to make sense of the behaviour and to develop the capacity to think and respond to rather than react to the behaviour, within a wider context of attending to relationships, then the self-harming behaviour may fade or appear in a more understandable pattern. This is a highly complex task, which may require outside support.

An important part of this task involves the adults developing a greater understanding of how and why they find themselves pulled into unproductive cycles in their responses to the young person and their colleagues. These adults may be directly caring for the young person or may be involved in the wider network. We have seen many instances where polarisation in the wider professionals' group results in an undermining of the placement.

One helpful way of conceptualising this process is via the idea of 'role-locks', referred to earlier in this chapter. This approach comes from the work of Yvonne Agazarian. The systems-centered therapy she has developed gives an approach to working with groups, families and individuals that involves building a system from which it becomes possible to recognise how we develop reciprocal role relationships that keep us locked in a struggle within which we have few choices and the experience is one of mutual persecution. An important role-lock in the context we are describing is that of identified patient and caretaker.

> Undoing the identified patient–caretaker role-lock requires recognizing how one is volunteering for one of these roles and how a split-off part of the self is projected onto one's role partner. Thus, the caretaker of the identified patient re-experiences the part of the self that wants care, a desire that is manifested repeatedly by the tendency to volunteer for the same old role. Undoing the identified patient–caretaker defence requires recognizing defensive denial.
>
> (Agazarian, 1997: 235)

The goal of undoing such role-locks requires work at sufficient depth to allow for the recognition of the existence of reciprocal role arrangements and the exploration necessary to understand where they originated. This process requires regular and sustained work with staff groups or regular meetings with foster carers. The primary carer is the main resource for the child or young person and, as is the case for the children in their care, it is not possible for carers to manage difficult therapeutic work unless the wider context is safe and responsive. In our experience, a range of structures needs to be in place to support and value this complex role, including out-of-hours support, respite, connections with other carers, high-quality relevant training and supervision, and good communication between professionals. Against this backdrop, more focused therapeutic work may be done. Our approach to addressing issues of self-harm is to work at different levels in the system, with our focus on the underlying issues rather than the behaviour itself, the central aim being to support the child–carer relationship. We would not advocate specific intervention packages in isolation as the tendency to overly attach to a model when anxious can lead to a lack of sensitivity to wider dynamics.

In our work with carers, some of the following themes recur:

- attending to and managing the feelings that the behaviour evokes in the carer;
- recognising that it is impossible to bear these feelings all the time;
- exploring carers' own attachment patterns and how they dovetail into the repetitive cycles;
- exploring what old, defensive roles the carers are induced into by the self-harming they are exposed to;
- developing the capacity to recognise these old roles and the triggers that induce them;
- attending to the rupture and repair of attunement in the relationships;
- addressing issues of power and control;
- addressing group and context issues and how these influence the intensity and frequency of the behaviour;
- resisting taking things personally and blamefully;
- developing a greater understanding among the adults about the developmental impact of trauma. Internalised experiences will not stop just because a 'good' carer has been found and indeed overt behavioural expressions of distress may increase at times of therapeutic movement.

The shared focus of attention is on the relationship between the carer and child/young person; and the young people may be involved in family-based work. In our experience of working in practice, the most useful direct work with young people is often that focused on developing competencies, both in regulating emotions and in life skills (Kinniburgh *et al.*, 2005) in the context of a well-supported and supportive stable placement. The experience of an attachment relationship that survives may be the single most therapeutic factor of all: 'To experience someone who is prepared to "stay in there", wanting to understand what is happening, conveys the hint that what is being experienced might be manageable, might be understood, might not be a hopelessly destructive force with which no one can live' (Howe, 2005: 274).

CONCLUSION

Many relationships between adults and young people within residential and fostering settings can drift into a recurring experience of mutual deprivation (Ironside, 2004). When this reaches a peak, carers may feel that they can no longer continue with a placement. The organisational response to a call for support may be extremely influential to the outcome. In our experience, at these points of potential 'rupture', workers often react anxiously, for instance responding with bland reassurance (*'you're doing a good job'*) without hearing the carer's distress or precipitously concluding that a placement has broken down and focusing energies on a replacement.

A central task of parenting in a context of insecure and difficult-to-sustain relationships might be described as finding ways to sustain a flow of emotional interactions (rupture and repair of attunement; Hughes, 2007) at a tolerable level of intimacy for all concerned. This applies as much to those in the wider system as to the carers themselves. Messages like 'this child breaks all their placements' can be seen as a response to feelings of impotence and anger (the lower part of the interpersonal cycle described in Figure 4.1). While there are young people who are extremely difficult to parent and do repeatedly get caught in a cycle of relationship rupture (and for some young people the degree of intimacy and intensity in a family setting may be too much to bear), in our view there is much more that could be done to develop and support carers, and the system's capacity to make sense of and manage the development of the young people in their care.

In this chapter we have described the 'symptom' of the presenting behaviour as a potential trap, diverting resources from the source of the problem. The nature of the trap can be described as a 'role-lock', wherein the self-harming young person and the carer relate via defensive roles in a way that compounds the lock, within which life is experienced as persecutory for both. Our concern is that the prevailing culture encourages this. Carers and teams working within a psychological/therapeutic frame may find themselves isolated when the system within which they are working becomes anxious about the possible consequences of the behaviour, and who will be held responsible for these. At the very point when they may need containment themselves, it may not be there.

We believe that the most effective intervention is to help carers recognise when they are being induced into repetitive and locked cycles and to assist them back into a current reality-based role that is relevant to the goal of the work. This can only be achieved with skilled facilitation and within a context where adequate support is given to carers and there is a shared commitment to the therapeutic task. This is a difficult, skilled task, and an important one.

REFERENCES

Agazarian, Y. (1997) *Systems-Centered Therapy for Groups*, London: Karnac.

Fonagy, P., Gergely, G., Jurist, E.L. and Target, M. (2002) *Affect Regulation, Mentalization and the Development of the Self*, New York: Other Press.

Hacking, I. (1995) *Rewriting the Soul*, Chichester: Princeton University Press.

Howe, D. (2005) *Child Abuse and Neglect*, Basingstoke: Palgrave Macmillan.

Hughes, D.A. (2007) *Attachment Focused Family Therapy*, New York: W.W. Norton.

Ironside, L. (2004) 'Living a provisional existence', *Adoption and Fostering*, 28: 39–49.

Kinniburgh, K., Blaustein, M., Spinazzola, J. and van der Kolk, B. (2005) 'Attachment, self-regulation and competency: a comprehensive framework for intervention with childhood complex trauma', *Psychiatric Annals*, 35: 424–430.

Norris, V.C. (1997) 'Adolescent and staff experiences of self-cutting behaviour in residential settings', Unpublished doctoral dissertation.

Richardson, J. and Lelliott, P. (2003) 'Mental health of looked after children', *Advances in Psychiatric Treatment*, 9: 249–256.

Siegel, D.J. (1999) *The Developing Mind*, New York: Guilford Press.

Chapter 5

Self-harm and attachment

Elizabeth Grocutt

INTRODUCTION

This chapter describes the interpersonal processes that contribute to the development of an insecure attachment system. I discuss early disruptive and abusive experiences of care as representing a contributory risk factor for developing an insufficient and fragmented sense of self. The destructive resolution of an individual's intra- and interpersonal conflicts can be displayed in violent acts directed towards the self or others.

An incoherent, chaotic sense of self is often observed in those who self-harm. Self-harm is a powerful form of non-verbal communication and expression. On an intrapersonal level, self-harm can provide a form of comfort or punishment in times of crisis. The relationship between an individual's self-harm and their attachment system is inextricably linked; self-harm can be understood as a response to the activation of conscious or unconscious interpersonal distress; it also re-creates or initiates interpersonal interactions. As attachment behaviours are often activated in times of heightened distress, this chapter explores the impact of working with clients in restricted mental health settings where relational needs may be easily triggered and observed when earlier, traumatic experiences of care are re-awakened. In these confined environments, clients are faced with a limited sphere of control and frequently find themselves as passive recipients of care, which may mirror or contribute to the re-enactment of their own disturbed earlier life experiences and relationship roles.

THE DEVELOPMENT OF AN ATTACHMENT

The formation of an attachment is a crucial component to an infant's development. The emotional exchanges between an infant and their caregiver provide a blueprint for interpersonal interactions that inform an individual's relationship expectations, their sense of self and perceptions of others throughout the lifespan.

The development of interpersonal relationships begins in childhood. John Bowlby pioneered research exploring the dynamics between infant and parent attachment relationships during the 1950s. His work focused on the effects of separation between caregiver and infant and the impact of attachment on psychological and emotional development in young children. Bowlby (1969) outlined the long-term implications of forging a secure reciprocal attachment, in which the infant's emotional and physical needs are identified, acknowledged and met. The sustained reliable, consistent and predictable interactions between a caregiver and infant create a mental representation of a 'secure base' that the infant will seek in times of uncertainty or distress.

Although an infant establishes multiple attachments relationships, Bowlby maintained that the principal caregiver, usually the mother, is the primary attachment figure. During an infant's first years of life, internal working models based on actual interactions are formed (Bowlby, 1969). These mental representations are a product of sustained interactions between an infant and their caregiver that provide a series of positive and negative appraisals of their attachment figure; as a reliable or unreliable, available or dismissive figure. Stemming from these interactions is the infant's developing sense of self as either worthy or unworthy of care. The emotional exchanges between caregiver and infant create a set of experiences and expectations that defines the emotional and physical security of that relationship. Over time, these sustained emotional dialogues are generalised and form the basis of the individual's expectations and assumptions for future relationships and influence their ability to develop reciprocal, empathic and supportive relationships.

As time progresses, these relational patterns become fixed and expectations of interactions derived from the caregiver are generalised to other interactions. Bowlby's research findings demonstrated not only the significance of a secure attachment, but also the impact of insecure attachments and separations for the infant's psychological development. Frequent or prolonged separations from caregivers instilled anxiety and fear of further abandonment; this experience of absence or loss resulted in a process of initial distress followed by grieving for the attachment figure who was no longer available to meet the relational needs activated in the infant's world. Infants often experience anxiety when faced with separation from their caregiver; however, those with a secure relationship will develop self-reliance and a sense of security from the knowledge that their parent will return. Infants with insecure relationships often display behaviours and responses that are out of context to the caregiving situation, therefore sporadic outbursts of aggression or distress in response to a non-threatening interaction may be observed as the infant battles with the parent's dual representation as both a fearful object and care provider.

Bowlby's (1973) model of separation anxiety was further developed and operationalised by Ainsworth *et al.* (1978) in the Strange Situation Experiment in which infants' protests to their mother's departure and the nature of their reunion were classified into specific attachment styles. An avoidant attachment style was demonstrated when the infant showed no distress when the parent left and did not actively seek out the caregiver on return. A secure attachment style, when the caregiver represents a secure base, was reflected by the infant's distress on departure but responsiveness and comfort at reunion. An ambivalent attachment style was characterised by an infant's clingy and distressed response to departure; at reunion, contact was sought but the comfort offered was rejected. The category of disorganised-insecure attachment style was later added (Main and Solomon, 1986) to include infants who showed an absence of clear attachment behaviours as defined by Ainsworth *et al.* (1978). These infants' actions and responses to their caregivers were often a mixture of ambivalent, avoidant and distressed behaviours. Ainsworth *et al.*'s (1978) research findings demonstrated that an individual's attachment system could be activated and observed in order to gain insight into the relationship between an infant and their caregiver and serve as a predictor for attachment styles in adulthood (Waters *et al.*, 2000).

Traumatic early life experience is a significant contributory risk factor to developing psychological difficulties in later life (MacMillan *et al.*, 2001). The formations of psychopathological difficulties, from an attachment perspective, are influenced by early problematic life care interactions that convey hostile and critical expectations about the self, others and how they feel they are perceived. Early life traumas involving separation, loss, violence or neglect can be re-activated and observed in subsequent interpersonal situations across the lifespan, ranging from an infant's reactions to separations and reunions with its caregiver, difficulties deriving sufficient comfort or reassurance from a parent, to problems tolerating, regulating and recognising emotional states within themselves and others. These difficulties can also be observed in the formation and maintenance of personal relationships, especially when earlier interactions have evoked feelings of fear and anxiety.

Insecure attachment difficulties can be observed through an infant's behavioural problems, including repetitive violent acts directed at the self, such as biting or head-banging. In relationships, these children may appear as indifferent to social cues or as hostile and intrusive with peers. Attachment difficulties are later revealed in adulthood; there is evidence that previous relationships characterised by inconsistent care, violence or rejection are re-enacted in adulthood (Miller, 1994). When these adults become parents, problems can emerge when their own sense of security and reassurance is sought from the infant; alternatively, the caregiver may draw on their own fragmented experiences of being cared for to recreate a familiar parent and child dynamic. In adulthood, an individual's interpersonal style and personality functioning can be elicited from interview-based attachment measures such as the Adult Attachment Interview (AAI) (George *et al.*, 1996). The individual's recollection of their early life experiences is evaluated in relation to the coherence of their childhood attachment narrative; unconscious aspects of the attachment system are revealed through the discourse. The application of the AAI demonstrates how early attachment experiences continue to influence how individuals seek out, appraise, interpret and sustain personal relationships across the lifespan.

DEVELOPING A THEORY OF MIND

The development of a theory of mind involves the capacity to have a clear sense of one's own mental states, which is largely achieved through the process of mirroring between an infant and its caregiver. The capacity to have a sense of one's own mind, feelings and thoughts is a prerequisite for having a sense of another's mind and to differentiate between the self and another's cognitive and emotional world (Fonagy and Target, 1997). This process involves conceptualising others' attitudes, feelings, hopes and responses. The ability to accurately 'read others' minds' enables potential scripts to be developed and referred to in future social interactions. As an infant develops, perceptions and encounters with others are internalised and the infant begins to learn that they are able to identify, interpret and predict responses within interpersonal exchanges. If caregivers fail to reflect emotional states to the infant, this can contribute to the development of an unstable and fragile sense of self, demonstrated through incongruent, inconsistent appraisals or responses to others.

Fonagy *et al.* (1998) have termed this capacity to conceptualise one's own state of mind an ability to 'mentalise', and consider this to be a strong predictive measure of a secure attachment relationship and psychological well-being and is notably absent in those with recollections of early traumatic experiences of care. An individual's difficulties in separating others' views and concerns from their own, empathising with others and distinguishing between thoughts and feelings, are characteristics associated with mentalising (Fonagy, 1989). The concept of mentalisation has been operationalised as reflective functioning (Fonagy *et al.*, 1998) and is developed from the parent's ability to be reflective in the context of confusing, emotionally uncertain situations, thereby enabling the infant to know their own state of mind. Reflective functioning is measured by an individual's ability to recall and identify emotional states and thought processes in themselves and their caregivers. This process also involves understanding how their own behaviour stems from their emotional states (e.g. I became angry because I felt hurt).

Developing a sufficient theory of mind involves the ability to mentalise, which in turn is associated with having experienced a secure emotional attachment bond (Allen, 2003). The skills involved in mentalisation are reflected through an individual's ability to recognise and interpret their own thoughts, feelings and needs along with those of others, on both a conscious and an unconscious level. This process begins during the developmental stage of infancy when, for example, the infant looks at their mother with hunger; the mother tells the infant they are hungry. In response, the mother soothes or feeds the infant, therefore reflecting the infant's feelings, prior to the development of language. These reciprocal interactions provide the infant with a coherent sense of their internal state and individuality separate from their caregiver and contribute to the development of self-confidence and autonomy.

DISORDERS OF MENTALISATION AND IMPULSE-RELATED VIOLENCE

An inability to mentalise therefore stems from a fragile sense of self and can be observed when individuals fail to differentiate external and internal interpersonal situations, or seem unaware of how to regulate their own thoughts and feelings. In response to this internal emotional confusion, overwhelming or heightened distress can be expressed externally through violence, either against oneself or towards others. Bateman and Fonagy (2004) stress the importance of an infant's experience of attachment relationships to the mentalisation process. However, mentalisation also involves complex interactions within an infant's social, neurological and environmental world and the process is heavily influenced by how the individual interprets their experiences.

People who self-harm often have an insecure sense of self (Bateman and Fonagy, 2004). It is not unusual for this fragility to be shown through the individual's confusion in differentiating and separating their emotional states from others. The problematic internal conflict observed with self-harming adults can be understood developmentally, as the infant who became attached to those who inflicted pain and suffering continues to maintain the attachment relationship to the internalised parent in later life, through self-inflicted violence. A fragmented sense of self is often observed through difficulties identifying, maintaining and protecting personal boundaries, stemming from the uncertainty about where their own sense of being ends and another person begins, in both a physical and psychological context. Self-harm can be seen as an attempt to establish the personal boundary between the self and others through the physical marking of the skin.

THE ABSENCE OF A SECURE BASE

Attachment theory considers self-harm in adulthood to be primarily a consequence of the experiences of early life relationship disruptions (Holmes, 2001). The absence of a safe, containing and reliable attachment figure prevents an infant from experiencing a secure base in which to explore their surroundings confidently or derive sufficient comfort in times of need. The loss of a consistent caregiver prevents the development of an internal mental representation of a secure base. In times of distress or uncertainty, the individual has an insufficient form of internal security or mental representations of containment to draw on. In response, self-harm can provide a paradoxical function that involves both attacking the self while simultaneously offering a self-soothing response to distress.

Self-harm can provide a physical resolution to the experience of internal chaotic states of anger, guilt and frustration. The individual with inconsistent experiences or abusive recollections of a secure base is likely to struggle with tolerating or containing internal feelings or seeking comfort or reassurance from others in times of need. The fear of rejection, abandonment, abuse or violence is a reflection of their fragile identity, stemming from incongruent experiences of early care. The powerful feelings from early life traumas are expressed violently towards the self and provide a form of comfort and control; this is a visible signal of internal chaos.

For individuals who have experienced early relationship traumas or separations, conscious and unconscious feelings of anger, loss and anxiety may be reactivated within particular interpersonal exchanges. These powerful feelings, stemming from anxiety, can be interpreted and expressed as anger and directed towards the self through violence. Within this context, self-harm can provide an immediate physical and visible resolution to the expression of longstanding, internal and overwhelming distress.

DEVELOPMENT OF SELF HARM IN ADOLESCENCE[1]

Self-harm often starts in adolescence and can emerge through a range of self-destructive behaviours, including substance misuse, cutting, overdoses and eating disorders. During this transitional stage of development between childhood and adulthood, self-harm can be understood as the expression of earlier losses, anger and fear being displayed on the body. Adolescent self-harmers frequently present with similar experiences of early histories of abuse, disruptive home environments and psychosocial stressors (Sansone *et al.*, 2004). Yates *et al.*'s (2008b) research highlights how a sense

1 See Chapter 4 for further discussion.

of parental criticism and alienation contributes to adolescents turning to their bodies as opposed to others, using self-inflicted violence to resolve conflicts. The presence of self-harm in adolescence highlights the difficult interpersonal transitions between childhood and adulthood relationships with peers, parents and the home and school environment. The work of Yates *et al.* (2008a) also explores the different manifestations of self-harm dependent on the nature of the abuse suffered, whether sexual or physical.

CASE EXAMPLE

Dominic, a 17-year-old boy, had experienced multiple episodes of sexual abuse from older male relatives from the age of seven before being taken into care. His childhood experiences of care were characterised by inconsistent, contradictory and violent interactions.

Dominic was admitted to an inpatient unit, due to his prolific self-harming. His self-harm was impulsive, desperate and frequent. He would use any available breakable object to repeatedly attack his body. When he was unable to self-harm, he would initiate an assault that would result in a physical restraint. The impact of this imposed physical containment often resulted in re-enactments of previous abusive experiences through being overpowered by men. In response, Dominic would become more isolated, angry and violent towards his body.

Dominic rarely spoke and never initiated conversation. He often hid beneath his baseball cap and never maintained eye contact. His minimal interactions made it difficult to form or establish a rapport with him. His behaviour kept staff at a safe distance and prevented a relationship developing that may invoke feelings of fear, abuse or rejection. Attempts at engaging him in conversations and activities often resulted in Dominic disengaging or rejecting what was offered. This led to feelings of helplessness and anger within the team that, despite continuing attempts, nothing was 'good enough' for Dominic.

Over many months of Dominic rejecting attempts to engage, he was able to develop some trust within the staff team. Initially his relationship with his male named nurse was continually attacked and rejected as Dominic sought to test out whether the therapeutic boundaries were safe, genuine and containing. Dominic's fears about engaging in a trusting relationship were linked to his previous experiences of being betrayed and attacked. His anxieties and need for control were demonstrated through his disengagement and re-engagement within relationships. His feelings of anger, self-loathing and guilt continued to be expressed through self-harm. As time developed he was able to recognise these feelings and talk about the confusion, anger and shame that had previously been expressed on his body. The development of a secure base took considerable time for someone who had experienced a damaging and abusive form of care in the past. Despite ongoing team debate about whether his nurse should be changed to a female key worker, the development of a therapeutic relationship with a man, which was neither abusive nor controlling, but instead, containing, robust and safe, was a significant symbolic step for Dominic in moving away from his abusive past.

THE INTERPERSONAL DYNAMICS OF SELF-HARM

Destructive or maladaptive behaviours directed at the body can be understood as non-verbal communication of unmet relational needs or the expression of difficulties that are too painful or overwhelming to speak about (Motz, 2001). If self-harm is understood as a form of violent communication and the expression of internal emotional conflicts, a verbal dialogue needs to be established to facilitate a shared understanding of these actions.

Self-harm can provide a form of affect regulation (Favazza and Conterio, 1989) especially in response to the activation of attachment needs such as loss, abandonment or rejection, which may be salient to an individual's earlier life experiences. Self-harm can also represent the re-enactment and continuation of violence (Miller, 1994), reflected by an individual's body remaining the target of ongoing abuse. Attacks to the self may also be understood as a conscious or unconscious response to experiencing traumatic memories (Van der Kolk *et al.*, 1991) and a strategy for processing, adjusting and communicating the complex feelings that arise from change and loss (Low *et al.*, 2000). Self-harm has also been interpreted as a symbol of survival and a positive method of coping with distress (Burstow, 1992). The individual who self-harms can be viewed as taking control of their lives and releasing their difficulties through marking but not destroying the body (Burstow, 1992).

Self-harm is a problematic, complex and often hidden behaviour that is frequently an indicator of further underlying emotional difficulties (Gardner, 2001). When physical, emotional or sexual abuse has occurred, subsequent attacks to the body can represent earlier psychological or physical wounds that were inflicted on the individual. In later life, the body can be used to expel the distress, anger and shame that are evoked by traumatic memories. This complex internal conflict is heightened if a caregiver also perpetrated the abuse, thereby producing conflicting and incongruent representations of care.

SELF-HARM, TRAUMA AND ATTACHMENT RESEARCH

Research studies have identified early potential predictive risk factors and life experiences that may contribute to individuals' likelihood to self-harm in adulthood, for example, disrupted attachments, violence, emotional neglect and sexual abuse (Van der Kolk *et al.*, 1991). Psychoanalytically informed mentalisation treatments have been found to reduce episodes of self-harm, anxiety, depression and symptom severity (Bateman and Fonagy, 2004) with individuals presenting with severe and complex emotional and relational difficulties.

Van der Kolk *et al.* (1991) study used historic and projective data of 74 participants who were monitored over four years. Self-harm rates were correlated with self-report questionnaires on, for example, childhood trauma, disassociation and disruptions in parental care. The results highlighted how childhood sexual and physical abuse, along with neglect and separation from caregivers, were significant predictors of self-harming in later life. During the two-year follow-up, those who experienced severe separation and neglect in childhood were more likely to self-harm in response to experiencing difficulties. The findings showed how childhood trauma played a contributory role to self-harming; while disruptions experienced in earlier attachments served to maintain the self-harm. Incidents of self-harm were often triggered by childhood memories of neglect and the re-enactment of abandonment. This important research provided the basis for further exploration of the link between early childhood trauma and self-harm in adulthood.

Low *et al.*'s (2000) study divided female inpatients into three groups: frequent, infrequent and non self-harmers, as defined by the levels of self-harm observed and recorded by staff. Individuals who self-harmed reported heightened levels of anxiety, internal irritability and disassociation. The results demonstrated a clear association between early sexual abuse and self-harming behaviours in later life and identified how disassociation may potentially lead to or contribute to self-harm. A path analytic model was used to explore the relationship between self-harm and early trauma. One pathway linked early childhood experiences to increased dissociative experiences and self-harm. The alternative pathway linked childhood experiences to lowered self-esteem and self-harm.

Women's personal accounts of what led to their self-harm, their perceptions of maintaining factors and staff responses were explored in a secure hospital (Liebling *et al.*, 1997). Many women attributed the development of their self-harm to their early traumatic life experiences of physical, sexual and emotional abuse and family stress. In adulthood, self-harm provided a coping mechanism for expressing and releasing earlier and current emotional difficulties. Many women spoke of wanting an empathic and supportive response when they self-harmed. This wish appeared to represent a form of care they had limited experience of from their own lives. The study highlighted the difficulties women experienced in tolerating their distress and deriving sufficient support from others. Often their actions resulted in mixed, inconsistent and at times critical responses from staff; these messages served to perpetuate feelings of isolation and reinforced a sense of rejection. How an individual's self-harm is responded to can serve to heighten distress or feelings of rejection that may not be otherwise verbalised, or unconsciously re-establish previous relationship patterns and roles, or in contrast a dialogue can emerge to promote a form of tolerance and understanding.

SELF-HARM AND ATTACHMENT IN INSTITUTIONAL SETTINGS

Women in psychiatric hospitals have an increased likelihood of experiencing early trauma, abuse and disturbed attachment styles, and as a result, their difficulties are often reflected through self-harming behaviours (Agrawal *et al.*, 2004). Women are also more likely to direct anger towards the self than to externalise these feelings (Motz, 2001, 2008). A secure environment may provide a sense of safety and containment, not experienced otherwise

(Liebling and Chipchase, 1996) or in contrast may reinforce an individual's perceived helplessness and loss of control. Liebling *et al.* (1997) identified antecedents and precursors in childhood that could lead to self-harming in later life, including early relationship problems, physical and sexual abuse, bullying and loss. Ward structures within secure settings can easily mirror the powerful dynamic between care-provider and care-receiver – mother and infant – and therefore past attachment relationships and interactions are more likely to be reactivated and acted out. For individuals who have experienced abusive early experiences, the probability of forming toxic attachments and the re-enactment of violent interactions increases significantly (Adshead, 2004).

Self-harming behaviours can also evolve as a shared currency for communicating distress. Within institutional settings, this powerful form of expression can serve to initiate the provision of enhanced levels of physical and emotional care that may otherwise not be available. The consequences of self-harming can result in one-to-one observations, thereby providing a sense of emotional and physical containment and recognition of distress. However, when this input is provided it may be experienced as overwhelming, threatening and intrusive. For those who do not self-harm, the perceived additional support bestowed on those who self-harm can create envy and anger.

Self-harm is a powerful action that not only facilitates the expression of an individual's emotional needs but also affects the immediate social systems operating within that person's sphere. In secure institutional settings, individuals' past interactions can be re-enacted through the relaying of familiar relationship scripts and enmeshed experiences. Previous abusive or unreciprocated relationships are often re-enacted unconsciously between an individual and a particular staff member or by a team's response to the individual. Self-harm can serve to project an individual's unconscious guilt and anger onto the staff team, to initiate particularly rejecting or controlling responses that may mirror their earlier child and parent interactions.

WORKING WITH WOMEN WHO SELF-HARM

Working therapeutically with those who self-harm requires the formation of an alliance that facilitates understanding, trust and containment, this may not have been experienced before. This relationship may be simultaneously sought yet rejected, tested and sabotaged as a sign of an individual's relational anxieties. Individual-based attachment psychotherapy focuses on building a secure base with the client within the sessions, which then enables past relationship patterns to be explored in order to understand how these interpersonal dynamics maintain self-harming behaviours (Holmes, 2001). The focus of therapy involves establishing a positive 'good-enough' attachment relationship and to avoid the dangers of representing an idealised care figure or the re-enactment and projection of past attachment figures. The therapy remains boundaried, time limited, robust and containing, while providing the client with fundamental skills in the recognition, acceptance and understanding of their own mental states and experiences.

The emphasis on creating clear, transparent relational boundaries is fundamental to the formation of a secure base with those who experience difficulties observing and maintaining the distinctions between themselves and others. Furthermore, these imposed relational boundaries prevent toxic, enmeshed attachments developing that can be displayed through polarised or inconsistent responses to the individual.

Self-harm has a powerful emotional effect on those who observe such violent acts and provide care to the individual. It can trigger a multitude of responses ranging from the need to protect and care for the individual to feelings of anger, horror and helplessness. An individual's act of self-harm draws others into their violent and chaotic world. The emotional impact of working with those who direct violence towards themselves cannot be underestimated. It is as important for staff working with those who self-harm similarly to have access to a secure base and to feel supported as a team. A protected space, provided within a supervision context, facilitates the discussion and acknowledgment of the impact and effect of working with self-harming individuals. Staff teams who provide emotional containment also need to feel contained and supported, in order to provide care in a challenging and unpredictable environment.

The projection of clients' emotional needs and distress onto staff members can evoke an expectation of presenting as an all-encompassing emotional container who will provide a positive and stable attachment figure. Alternatively, feelings of rejection and anger can be experienced by the therapist or staff member and lead to self-doubt about whether the relationship is a containing or sufficient experience. Clients' unbearable levels of expressed distress, sense of neediness and fear of rejection can contribute to the re-enactment of earlier abusive care experiences and staff members can easily be drawn into these roles.

The process of providing a secure relationship for the client involves tolerating and accepting self-inflicted violence and providing care that is supportive but not rejecting. The balance between promoting responsibility from the individual and providing a sense of containment within the relationship is a complex and changing dynamic. Self-harm can fulfil a purpose or a multitude of functions within relationships at different times. Several questions need to be asked about the function of these violent acts: Is it to initiate care? Is it a response to rejection or fear of abandonment or an expression of anger? Is the violence stemming from a sense of feeling overwhelmed or out of control? Is self-harm serving to maintain the levels of care within the relationship through regulating the amount of contact and concern received? The personal role that self-harm serves needs to be understood in conjunction with the client's personal history and their experience of care, to make sense of these violent actions. The underlying factors that serve to maintain self-harm can be overwhelming and distressing and may be unconsciously avoided in the hope that, if they are not discussed, they may disappear. Similarly, focusing on the physical care and containment of the individual who self-harms can shift the focus away from trying to understand the unresolved factors driving this behaviour to more reactive emotional and immediate responses. These procedural patterns of responding to self-harm are easily activated and often provide an artificial sense of control and containment in times of chaos.

It is not unusual for individuals to re-create and re-enact past abusive relationship patterns unconsciously. Clients can idealise health professionals as the perfect emotional container and individuals may find themselves being perceived as a mother or father figure. The idealised image is fragile and easily destroyed when unrealistic expectations are not met and the subsequent disappointment serves to confirm past care experiences and expectations. An individual's projection of an idealised carer reflects their inadequate boundaries and vulnerabilities that are overtly displayed in the quest to create and experience a form of care that was absent in their earlier lives. Interpersonal anxieties are often reflected in ambivalent interactions with staff members. These inconsistent patterns of seeking contact and then pushing people away reflect the client's process of testing whether the individual can be trusted as a secure base and will not conform to past experiences of instilling feelings of rejection and abandonment.

By aiming to develop a 'good-enough' secure attachment relationship, the staff can reduce unrealistic expectations and hopes for the client that will only serve to reinforce past emotional attachments, through being overwhelming, rejecting or disappointing. The process of establishing emotional attunement with the client provides the foundations for further interpersonal skills and trust to develop. Within the therapeutic relationship, ongoing difficulties can be addressed, including identifying and naming mental states, remaining boundaried yet robust and acknowledging and facilitating the mourning of potential losses. All these processes assist in the development of a stable, positive sense of self. These sustained and consistent interactions can help the formation of a safe base, physically within the ward and intrapsychically within an individual, providing an internal and external perception of safety and containment.

CASE EXAMPLE: TESS

Tess experienced a difficult childhood and was raised in care for much of her early life. She had sporadic contact with her mother and rarely saw her siblings. Tess's contact with her mother was inconsistent: at times she was lavished with gifts or alternatively her mother would ignore her for months at a time. Contact was initiated and ended on her mother's terms.

Tess's chaotic adult lifestyle and reliance on alcohol led to her frequent hospital admission. Without her usual coping mechanisms, she frequently self-harmed to manage her feelings of frustration and sense of isolation. Her interactions with staff members would involve long discussions about her past and she would follow staff around the ward to spend more time with them. Her level of need and wish to be cared for often resulted in staff finding it difficult, draining and tiring to spend time with her. Staff tried to either avoid her or spend significant periods of time with her; a response that unconsciously re-enacted Tess's previous relationships. Despite the time staff spent with Tess, she reported that it was insufficient and in response she would threaten to self-harm.

This sense of feeling abandoned led to her feeling in need of more care and would result in Tess seeking out particular members of staff. Her relational difficulties and needs were demonstrated through Tess calling members of her care team 'mum' and initiating and displaying physical affection. When some staff challenged Tess about these inappropriate gestures, she would respond angrily and isolate herself and, in an attempt to manage her sense of rejection and sadness, self-harm. Self-harm provided the re-establishment of contact and physical care, which she craved.

Therapeutic input with Tess involved supporting her to use the allocated time with staff to explore, monitor and understand her feelings and to move away from uncontained interactions that reinforced her sense of abandonment. The cycle of Tess seeking care, feeling rejected and subsequently self-harming was sensitively explored with her and used as a starting point to consider alternative, less destructive, options. A structured time-limited appointment with an agreed agenda and allocated space to think about managing potentially difficult situations in the interim period, helped prevent a sense of abandonment and provided a focus for Tess. In between sessions, Tess used a diary to monitor her patterns of interactions and difficulties. It became an adjunct to the sessions that enabled her to monitor, check and challenge her self and enhanced her own identity. The diary also facilitated a process of shared and private reflection and exploration within and beyond the sessions. Over time, Tess was able to acknowledge and talk about her sense of loneliness and the role of alcohol in managing her painful feelings when she had no access to her usual method of coping. Outside of the sessions, Tess was also encouraged to engage with other staff members on the ward to prevent toxic attachments developing between Tess and particular female members of staff.

CONCLUSIONS

Early attachment experiences are crucial in serving as a template that not only informs expectations and assumptions for future relationships but also impacts on the development of an individual's sense of self and perception of others. Attachment theory provides a developmental framework in which self-harm can be interpreted and understood from an individual's early life attachment system and subsequent experiences of care. Although an unpredictable and inconsistent attachment system does not necessarily result in the development of interpersonal difficulties in later life, it is certainly a significant risk factor. How an individual understands and appraises their situation and surroundings remains an important factor in the formation of psychological intra- and interpersonal problems in adulthood.

In times of uncertainty, individuals' attachment-seeking behaviours will be triggered to initiate a soothing response to the activated internal distress. Those with predominantly incongruent experiences of care are more likely to struggle with containing and resolving their internal emotional states. Self-harm can provide a physical resolution to the toleration and regulation of unbearable or overwhelming feelings.

In restricted institutional settings, the purpose of self-harm is often complex and will invariably provide a multitude of intra- and interpersonal functions, frequently providing a dual role of comfort and self-punishment.

The process of establishing and experiencing a positive, boundaried, secure 'good-enough' attachment relationship is important to those who have predominantly experienced abusive, violent and unpredictable forms of care. Furthermore, a robust therapeutic alliance can offer the space and opportunity to explore and understand links between previous relationships and ongoing interpersonal dynamics. This relationship can provide a safe base and allow the exploration of the reasons for self-harming, thus reducing the need to do so.

REFERENCES

Adshead, G. (2004) 'Three degrees of security: attachment and forensic institutions', in F. Pfafflin and G. Adshead (eds) *A Matter of Security: The Application of Attachment Theory to Forensic Psychiatry and Psychotherapy*, London: Jessica Kingsley Publishers.

Agrawal, H.R., Gunderson, J., Holmes, B.M. and Lyons-Ruth, K. (2004) 'Attachment studies with borderline patients: a review', *Harvard Review of Psychiatry*, 2: 94–104.

Ainsworth, M.D.S., Blehar, M.C., Waters, E. and Wall, S. (1978) *Patterns of Attachment: A Psychological Study of the Strange Situation*, Hillsdale, NJ: Lawrence Erlbaum Associates, Inc.

Allen, J.G. (2003) 'Mentalizing', *Bulletin of Menninger Clinic*, 67: 91–112.

Bateman, A. and Fonagy, P. (2004) *Psychotherapy for Borderline*

Personality Disorder: Mentalization Based Treatment, London: Oxford University Press.

Bowlby, J. (1969) *Attachment and Loss. Volume 1: Attachment*, London: Hogarth Press.

Bowlby, J. (1973) *Attachment and Loss. Volume 2: Separation: Anxiety and Anger*, London: Hogarth Press.

Burstow, B. (1992) *Radical Feminist Therapy: Working in the Context of Violence*, London: Sage Publications.

Favazza, A.R. and Conterio, K. (1989) 'Female habitual self-mutilators', *Acta Psychiatrica Scandinavica*, 79: 283–289.

Fonagy, P. (1989) 'On tolerating mental states: theory of mind in borderline patients', *Bulletin of Anna Freud Centre*, 12: 91–115.

Fonagy, P. and Target, M. (1997) 'Attachment and reflective function: their role in self-organisation', *Development and Psychopathology*, 9: 679–700.

Fonagy, P., Target, M., Steele, H. and Steele, M. (1998) *Reflective-Functioning Manual, Version 5.0 for Application to Adult Attachment Interviews*, London: University College Press.

Gardner, F. (2001) *Self-Harm. A Psychotherapeutic Approach*, Hove: Brunner-Routledge.

George, C., Kaplan, N. and Main, M. (1996) *Adult Attachment Interview*, Berkeley, CA: Department of Psychology, University of California.

Holmes, J. (2001) *The Search for the Secure Base: Attachment Theory and Psychotherapy*, Hove: Brunner-Routledge.

Liebling, H. and Chipchase, H. (1996) 'Feminist group therapy for women who self-harm: an initial evaluation', *Feminism & Psychology*, 2: 24–29.

Liebling, H., Chipchase, H. and Velhangi, R. (1997) 'Why do women harm themselves? Surviving special hospitals', *Feminism & Psychology*, 3: 427–437.

Low, G., Jones, D., MacLeod, A., Power, M. and Duggan, C. (2000) 'Childhood trauma, dissociation and self-harming behaviour: a pilot study', *British Journal of Medical Psychology*, 73: 269–278.

MacMillan, H.L., Fleming, J.E., Streiner, D.L., Lin, E., Boyle, M.H., Jamieson, E., Duku, E.K., Walsh, C.A., Wong, M.Y.-Y. and Beardslee, W.R. (2001) 'Childhood abuse and lifetime psychopathology in a community sample', *American Journal of Psychiatry*, 158: 1878–1883.

Main, M. and Solomon, J. (1986) 'Discovery of a new, insecure-disorganized/disorientated attachment pattern', in T.B. Brazelton and M.W. Yogman (eds) *Affective Development in Infancy*, New York: Ablex.

Miller, M. (1994) *Women who Hurt Themselves. A Book of Hope and Understanding*, New York: Basic Books.

Motz, A. (2001) *The Psychology of Female Violence: Crimes Against the Body* (first edition), Hove: Routledge.

Motz, A. (2008) *The Psychology of Female Violence: Crimes Against the Body* (second edition), Hove: Routledge.

Sansone, R.A., Levitt, J.L. and Sansone, L.A. (2004) 'An overview of psychotherapy strategies for the management of self-harm behavior', in J.L. Levitt, R.A. Sansone and L. Cohn (eds) *Self-Harm Behavior and Eating Disorders: Dynamics, Assessment, and Treatment* (pp. 121–134), New York: Brunner-Routledge.

Van der Kolk, B.A., Perry, J.C. and Herman, J.L. (1991) 'Childhood origins of self-destructive behaviour', *American Journal of Psychiatry*, 148: 1665–1671.

Waters, E., Merrick, S., Treboux, D., Crowell, J. and Albersheim, L. (2000) 'Attachment security in infancy and early adulthood: a twenty-year longitudinal study', *Child Development*, 71: 684–689.

Yates, T.M., Carlson, E.A. and Egeland, B. (2008a) 'A prospective study of child maltreatment and self-injurious behaviour in a community sample', *Development and Psychopathology*, 20: 651–672.

Yates, T.M., Tracy, A.J. and Luthar, S.S. (2008b) 'Nonsuicidal self-injury among "privileged" youths: longitudinal and cross-sectional approaches to development process', *Journal of Consulting and Clinical Psychology*, 76: 52–62.

Part 3

Women and self-harm

Chapter 6

Speaking with the body

Pamela Kleinot

Vignette 1

Kay's mother left her when she was aged two, taking her sister and brother with her to another island in the Caribbean. She was left in the care of her father who went to live in the UK when she was five, leaving her with her aunt who used to beat her. Both parents remarried and had other children. She was sexually abused by a neighbour at seven. She began slashing her body when she was 12 and took her first overdose at 13. She had periods of anorexia, alternating with binging and drinking herself into a stupor, from the age of 15 and had a son when she was 16. Kay, aged 23, was serving a three-year sentence at a women's prison for smuggling cocaine into Britain hidden in her vagina. Two years before the offence she drank bleach while pregnant and the baby died in her womb.

Kay's story encapsulates the essence of self-harm and murderousness which entails using the body violently to express emotional distress. It is a psychic symptom that is autistic because it appears not be able to be spoken or thought about. The person seems to lack the ability to self-soothe. In my conceptualisation, suicide and self-harm, including disfiguring the body through eating disorders and excessive drinking, are driven by the same impulse. Violence is used to protect against psychic pain. It is a frantic attempt to assuage overwhelming trauma that an individual cannot process. There is a compulsion to act, not think, as tension builds up and the person becomes flooded with feelings. There is an unconscious dread of falling apart. The torment is linked to early psychic trauma that remains raw and undigested. What is upsetting must be got rid of. This is commonly known as acting out.[1] It is as though signal anxiety has gone awry, unable to register a danger signal and make use of suitable defences. The purpose of psychotherapy is to decode the signals and provide an internal container for the digestion of intolerable affects, and for transforming the unthinkable into the thinkable (Bion, 1967).

In this chapter I discuss a psychoanalytic model for understanding and treating self-harm, which should be viewed in a social-relational context. I focus on the more extreme self-harm, which includes physical injury, as the person acts on intolerable experiences rather than thinking about them. This is due to an inability to mourn early loss. Difficulties in thinking and mourning are linked to failures to symbolise properly following breaches in early containment. I distinguish between suicide and physical self-harm and use case material based on an amalgam of several years' experience of working with such patients in a women's prison in the UK. I suggest that self-harm is linked to a deep feeling of not being wanted and the shame associated with it.

I explore the link with borderline personality states and in case illustrations I examine my experience of an inner deadness in patients who self-harm, which evokes a powerful drowsiness in me as though I am being anaesthetised and drawn into the patient's unconscious world of blocking out pain. I have come to understand the symptom as alexithymia, a term coined by Sifneos (1973) to express the idea that without words we can neither think nor know what we feel. The word alexithymia is derived from Greek meaning 'without words for feelings'. I suggest that self-harm and alexithymia may be seen as a defence against annihilation and falling apart. The terror of abandonment is the inflammatory wound. I discuss the therapeutic task of containing and metabolising the patient's experience to help them to understand the meaning of their behaviour and move from action (wounds) to talking (words). The most important job for a therapist is to pay

1 Acting out is a defence used to express unconscious feelings or conflicts through actions rather than words. It is a maladaptive coping mechanism, which includes using alcohol, drugs and self-harm to expresses painful, angry or confusing feelings that a person cannot verbalise.

attention to countertransference as they attempt to process the toxic material from the patient's past and try to remain thinking under provocation.

I suggest that the repetition compulsion is a key factor in self-harm as it becomes an habitual way of attempting to block out psychic pain by inflicting physical wounds. Psychoanalyst Paul Russell (1991), an inspiring teacher whose many papers remained unpublished in his lifetime but whose mentorship and prescient ideas influenced the writing of several leading relational analysts in the United States, wrote with insight about the repetition compulsion 'as if drawn to some fatal flame', which he considered to be one of Freud's greatest legacies. Russell regarded it as being a search for a lost relationship and the cost of that unmourned loss, which was like an addiction, 'as if governed by some malignant attraction which one does not know and cannot comprehend or control' (1991: 4).

My understanding of physical self-harm has also been influenced by Fairbairn (1952), who challenged Freud's drive theory that man was object-seeking not pleasure-seeking, postulating that our need for emotional contact was the basis of mental life; Bowlby (1958) who reframed defences in terms of attachment theory, highlighting our need to belong and the traumatic impact of separation and loss; and Foulkes (1948), the founding father of group analysis in Britain, who believed in the sociality of man and described an autistic symptom seeking to communicate and be understood – a key striving in borderline personality states.

CLINICAL DISCUSSION

Kay was one of many women whose violence follows the trauma of sexual abuse and early separation. Her name could be added to the long list of Jamaican drug mules crowding UK jails who attempt to transform their lives through drug dealing. She was born into a dislocated and impoverished family with a legacy of slavery. She had suffered extreme deprivation and had self-harmed for much of her life. It had become an addictive way to channel her distress. Mahatma Ghandi suggested that poverty was the deadliest form of violence (quoted in Gilligan, 1996).

Kay was referred by her probation officer because she was a high suicide risk. I saw her for once-weekly individual psychotherapy for 14 months. Kay was abandoned and repeated history by abandoning her own child – leaving him in Jamaica – by being in prison thousands of miles away. She said she felt like she was an undesirable package passed around from her mother to her father and then her aunt. The scars on her arms were testimony of her inner wounds. Kay lacked the capacity to symbolise. I often struggled to stay awake in her presence as waves of exhaustion engulfed me. She was disconnected from her own emotional state as she talked about her life and did not have the words or language to describe her distress. It seemed she was terrified of contact and the possibility of being left yet again. The only way she could convey it was to make me feel it through projective identification whereby a person projects unwanted feelings into another person (Klein, 1946). It was as though she was numb and mute (alexithymic). Kay gave me the experience of what it was like to feel unwanted (unloved), a shameful feeling of being grubby and repellent. There were times when I felt as though I was being anaesthetised in her presence and drawn into her void. She was sad and lonely. I could sense her desolation and emptiness as though there was nothing inside her. In my countertransference I felt lost and useless. I imagined that she felt like a blob without any colour or shape, trapped in a dark, locked space where nothing grew as if she was in a black hole (Tustin, 1986). I found it hard to connect to her and for us to think together about what had happened to her and make sense of her behaviour.

My understanding of Kay is that she suffered from an absence of a caregiver having been abandoned by her mother, then her father into the cruel hands of her aunt who gave her no warmth or love. She had no one to whom she could attach herself as a baby. There was no mother to soothe her, to gently disillusion and frustrate her, so she turned in on herself. I suggest that Kay's severe traumas caused her to suffer psychic annihilation or 'soul murder' as Shengold (1989) termed it. In psychoanalytic terms, I understand her self-harming to be linked to the first few months of life where her ego fragmented and she regressed to an unintegrated state as the 'environment mother' had failed to hold (Winnicott, 1960) or contain (Bion, 1962) her. Such a serious disruption in her care caused her to regress to the Basic Fault Level (Balint, 1968). Kay died psychically in early infancy (Winnicott, 1974). Her predicament was not about a bad object but being in a world of no object, ruled by emptiness with no one to mirror her, soothe her or value her talents. She was not able to develop the capacity to symbolise and link her self-harming to her childhood. In Freud's (1917) seminal paper on mourning and melancholia, he describes how the patient incorporates the lost object and identifies with it, effectively turning against the self in hatred.

Kay was constantly replaying her early trauma of abandonment by attacking her body, which was a symbolic representation of her mother. Her suicide attempts may be seen as a way of trying to kill herself off by destroying the mother within. She was trying both to eliminate and to torture her mother by these assaults. Suicide may be understood symbolically as murdering the mother, self-mutilation torturing the mother and anorexia starving the mother. In all three cases, it is important to have a body split off from the mind that becomes triumphant, according to Campbell and Hale (1991), who have identified unconscious suicidal motivation in self-harm that includes a fantasy of 'elimination' in which bad bits of the self can be evacuated through attacks on the body.

Individuals like Kay are often referred to as 'difficult patients' and diagnosed with borderline personality disorder because of such chronicity, impulsivity and chaotic relationships. Like Kay, they may show 'psychotic' features when talking about hurting themselves in response to 'voices'. Kay insisted that her abuser, Charles, had told her to harm herself. As Charles was long dead, it became clear that this 'voice' represented Kay's abuser and was part of her – the part she hated – her split-off rage that she could not access. She did not have the language and often looked at me blankly. Kay was in fact dissociating, a psychological mechanism used to block out memories. Self-harming seemed to help deflect from her pain and provided relief from unbearable tension.

Kay's charge of smuggling cocaine to make money could be seen as the perfect crime to change her life by bringing wealth and happiness – the search for an object relation that is associated with ego transformation and repair (Bollas, 1992). Her transgression may be seen as an unconscious way of seeking help. Winnicott (1956) refers to the antisocial tendency, not delinquency, which is an expression of hope that the individual is adamant that the environment must make something up to them – something good that has been lost.

Vignette 2

Ana was born a year after her brain-damaged brother died. The family home in Brazil was filled with memorabilia of the dead baby – clothes, photographs and boys toys – but no one ever spoke about him. Ana said that her mother always hated her. She began to cut herself from the age of nine. She was promiscuous and began taking drugs when she was 13. She had an abortion at 15, the first of many. She stumbled from one abusive relationship to another and had two children who had been taken into care. She had persistent headaches and stomach pain. Ana, aged 26, was convicted of fraud and deception.

'I never felt I existed,' said Ana, who appeared to grow up feeling not wanted or loved for herself. She hated her birthdays, saying she had nothing to celebrate. As a replacement child it seemed she did not feel entitled to live, she was not the 'real' thing but a replacement, a fraud, which in some way explains her crime of defrauding social services.

Ana's experience of hateful early contact may have been impossible to process mentally. The message engraved on her arms and legs was violent, which appeared to reflect her inner wound of being a replacement child and not feeling wanted. She could not think about what happened to her. I experienced Ana as wooden and lifeless in sessions, which sometimes aroused an intense and sudden sleepiness in me. She had developed a pseudo-independence and it seemed she could not tolerate any connection for long with partners, parents or even her own children. She was frightened of closeness and always expected to be let down. In a thought-provoking paper on drowsiness in the countertransference, Dennis Brown (1977) describes self-sufficiency as a defence against total regression to a longed-for but dreaded dependence and merging, and thus both abandonment and loss of self. He quotes Dickes (1965) as describing a hynoid state (usually termed fatigue, drowsiness or sleepiness) as representing a defence against unacceptable sexual and aggressive impulses related to repressed memories.

Ana's distress was somatised, that is, expressed through the body, as she could not put into words what she was feeling. Her headaches may be understood as her way of not engaging with her thoughts while her stomach pains may reflect her difficulty trying to metabolise or stomach such undigestable experiences. This form of alexithymia accounts for the common currency of expression in women's services (Aiyegbusi, 2004). I found it difficult to stay awake in her sessions. The only flicker of life was when her face lit up as she described the relief after she had cut herself. Cutting can induce euphoria with the release of the body's own morphine-like substances, known as endorphins.

Ana's visceral description of the excitement (arousal) and release from tension was as though she was experiencing an orgasm from her assaults on her body, which verifies Welldon's (1992) idea of self-injury as a perversion rooted in a woman's experience of being mothered in infancy.

Ana's promiscuity and killing her babies through abortions also accords with Welldon's notion of a woman's perversion to use her whole body, including reproductive capacities. The dead babies may reflect Ana's deep feeling of not being wanted by her mother and trying to kill off her baby self through repetitive abortions. I suggest that she may be envious of her own capacity to become a mother and the care she might be able to give an infant, which was lacking in her own life. Her many abortions may also be seen as failed attempts to replay her own early trauma of being a replacement child who could never make up for the idealised brother that was lost to her parents.

RELATIONAL CONTEXT OF SELF-HARM

Both Kay and Ana illustrate how self-harm viewed as a perversion stems from a disturbed infant–mother relationship, which ranges from lack of containment (Bion, 1962) to coldness, cruelty or indifference. Both patients longed for connection but were terrified of intimacy. I have found Henri Rey's (1994) idea about a claustro-agoraphobic dilemma useful in understanding patients like Kay and Ana who are unable to find security either with or away from their objects. Rey suggested that this anxiety was common to borderline and psychotic patients who felt trapped and developed a claustrophobic reaction when too close to their objects while agoraphobic when they tried to escape because they were terrified of the empty space that threatened them with disintegration. He further posited that patients who had not achieved a 'psychological birth' were unable to develop a separate mental life from their primary object. It was as if they were in a 'marsupial space' like a baby kangaroo in its mother's pouch, neither inside nor separate. Patients who inhabit this space feel that their selves reside in the other and live in fear of being engulfed and losing themselves in the other. Rey's ideas were further developed by Glasser (1979), who wrote about the 'core complex', which is basically a survival technique to defend against early anxieties of helplessness and fragmentation.

Taking refuge in a dead world as Ana and Kay have done can be seen as a protection against further loss and a fear of fragmentation. We are born wholly dependent on another for survival – usually a mother who regulates distress and protects her baby from impingements in the environment. Object-loss is a fundamental moment in the structuring of the human psyche. The repetition compulsion is a key feature of such early loss. Russell (1987) suggested that the repetition compulsion represented the interruption of some important early relationship, which carried with it a stunting, an arrest of the development of the capacity to feel. A memory, he suggested, masqueraded as a present-day event and was 'functionally suicidal with every repetition containing a nucleus of hate' (1987: 9). 'The repetition compulsion is the scar tissue of the injury to the capacity to feel. We learn to feel in relationships, and the loss of relationship is the loss of something we need to feel' (1987: 10).

The word 'trauma' is derived from Greek, meaning to wound or pierce. This happens during the baby's delicate stage of forming a self when the ego is vulnerable and totally depends for its survival on the mother, who serves as a supplementary ego (Heimann, 1956, cited in Bollas, 1987), facilitating environment (Winnicott, 1963) and container (Bion, 1962). Sensations are the beginning of psychic life as the baby is fed, bathed and changed by anOther. Bowlby (1958) followed Freud's (1920) idea that traumatic events breached the 'protective shield' that guards the ego from being over-stimulated. The mother in her caretaking role provides a filtering function to protect her baby from extremes of experience. She manages the baby's arousal by acting as a protective shield but when this becomes overwhelming, it sets in motion defensive measures, particularly the repetition compulsion, whereby the ego seeks mastery over the intolerable arousal by re-experiencing it. The essence of a traumatic experience is the ego's experience of 'helplessness' when over-stimulated (Freud, 1926).

Vignette 3

Paula was adopted as a baby. Her parents constantly argued until her adoptive mother abandoned her when she was 11. Paula was left in the care of her alcoholic father, who raped and beat her regularly. She began burning herself with cigarettes at 14. Her life of crime began soon after she started taking drugs and dropped out of school. She worked as a prostitute and shoplifted to finance her heroin habit. Paula's three children were taken into care by social services. She had been in and out of prison for the past 15 years for various offences including grievous bodily harm for stabbing a taxi driver to steal his cash. I met her when she was 33, awaiting trial on a charge of murder.

Paula's attacks on herself and others appeared to reflect her broken violent attachments and deep feeling of rejection. She was referred for once-weekly psychotherapy because she was burning herself profusely. I was struck by her appearance when I first met her: dishevelled, with missing teeth and scars all over her face, looking battered by life and much older than her 33 years. Paula was expecting a life sentence after injecting one of her clients with heroin. He passed out and although his lips turned blue, a visible sign that he was dying, she did not call an ambulance. She sat beside him and smoked a pipe of heroin before snatching his wallet and car keys and setting off for a nightclub.

Paula had spent much of her life anaesthetising her pain with drugs, drink and sex to negate the self that suffers. I felt paralysed in her early sessions, at times useless and speechless, which I thought was her projection of helplessness and despair. She related to me anorexically as she struggled to take anything from me. It was as if she had to hold herself together tightly and could not bare the humiliation of being 'helped'. However, in one session after about five months it seemed we had made contact as she reflected on her life and spoke with regret about 'terrible' things she had done and how ashamed she felt. Foremost was how she treated her children. 'How could any human being behave like that,' she said. We talked about her vulnerable and murderous sides. For the first time I felt a warmth towards her. The following session she was furious and after about five minutes let rip. In summary, she exploded; she verbally attacked me, saying she wouldn't harm an insect and insisted she was not a murderer. She was shaking and her face became flushed. As her voice became louder, my palms became clammy and my heartbeat raced. I was anxious and feared she would physically assault me. I struggled to think under this onslaught. There was no panic button in the room. I told her we needed to slow down and think about what was happening. She went silent. I was relieved. After a few minutes, we began to talk about her rage and before she left she said she had wanted to hit me and run out of the room.

What happened between Paula and myself was extremely complex. My difficulty in being with her in the room helped me understand her own early experience of not feeling wanted. Her nonchalance was a façade. I had previously been aware of feeling under enormous pressure to react sadistically to her, which I understood to be her defence against an inner state of helplessness and panic. I understood her anorexic way of relating as linked to her unmet needs, which were insatiable. Her needs and constant rejections became conflated. I suggest that her needs, which were overwhelming, made her feel greedy and shameful. It seemed safer for her to deny her appetite, withdraw into herself and starve. Anything she took from me had to be repudiated. Her life was filled with destruction, abuse and self-hatred. I suggest that making contact with me the previous week and getting in touch with her tenderness felt intolerable: it awakened a deep feeling of being unlovable and it seemed she could not bear to feel the sadness of her losses and regrets. Although she longed for connection, she was terrified (Glasser, 1979; Rey, 1994).

Paula did not have a caretaker to mirror her and help negotiate early feeling states. It was easier for her to ward off psychic pain than to face it. She had no internal template of a relationship. I suggest that she had suffered 'psychic death' as a baby (Winnicott, 1974; Green, 1980). She was emotionally crippled by a life filled with rejections: first by her birth mother, then her adoptive mother, passed into the cruel treatment of her father who used her for his own gratification. She defended herself from falling apart through her lifestyle of addiction, prostitution and crime. It seemed the only way she could feel alive was the temporary high she got from heroin and from abusing her body.

THE SKIN AS CONTAINER

I have found Bick's (1962) concept of a psychic skin as container to hold the personality together useful in understanding the link between Paula's early ruptures and her self-harm. This psychic skin as container is achieved in the sensuous interplay between mother and baby during the suckling phase as the nipple, breast and mother are fused. The nipple seals the hole in the boundary between mother and baby (primary skin formation). When the process of primary skin sensation goes wrong, the infant forms a 'second skin sensation' to keep the personality intact and contain them from the fear of 'falling into pieces'. The second skin sensation is 'the inappropriate use of certain mental functions, or perhaps innate talents, for the purpose of creating a substitute for this skin container function' (Bick, 1968: 56). Bick's concept of 'adhesive identification' whereby the baby appears to 'stick to' the object rather than having introjected a space (the primary object) has particular relevance to self-harm where no space exists as the cigarette burns the flesh or the scissors cut the skin. Bick's ideas were further developed by the French analyst Anzieu (1989), who saw the skin ego as a psychological body envelope that separates self from object. The skin encapsulates a sense of self and separates itself from an external object.

Paula's early damage as an infant made it hard for her to have any form of relationship or intimacy. She could only attack herself and her thinking was concrete, making it difficult to graft meaning on to her experience. She coped by dissociating and encapsulating the affects in autistic enclaves (Mitrani, 1996) and numbed her pain with drugs, which were readily available, whereas people were not. Nothing I did or said enlivened the deadness I experienced in the room. Encapsulation as 'a defence against annihilation anxiety through which a person attempts to enclose, encase and to seal-off the sensations, affects and representations associated with it' has been defined and documented by Hopper (2003: 1999). I felt challenged by Paula to grasp the minute hope in our sessions, mindful that she had asked for therapy, perhaps indicating a longing for contact or perhaps it was just relief from pain. I saw Paula for once-weekly psychotherapy for eight months before she was convicted; her murder charge was converted to manslaughter and she was abruptly transferred to another prison.

Vignette 4

Sophie was strikingly beautiful with long blonde hair and green eyes. She had scars on her arms from cutting. She and her younger brother were brought up by her impoverished mother who worked as a prostitute and brought various 'uncles' home from the pub. She was sexually abused by her mother's boyfriend, who lavished the family with gifts. Sophie's mother often became so drunk that she used to soil herself and Sophie had to clean her up and put her to bed. She began cutting her face and arms when she was 10. Her mother told her to stop telling lies when she disclosed the abuse. Sophie ran away from home at 11, slept rough and was taken into care for four years. She began taking drugs and drinking heavily at 14 and was prone to violent outbursts. She found intimacy intolerable. I met her when she was 20 while serving a four-year sentence for grievous bodily harm against a man who 'slighted' her in her local pub.

I saw Sophie for once-weekly psychotherapy for 15 months before she was unexpectedly transferred to another prison. She was referred by a prison officer because of her depression and persistent cutting. I found her mercurial. Her moods changed rapidly in a single session. She had psychotic episodes and her defences were easily unsettled. She often experienced explorations as criticism and her violent states of mind were palpable. I always sensed that her finger was never far from the self-destruct button. I got a flavour of how swiftly she felt shamed and lost control, which helped me make sense of her crime: she cut a man's right eye with glass when she felt he had insulted her. He lost the sight of that eye. I understood Sophie's self-harm and violence towards others as a response to shame. The notion of shame as a pathogen that causes violence has been conceptualised by James Gilligan (1996), who has compared its specificity to the tubercle bacillus, which causes tuberculosis. Gilligan describes how this deadly emotion drives people to destroy others and themselves.

As Sophie spoke about her losses she aroused strong feelings in me, from sadness to dread. At times I found it hard being in the room with her, particularly when she became blank as though there was a huge gaping hole inside her. I struggled to make sense of the nothingness that filled the space between us. It was like touching a void. Sophie did not have the equipment to process or even describe what she was feeling. It was as though she was getting rid of psychic lumps of what Bion (1967) called beta elements. I often felt detached in her sessions and struggled to enter her experience. I came to understand my drowsiness and this emptiness as standing in place of meaning, the helpless child unable to articulate her experience of a switched-off mother – her early trauma of disconnection from her mother, which remained raw and unprocessed. My drowsiness may also have been an unconscious attempt on my part to ward off Sophie's painful material and resist the projections of her dreadful trauma.

Sophie attended her sessions regularly for several months until one session after an Easter holiday when I had to take an unscheduled break for a month. When I returned she told me she thought I would never come back. She started missing sessions and acting out in various ways. Evidence pointed to her returning to drugs as she was exhausted and cut off during most of her sessions. I felt drained after these encounters.

Despite her deadness, she had considerable charm and in a perverse way had learnt to get what she wanted from people. She was adept at manipulating her environment by being seductive, which she had mastered while in care. In the prison context she used her beauty and seductive skills to nudge officers into breaking the rules. Sophie got away with the most incredible things with the collusion of prison staff. On one occasion, drugs had been posted to her in prison. She was suspended from her job and stripped of her status. She decided that the woman opposite her cell had posted the drugs. She beat her up and told me how a group of officers clapped and cheered her on. The following week, Sophie was back at work; her privileges had been reinstated.

BOUNDARIES AND TRANSGRESSIONS

Sophie subsequently got away with testing positive for morphine during a routine urine test. She told the prison staff that her tea had been spiked by an inmate. About a month later I went to collect her for her session and was told that she had been transferred. I spoke to a senior officer with whom she had a 'special relationship'. The officer said: 'I've protected her for too long. I just couldn't do it this time. She came to me because she was in trouble. She had a urine test after smoking heroin in the room with the girls. I managed to get her shipped out before the test results came back. I couldn't go on protecting her. I felt betrayed'.

It seems that the prison officer lost her boundaries because of her own neediness. On the surface she seemed caring and protective but Sophie eventually had to be transferred to another prison because of her drug dealing. This was a classic example of destructive behaviour masked as protectiveness. It is important to note that there was a lack of supervision and support for prison officers who often mirror the prisoners by acting rather than thinking.

Although Sophie used her charm to seduce and had spent much of her life winning people over, she was repeatedly rejected and thrown out of places. This got played out in the prison where she was 'spoilt' by prison staff who turned vindictive when she got too much and evicted her. This case highlights the difficulty with boundary issues, particularly with this vulnerable patient group who pose a high risk to professionals as their sexuality has been intertwined with care. They crave intensity and emotionally charged relationships. The patient may idealise the carer and long to be 'special' (Main, 1957), initially gratifying the carer but often ending up being rejected as the carer collapses under such insatiable demands. Enactments are inevitable in all therapeutic relationships and it is imperative to have a space to talk about this work. At times, therapists walk a tightrope with borderline patients, balancing their need to protect and desire to retaliate under provocation. Borderline patients have a propensity to evoke powerful feelings, which, if not processed, pose a threat to the therapeutic space. It can become a slippery slope as boundaries become distorted, ranging from minor transgressions to actual sexual relations. Therapists have their own blindspots and the lure of vulnerablility, including the unconscious attraction of particularly one so beautiful as Sophie who at times seems so tender and helpless, poses a danger to an inadequate therapist's hungry need to feel worthwhile or merely have their narcissistic needs gratified.

I learnt how difficult it was to maintain my therapeutic role with patients who act out and put obstacles in the therapy. Many patients in secure settings experience 'care' as a provocation (Adshead, 1997). They yearn for an idealised soothing carer who will take their torment away but, in reality, no care can be good enough and attempts to provide care are denigrated. Adshead warns that by accepting the caring role, the professional unconsciously engages in a traumatic re-enactment, playing the part of both the abusing carer and the carer who fails. I understand that the early environmental failure and level of deficit can never be undone.

GENERAL DISCUSSION

Kay, Ana, Paula and Sophie's violence towards themselves substantiates Welldon's (1988) notion that self-harm is a typically female act of violence where the aggressive impulse is turned inwards on their own bodies or babies. Other clinicians have grappled with this subject and made various attempts to understand and treat the underlying motivation of people who deliberately hurt themselves. The idea of physical forms of self-harm having both a private and a public meaning has been formulated by Kroll (1993). The view that crimes committed against the body are a painful way of saying 'I hurt' and may disguise a wish to harm others has been suggested by Motz (2001). Self-harm has also been referred to as the psychic wound written on the body (Adshead, 1997) and signing with a scar (Straker, 2006). Self-harm may also be understood as a cruel attack on the body – a form of self-murder, according to Campbell and Hale (1991), who also see it as an attack on the minds of therapists and those who care for them.

Prison is generally a highly charged atmosphere where the use of drugs is rife and sex is used to ward off pain. All the patients I saw while working there over several years had experienced extensive abuse and deprivation. Their lives were filled with undigested traumas and one of the main ways they knew how to relate in the world was to act out, which provided a temporary relief from their anguish.

It is a challenge trying to offer psychotherapy in a prison where the line between treatment and punishment is blurred. Apart from the difficulties of engaging with deprived and damaged patients, psychotherapists also have to deal with the impingement of a traumatised institution on the work – an institution that is completely unthinking. The patient and the institution, singly and in combination, at times employ impenetrable defences and it is difficult to navigate around this fortress. There have been some changes in the prison since I worked there many years ago, when several of my patients were sent to the punishment block when they self-harmed. Changes took place when care came come under the auspices of the National Health Service. However, prison staff often lack understanding of the acting-out behaviour that communicates particular individual and societal conflicts.

SOCIAL CONTEXT

The majority of prisoners come from impoverished backgrounds and have suffered extreme deprivation and social exclusion. Their violence towards themselves and others rooted in a fear of abandonment should always be viewed in a social context. Foulkes and Anthony (1957 [1965]) viewed individuals as nodal points in a communicational network in which the social permeated the individual to the core. They defined health as the free flow of communication through the network (the community). Ill-health was a blockage in the system, which they termed the 'autistic symptom': 'It mumbles to itself secretly, hoping to be overheard' (Foulkes and Anthony, 1957 [1965]: 259).

Social exclusion is a fundamental cause of mental illness. Sociologists such as Durkheim (1897) and Sainsbury (1955) believed that social isolation rather than economic status was the major determinant of self-destructive behaviour. In a groundbreaking study of suicide during the industrial revolution, Durkheim described it as an aspect of one's under- or over-social integration with society. Self-harm is common in human societies and self-harming activities such as ritual markings, body piercing and tattooing are tolerated. I suggest that political acts of violence such as suicide bombing in the Middle East stems from a deep feeling of shame. Although suicide bombing is not a psychological attack on the self, it may be understood as a desperate attempt to be recognised and transform powerlessness by a deed which speaks louder than words and to kill the hated Other. It is difficult to comprehend how women, the bearers of life, turn into killing machines with bombing devices strapped to their wombs. Gaza psychiatrist Eyad Sarraj (2004) points to the social environment that produces human bombs and suggests that the honourable Arab rejects shame and dies in dignity. He suggests that the long history of military occupation in which children have witnessed the humiliation and helplessness of their parents is the underlying motivation. In her research on women suicide bombers, journalist Victor (2003) suggests that women who become 'martyrs' differ from their male counterparts in that they have personal problems that make their lives untenable within their own culture, which pushes them over the edge.

CONCLUSION

Working in a prison with patients who self-harm constantly tested my skills. It is a challenge being in a room with someone who cannot put their pain into words and particularly tough trying to be a psychotherapist in an environment that oscillates between control and containment and where understanding is not part of the culture. Attempts to help are often made with good intentions but without reflective spaces these easily become collusive or perverse. The prison can become a perversion of containment when staff react in an excessively disciplinary way or just destructively. I was struck each time a patient was abruptly transferred to another prison with no chance to have an ending to their therapy or even say goodbye. It repeated the patient's early ruptured attachments and denigrated the psychotherapy work. On the positive side of working in a prison, the containment is very helpful – often referred to as the 'brick mommy'. The idea of the 'brick mother' was described by Rey (1994) as a container for broken-down selves.

All the patients I worked with who self-harmed caused me to feel drowsy through projective identification of alexithymia. I initially felt uncomfortable about my sleepiness in sessions, which impinged on my function as a psychotherapist and my possible usefulness to such patients. In time, I learnt how meaningful such a powerful countertransference experience could be, which gave me a greater understanding of my patients' internal world as well as insight into their early life experience and terror of abandonment.

I would like to end this chapter with a final vignette of how the containment of prison facilitated therapy.

Vignette 5

Goldie was abandoned by her mother at birth. Her father won custody after her parents split up while her mother was pregnant. She was neglected and sexually abused at eight. She began cutting her arms when she was 12 and jumped off the roof of her house in a rural village in Brazil when she was 14, breaking her legs. Several suicide attempts followed. She also had long periods of anorexia. Goldie, aged 23, was serving a four-year sentence for smuggling cocaine into Britain by swallowing 86 condoms filled with the drug.

Goldie was on remand waiting to be sentenced for drug dealing when she was referred to me for therapy by a psychologist because of her cutting and burning. Goldie created so many obstacles to therapy that I felt challenged. The first major hurdle that I had to face was having to collect the patient. She was never in her cell as arranged and I had to run around the prison looking for her. When I finally found her week after week, she kept me waiting while she took her time changing from her gym clothes or swimming costume, or while she cleaned up from her art class. She always waved to other inmates as we left together. I could not fathom what was going on. I felt very lost and alone in the prison when I began seeing Goldie. She was my first patient in prison and I was struggling to grasp the magnitude of what I had taken on as I had to walk through long corridors, up and down staircases, locking and unlocking many doors.

I had seen Goldie for six sessions before a Christmas break. When I returned, Goldie told me that she had tried to hang herself in my absence. The marks were still visible on her neck 10 days after an officer had cut the sholaces in the bathroom. She had also been cutting herself and not eating. Although she had made three suicide attempts since her arrest, this time was different because she was in therapy. I suggest that I had represented a smidgen of hope for her but she may have felt betrayed once again in her life because due to the Christmas break I wasn't around when she was sentenced in court for her crime. Goldie tried to hang herself an hour after she was 'falsely accused' by an officer of physical violence. She was furious.

Goldie continued to give me the run-around for the next month. I was not trained to look for patients in this way. I went through a considerable struggle within myself and began to think it was futile seeing such a patient who kept playing hide and seek with me and self-harming. I wrestled with myself about chasing after her. I felt compromised. In session after session I tried to interpret her ambivalence and everything I could possibly think of, but nothing seemed to work. I gave up trying to understand and looking for an answer in various theories. I felt useless and abandoned, which helped me understand what Goldie's early experience might have been like for her. One day, after about three months of this frantic search, I realised that Goldie's therapy began the moment I started looking for her. She was probably frightened and hid away from me. The only way she could communicate her early experience for which she had no words was to make me experience what it felt like to be lost and rejected. I was reminded of Winnicott's (1963: 186) paper 'Communicating and not communicating' in which he said: 'It is a joy to hide but a disaster not to be found'.

I was amazed that when I resolved this conflict within myself, there was a major shift in Goldie. She was on time at the agreed place from then on. We were able to connect and explore her lack of compassion for herself and destructive way of coping with difficult feelings. One of the main things Goldie seemed to take from therapy was that she could think about things and not feel crushed by them and just act. In the Easter break I arranged for Goldie's probation officer to see her. When I returned she told me that she had blades, was tempted to cut herself in the break but threw them away because she did not want to disappoint me by cutting herself. It seemed she could be 'held' externally by thought.

Her therapy progressed well in the next six months as she talked openly about her painful experiences. On one occasion I went to collect her from the kitchen where she was working and the head chef told me that Goldie could not come to therapy that day because they were short-staffed. I stood my ground and insisted that it was important for her to come for her therapy. As her session began, Goldie said: 'I am so pleased you fought for me because my mother never did. I always wished my mother would have been there. Why didn't she fight for custody of me? We never bonded. My grandmother told me that I never ever sucked my mother's breast. I was brought up on formula'. I realised that I represented her 'formula mother' (substitute for mother's nutritious milk) as I saw her for 50 minutes once a week.

That was in fact the last time I ever saw Goldie as she was transferred to another prison before my summer break. I was in turmoil about her sudden departure with no possible ending. Before this break, Goldie kept telling me that I was taking double the time I had previously taken, four weeks instead of two. It was a great surprise to me when I went to collect her in the penultimate session before this break and she was gone. Her probation officer told me she had lodged a complaint about the racism in the kitchen and was, to use the prison jargon, 'shipped out', which is customary when complaints are made. It seemed she had opted to avoid the pain of saying 'goodbye'.

I was initially incensed at the insensitivity of the prison authorities who work countertherapeutically. However, I looked a little deeper and realised that Goldie had re-enacted something from her past by abandoning me before I could abandon her. She stayed the full term – nine months, as she had in her mother's womb. She was whisked away from the prison and her therapy in the same way she was snatched away from her mother when she was born. She took control this time.

Although Goldie left abruptly before we could do further work, the containment of prison enabled me to find her and penetrate the deadness to make some form of intimacy possible. I suggest that I touched Goldie's longing for recognition and to be appreciated for herself as she sensed that I was deeply affected by her. I believe we made contact on the basis of what Jessica Benjamin (2006) refers to as 'Thirdness', that intersubjective mental space that emerges from our capacity to surrender, to let go of self and take in the other's view or reality. Co-construction of this third allows for mutual recognition and an acceptance of being unconsciously drawn into enactments of early ruptures in the patient's life.

It is important to enter into the patient's experience and strive for a different outcome. Holding involves collaboration, as the patient must allow the unbearable aspects of themselves to be 'held' by the therapist until they are more adequately equipped to think about these difficult issues and explore their meaning. When therapists are able to contain the patient's intolerable feelings, the patient learns that the 'nameless dread' will not annihilate them and that eventually they will be able to bear this themselves.

I want to acknowledge my indebtedness to my patients who have taught me about the complexity of self-harm and given me the privilege of entering their experience.

REFERENCES

Adshead, G. (1997) 'Written on the body: deliberate self-harm and violence', in E.V. Welldon and C. van Velsen (eds) *A Practical Guide to Forensic Psychotherapy*, London: Jessica Kingsley Publishers.

Aiyegbusi, A. (2004) 'Nursing under fire', in N. Jeffcote and T. Watson (eds) *Working Therapeutically with Women in Secure Mental Health Settings*, London: Jessica Kingsley Publishers.

Anzieu, D. (1989) *The Skin Ego*, New Haven, CT: Yale University Press.

Balint, M. (1968) *The Basic Fault: Therapeutic Aspects of Regression*, London: Tavistock.

Benjamin, J. (2006) *Our Appointment in Thebes: Acknowledging the Analyst's Fear of Doing Harm*, New York: University Post-Doctoral Programme.

Bick, E. (1962) 'Child analysis today', in M. Harris Williams (ed.) (1987) *Collected Papers of Martha Harris and Esther Bick*, Strathtay, Perthshire: Clunie Press.

Bick, E. (1968) 'The experience of the skin in early object-relations', in M. Harris Williams (ed.) (1987) *Collected Papers of Martha Harris and Esther Bick*, Strathtay, Perthshire: Clunie Books.

Bion, W.R (1962) *Learning from Experience*, London: Heinemann.

Bion, W.R. (1967) *Second Thoughts*, London: Heinemann.

Bollas, C. (1987) *The Shadow of the Object: Psychoanalysis of the Unthought Known*, London: Free Association Books.

Bollas, C. (1992) *Being a Character: Psychoanalysis and Self Experience*, first published in the US by Hill & Wing in 1992, London: Routledge.

Bowlby, J. (1958) 'The nature of the child's tie to his mother', *International Journal of Psychoanalysis*, 39: 350–373.

Brown, D. (1977) 'Drowsiness in the countertransference', *International Review of Psychoanalysis*, 37: 344–346.

Campbell, D. and Hale, R. (1991) 'Suicidal acts', in J. Holmes (ed.) *Textbook of Psychotherapy in Psychiatric Practice*, Oxford: Churchill Livingstone.

Donne, J. (1612) *The Second Anniversary of the Progress of the Soul.*

Durkheim, E. (1897) *Le Suicide*, Paris: Alcan.

Fairbairn, W. (1952) *Psychoanalytic Studies of the Personality*, London: Routledge.

Foulkes, S.H. (1948) *Introduction to Group-Analytic Psychotherapy:*

Studies in the Social Integration of Individuals and Groups, London: Heinemann.

Foulkes, S.H. and Anthony, E.J. (1957 [1965]) *Group Psychotherapy: The Psychoanalytic Approach*, Harmondsworth: Penguin; reprinted 1984, London: Karnac.

Freud, S. (1917) 'Mourning and melancholia', in *On Metapsychology: The Theory of Psychoanalysis*, vol. 11, Harmondsworth: Penguin.

Freud, S. (1920) 'Beyond the Pleasure Principle', in *The Complete Psychological Works of Sigmund Freud*, vol. 18, London: Hogarth Press.

Freud, S. (1926) 'Inhibitions, symptoms and anxiety', *The Standard Edition of the Complete Psychological Works of Sigmund Freud*, vol. 20, London: Hogarth Press.

Gilligan, J. (1996) *Violence: Reflections on our Deadliest Epidemic*, London: Jessica Kingsley Publishers.

Glasser, M. (1979) 'Some aspects of the role of aggression in the perversions', in I. Rosen (ed.) *Sexual Deviation* (third edition), Oxford: Oxford University Press.

Green, A. (1980) 'The dead mother' (La Mere Mort), in *Narcissisme de Vie, Marcissisme de Mort*, Paris: Paris Editions de Minuit, pp. 222–253; later in Green, A. (1986) *On Private Madness*, London: Hogarth Press and the Institute of Psychoanalysis.

Hopper, E. (2003) *Traumatic Experience in the Unconscious Life of Groups: The Fourth Basic Assumption: Incohesion: Aggregation/Massification or (ba) I:A/M*, London: Jessica Kingsley Publishers.

Klein, M. (1946) 'Notes on some schizoid mechanisms', *International Journal of Psycho-Analysis*, 27: 99–110.

Kroll, J. (1993) *PTSD/Borderline in Therapy*, London: W.W. Norton.

Main, T. (1957) 'The ailment', *British Journal of Medical Psychology*, 30: 129–145.

Mitrani, J.L. (1996) *A Framework for the Imaginary*, New Jersey, NJ: Jason Aronson.

Motz, A. (2001) *The Psychology of Female Violence: Crimes Against the Body* (first edition), Hove: Routledge.

Rey, H. (1994) *Universals of Psychoanalysis in the Treatment of Psychotic and Borderline States*, London: Free Association Books.

Russell, P. (1987) 'The role of loss in the repetition compulsion', Unpublished manuscript.

Russell, P. (1991) 'Trauma, repetition and affect', Unpublished manuscript.

Sainsbury, P. (1955) *Suicide in London*, London: Chapman & Hall.

Sarraj, E. (2004) Faculty for Israeli–Palestinian Peace conference, Jerusalem.

Shengold, L. (1989) *Soul Murder: The Effects of Childhood Sexual Abuse and Deprivation*, New Haven, CT: Yale University Press.

Sifneos, P. (1973) 'The prevalence of alexithymia in psychosomatic patients', *Psychotherapy and Psychosomatics*, 22: 255–262.

Straker, G. (2006) 'Signing with a scar: understanding self-harm', *Psychoanalaytic Dialogues*, 16, New York: The Analytic Press.

Tustin, F. (1986) *Autistic Barriers in Neurotic Patients*, London: Karnac.

Victor, B. (2003) *Army of Roses: Inside the World of Palestinian Women Suicide Bombers*, London: Robinson.

Welldon, E.V. (1988) *Mother, Madonna, Whore: The Idealisation and Denigration of Motherhood*, London: Karnac.

Welldon, E.V. (1992) *Mother, Madonna, Whore: The Idealisation and Denigration of Motherhood*, London: Karnac.

Winnicott, D.W. (1956) 'Primary maternal preoccupation', in *Through Paediatrics to Psycho-Analysis*, London: Hogarth Press, 1982.

Winnicott, D.W. (1960) 'The theory of the parent–infant relationship', in (1990) *The Maturational Processes and the Facilitating Environment*, London: Karnac.

Winnicott, D.W. (1963) 'Communicating and not communicating leading to a study of certain opposites', in (1990) *The Maturational Processes and the Facilitating Environment*, London: Karnac.

Winnicott, D.W. (1974) 'Fear of breakdown', *International Review of Psycho-Analysis*, 1: 103–107.

Chapter 7

Absences, transitions and endings

Threats to successful treatment

Lynn Greenwood

Debbie was anticipating a two-week business trip to Brazil. Her tone combined anxiety and triumph:

> 'I'd never have done something like this three years ago; I'd have found an excuse not to go. But then three years ago, I wouldn't stand up to people at work: they'd be walking all over me and I'd end up bingeing and vomiting. And if I *did* stand up for myself, I'd feel so guilty that I'd *still* end up with my head over the toilet. Then there'd be the risk that I'd continue the binge on my way home – probably after I'd been down the pub. Then there'd be the laxatives. . . . And then I'd feel so bloody awful about myself that I'd do some ironing – and burn myself accidentally on purpose, or get up in the middle of the night and cut. Even thinking about going to Brazil would've terrified me: it'll be a boozy trip and the food'll be strange and I'll be meeting lots of new people and Jerome [her colleague] can be a right pain in the bum. But I'm going. . . . Things may get a bit "hairy" but that doesn't mean I can't pull it round again.'

Debbie and I started working together just over four years ago when she was admitted as an inpatient to the eating disorder unit of a private hospital. Her self-damaging behaviours went much further than a simple diagnosis of bulimia nervosa and included:

- bingeing;
- vomiting;
- (food) restriction;
- laxative abuse;

- over-exercise;
- alcohol abuse;
- self-harm (cutting and burning);
- abusing caffeinated drinks and caffeine tablets;
- disinhibited sexual behaviour;
- over-work (at her desk by 6am, often not leaving before 8pm).

Debbie's eating disorder is at the core of a constellation of other self-destructive behaviours, a phenomenon that Lacey (1993) explored in a catchment area study. He found that 40 per cent of 112 normal-weight bulimic women reported self-damaging and addictive behaviours (drug and alcohol abuse, stealing, overdoses and cutting) in addition to bingeing and vomiting. Eighty per cent of this group reported a history of three or more such behaviours. Lacey (1993: 192) argues that his sample is 'representative of an urban British catchment area' and then defines the group as 'multi-impulsive bulimic'. In an earlier literature review of impulsivity in 'substance abuse disorders, eating disorders, classical disorders of impulse control, self-harm and personality disorders' Lacey and Evans (1986: 641) had concluded that the term 'multi-impulsive personality disorder' could be applied to a significant number of clients with a poor prognosis and formulated diagnostic criteria for the multi-impulsive form of bulimia (1986: 644):

1 Bulimia is associated with one or more of the following:
   gross alcohol abuse;
   'street drug' abuse;
   multiple overdoses;
   repeated self-damage;
   sexual disinhibition;
   shoplifting.

I believe we could add other behaviours to this list, including blood-letting; abuse of laxatives, caffeine tablets and caffeinated drinks; over-exercise; compulsive gambling; even excessive piercings and tattoos. Arguably, self-damaging behaviour also encompasses a marked lack of personal care. Lacey and Evans's diagnostic criteria continue:

2 Each behaviour is associated with a similar sense of being out of control.

3 Each of these patterns of behaviour may fluctuate, and they are interchangeable and impulsive.
4 The patient's affects are of depression and intense anger which are declared when the behaviours are controlled.

Lacey and Evans highlight the difficulty of treating each of the self-damaging behaviours in isolation. Controlling one symptom (perhaps drug abuse) may lead to an increase in, say, drinking or sexual disinhibition. Thus, stress, anxiety and other overwhelming feelings continue to find 'release' as the client moves from one self-destructive pattern to another.

This 'catalogue' of self-destructive behaviours is not unusual – particularly in inpatient or day-care settings. Eating disorders are notoriously challenging to treat – even more so when the individual uses several self-damaging coping mechanisms. Many people require multiple treatments (by specialist drug and alcohol as well as eating disorder services). However, 'wanting' help can diminish when the struggle to withstand what feel like deadly emotions becomes unbearable.

The financial constraints under which the National Health Service (NHS) operates make it almost impossible to provide the level of support that many of these individuals need. A client in a day hospital who, at 8pm, is highly distressed after a row with her partner, may not feel able to control her impulse for 12 hours until the unit opens. Furthermore, she may be reluctant to call a crisis line, staffed by – to her – strangers.

I worked with Debbie once a week throughout her admission (first as an inpatient and then in day care). Her husband was caring and supportive, but she chose to hide from him information about her condition that would have increased his vigilance when she returned home. Against advice, she returned to work as soon as she could (despite her condition, she was in a senior position in a major merchant bank) and continued to see me, twice a week, in my private practice. She struggled with the transition back to work and – as Lacey and Evans (1986) predict – her behaviours started to spiral out of control, her mood plummeted and her psychiatrist admitted her to a general psychiatric ward for eight weeks. After discharge, Debbie was determined to avoid another admission ('I'd rather die than go back into that place,' she said. I encouraged her to think how accurately that emphatic statement might describe her choices), yet she still found it impossible to keep her behaviours under control. To be accurate, she found it impossible to identify an alternative to damaging herself.

Transitions from one type of treatment (inpatient to day care to outpatient) present an enormous challenge as clients start once more to encounter day-to-day responsibilities. Even without movement through increasingly less intensive forms of treatment, they face the challenge of 'keeping themselves safe' when they have no easy access to the professionals they know and trust. Trust is not something that can be taken for granted; establishing attachments is often extremely hard for those who have experienced deprivation, neglect and abuse.

I am not suggesting that what I offer as (in this case) a psychotherapist in private practice can rival the multidisciplinary professional teams who work in specialist services. However, my work with Debbie (and other young women with similar difficulties) has led me to develop a particular approach that, I believe, may contribute to thinking about the treatment of this complex client group.

THE FUNCTION OF SELF-DAMAGING BEHAVIOUR

In this chapter, I am consciously choosing to use the terms 'self-damaging' or 'self-destructive' behaviour instead of 'deliberate self-harm'. The last of these generally describes attacks against the body: cutting, burning, blood-letting, head-banging or the insertion of sharp objects. Self-damaging behaviour is a far broader term, encompassing deliberate physical harm and other destructive acts (see Lacey and Evans's list above).

Women use self-destructive behaviour in order to try and contain and express extreme distress and rage: physical pain protects against and distracts from psychic anguish. Melanie Klein's (1946) concept of projective identification is useful in understanding the perceived need to damage the self. (Even her vocabulary communicates the force of these impulses.) This psychological process is at its most powerful during the paranoid-schizoid phase of development as one of two lines of attack on the mother. The first is the 'predominantly oral impulse to suck dry, bite up, scoop out and rob the mother's body of its good content' (1946: 8). The second:

> derives from the anal and urethral impulses and implies expelling dangerous substances (excrements) out of the self and into the mother. Together with these harmful excrements, . . . split-off parts of the ego are also projected . . . *into* the mother. These excrements and bad parts of the self are meant not only to injure but also to control and to take possession of the object. In so far as the mother comes to contain the bad parts of the self, she is not felt to be a separate individual but is felt to be *the* bad self.
>
> (Klein, 1946: 8)

In short, when a baby feels pain, distress or threat, she tries to 'put' these unbearable experiences into mother. Klein emphasises that projective identification is a form of communication. The mother's challenge is to empathise with her baby: to receive, contain and soothe overwhelming feelings. Where a mother (or father or care-taker) is unable to perform this role, it leaves the child with her original distress and a rage that she has no alternative but to turn on herself.

This is evident in Debbie's history. Her mother, Julia, was only 16 when Debbie was born – a few months after she had married Stewart, a couple of years her senior. The pregnancy was unplanned and the relationship did not last. Devasted when Stewart left, Julia took her young daughter to live with her mother and spent the best part of a year in bed, refusing to eat. When Debbie was five, Julia remarried. This was another unsatisfying relationship that lasted about ten years. Debbie remembers that her mother was constantly dieting. When she looks at photos from that period, she can see that Julia is underweight. She can also see that she herself is a healthy weight, although mother's constant criticism of her appearance 'implanted' a belief that she was fat. (This belief eventually became a reality.) Debbie felt that Julie wanted the perfect daughter: a high academic achiever, slim and well groomed, and a constant source of reassurance and support. Debbie started bingeing when she was eight. This increased significantly when she was 11 and her stepfather's job precipitated a move to the other side of the country – away from her grandmother, the one person who Debbie feels loved her for who she was rather than what she achieved or how she looked.

'There's nothing more wonderful,' she said recently, 'than being alone on the sofa with the door shut and a bag full of chocolate.'

The soothing effect of this is obvious: literally, eating on the feelings. However, by her mid teens, Debbie was bingeing *and* vomiting – which became her 'core' self-destructive behaviour. The emotional response to a difficult experience triggers compulsive eating to numb the anxiety, followed by hours of self-induced vomiting to get rid of the (by now) seemingly toxic food inside her. This violent evacuation leaves a short-lived feeling of emptiness and relief . . . until the cycle begins again.

Debbie's mother's anorexia turned into binge-eating. She loathed her body, went on constant (and unsuccessful) crash diets and berated her daughter when she gained weight. From the age of about 12, Debbie was convinced she was so repulsive that no man would ever find her attractive. It is hardly surprising that her first sexual experiences were all exploitative, abusive and even violent. Bingeing and vomiting were no longer enough to anaesthetise her misery. One by one, she introduced other coping mechanisms: laxatives, over-exercise, alcohol, cutting and burning.

Unlike many people who use self-damaging behaviour, Debbie suffered no childhood physical or sexual abuse but lacked the emotional engagement of her mother. Julia had difficulties of her own and was unable to provide her child with the psychological and emotional care that would have equipped her to manage unpleasant experiences. To distract herself from the enormous effort of maturing into a separate, individuated young person (Mahler *et al.*, 1975), Debbie started to use her own body to obliterate mental pain and express the rage towards a mother who was unable to reassure her and looked to her daughter to experience, then relieve, her own anxiety.

'YOU WANT TO TAKE AWAY MY SAFETY NET'

Debbie admits that, throughout her first hospital admission, she believed that the treatment would help her mood but that it would have little impact on her bingeing, vomiting and other behaviours. These were the only coping mechanisms she knew and she did not want to give them up. In my experience, this is not unusual. Women will want to recover from anorexia without gaining weight. Or they will want to stop cutting *quite so much*. Or they want to be able to choose to stop drinking after a couple of glasses. Or even all three. A decision to enter treatment is never unequivocal – and those who are admitted under the Mental Health Act may do their utmost to refuse it. Most treatments aim to provide the following:

- a safe environment (where access to, say, sharps is restricted or where staff supervise eating);
- opportunities for experiences, thoughts and feelings to be explored and understood;
- an understanding of triggers;
- alternative, healthy coping mechanisms;
- support with building a 'nourishing' lifestyle (friendships, work and leisure activities).

Some people (such as Debbie) start treatment in an inpatient setting. This permits a period of regression: clients have access to carers 24 hours a day, allowing them to return to a child-like state. Childhood is, of course, the appropriate time for such care. If the client continues to use self-damaging behaviours, she may be put on one-to-one observation – receiving a level of care she may never have had even as an infant. The aim is to help clients accept pseudo-parental care and relinquish self-destructive behaviours. For some, even this is not enough and they fight to hold on to familiar and destructive coping mechanisms.

There are advantages and disadvantages to day-care units. Clients remain in their homes and in contact with familial and social networks that may be part of the problem. During time on the ward, they can explore current tensions and difficulties and consider new ways to manage them. However, these clients often have few interests and lack the social and practical skills to fill their time. Evenings and weekends can seem interminable and a return to damaging but familiar coping mechanisms the only way to manage them.

Equally tricky is the transition to less intensive forms of treatment, which is often traumatic. The loss of intensive (24- or eight-hour or even one-to-one observation) care is also experienced as a loss of the longed-for maternal vigilance: not only is there the pain of the loss of the ward, the team and fellow clients, there is also the need to face external stresses and tensions once more.

In a qualitative study of 32 individuals, six months after their discharge from residential eating disorder treatment, Cockell *et al.* (2004) identified factors that facilitated and hindered recovery. Supportive factors fell into three broad categories:

- maintaining connections with social supports, including family, friends and professionals;
- applying cognitive and affective skills learned in treatment (for example, meal-planning, expressing rather than suppressing emotions and assertion);
- focusing beyond the eating disorder to concentrate on 'higher values' and make changes.

Similarly, factors that hindered recovery fell into three broad categories:

- loss of the structure provided by treatment and of specialist support. Clients also reported a 'sense of disconnection' (Cockell *et al.*, 2004: 531), having left a group of people who understood their difficulties;
- self-defeating beliefs, including unrealistic expectations and an emphasis on being in control;
- dealing with real life, including returning home where difficult issues often remain unresolved.

While the focus of this study was purely on those treated for eating disorders, I suspect that the findings would hold for the group I am discussing. At the very top of the list for Cockell *et al.* are factors concerning the maintenance or loss of sources of professional, social or personal support. A sense of abandonment is at its most acute when a client suddenly feels overwhelmed by fear, anxiety or distress. While there is often an external trigger for these powerful emotions, it can feel as if they come out of nowhere. More than this, the experience can be so unbearable that the client feels she must get rid of them immediately: all too often, self-damaging behaviour seems the only solution – largely because it is the most familiar.

When Debbie moved to day care, she found the empty hours extremely stressful. She had not stopped using behaviours and these quickly spiralled out of control. Work – or perhaps more accurately over-work – helped ease stress but was itself a stressor. Debbie was obsessive: checking and rechecking documents, bingeing and vomiting if she thought someone was going to be angry with her, and always telling me she was about to be fired. Unwittingly, her husband increased her anxiety. He believed her treatment had 'cured' her.

We had increased her psychotherapy sessions from two to three a week. At one level, Debbie worked hard: making links between childhood beliefs and experiences and current situations and relationships she found difficult. However, she often hid the behaviours she was using – particularly when she cut or burned.

FEAR OF LOSS AND ABANDONMENT: THE 'UNTHINKABLE ANXIETY'

As well as dealing with everyday pressures, abandonment was a key theme throughout the first two years of Debbie's treatment. She told me that when she was on her way to see me, she often worried that I would not answer the door. Similarly, in sessions leading up to a break, she would ask anxiously if I was really coming back. Cockell *et al.* (2004) underline the importance of loss as a factor inhibiting recovery, focusing on discharge from an inpatient setting. I believe that loss and abandonment – temporary or permanent, real or perceived – underlie the frequent relapses common in this patient group. For those being treated in day-care units, the weekend can feel like a terrifying void they must face alone – imagined evidence that 'carers' do not really care. Similarly, those whose treatment consists of only one or more hour-long sessions a week may believe that they are forgotten as soon as they walk out of the door.

In his paper 'Dependence in infant care, in child-care, and in the psycho-analytic setting', Winnicott (1963) reflects on the impact of breaks in treatment on one of his clients:

> My going away re-enacted a traumatic episode or series of episodes of her own babyhood. It was . . . as if I were holding her and then became preoccupied with some other matter so that she felt *annihilated.*
>
> (Winnicott, 1963: 249–50; italics in original)

This reflects his earlier thoughts on the role of parental care, emphasising that a small baby is:

> all the time *on the brink of unthinkable anxiety*. Unthinkable anxiety is kept away by [the] vitally important function of

> the mother at this stage, her capacity to put herself in the baby's place and to know what the baby needs in the general management of the body.
>
> (Winnicott, 1962: 57–58)

'Felt annihilated', 'on the brink of unthinkable anxiety': Winnicott expresses powerfully the experiences he locates in infancy but that are still an aspect of our clients' day-to-day lives. He also stresses the importance of the 'good-enough mother [who] starts off with an almost complete adaptation to her infant's needs' (Winnicott, 1951: 190). Debbie's mother failed to adapt to her daughter's needs. In fact, the process was often reversed: mother turned to daughter for comfort and reassurance – and to fulfil her own unfulfilled dreams and ambitions. Unsurprisingly, Debbie found it hard to rely on professionals to support her in relinquishing her self-damaging behaviours: not only might we prove to be as unreliable and demanding as her mother, we were – in her mind – likely to disappear altogether (just as the caring Julia disappeared and was replaced by the critical, demanding and dependent Julia).

Attachment theory provides a useful framework within which to consider the impact of our clients' early histories. Eight years after Ainsworth *et al.* (1978) had defined three discrete attachment styles (secure, anxious resistant and anxious avoidant), Main and Solomon (1986) observed a fourth in a group of children who experienced their parents as either frightened or frightening – both of which are anxiety-provoking for infants who come to see mother and/or father as a cause for alarm as well as a refuge from it. Clients with traumatic histories tend to form attachments that are overly rigid: profoundly secure, profoundly anxious or profoundly avoidant. They lack a fluidity that enables them to move through a series of responses as appropriate. Furthermore, in their personal relationships, they may choose frightened or frightening partners, thus repeating childhood patterns.

If it continues, this ambivalence can be an obstacle to successful treatment. First, a client may resist becoming too attached to members of the professional teams, anticipating abuse and/or abandonment. Then, if she manages to overcome her anxiety, she is likely to experience the transition (from residential to day-care and then to outpatient settings) as a series of rejections, losses and abandonments – exactly what she had most feared and what may well cause her to spiral into relapse.

Working on an eating disorder day unit, we face particular challenges with our client groups. There are particular challenges in working with those with a diagnosis of multi-impulsive bulimia or anorexia, especially where there is an underlying personality disorder. A brief discussion of such a client serves to highlight these. Sarah – a long-term user of mental health services – was diagnosed with multi-impulsive bulimia and borderline personality disorder. She had refused a referral to a specialist service and came to the day hospital to address bingeing, vomiting, burning, cutting and cannabis abuse.

Initially, Sarah was critical (and scared) of the programme and seemingly confused in groups and psychotherapy. She made sweeping generalisations about how people behave and treat each other – evidence of being abused psychologically, physically and sexually from a young age. Despite this, she gradually formed friendships and was clearly attached to members of the team – particularly the occupational therapist. During the early months of her treatment, she tended to unravel at weekends, when the unit was closed and her only source of support was the crisis line, staffed by people who were strangers to her.

Despite this, Sarah managed to bring her behaviours increasingly under control and completed her nine-month, day-care programme – a considerable achievement. We then discharged her to the outpatient phase of treatment: this lasts a year and comprises a weekly psychotherapy appointment (in Sarah's case, with me) and a transition group (which, as the name suggests, aims to support the move to more independent living). We liaised with her local Community Mental Health Team (CMHT), who organised two days at a general psychiatric day hospital and a couple of afternoons at a specialist support group for clients with personality disorders. Overall, our aim was to provide the support we thought Sarah needed.

Within three months, Sarah had started to decompensate. She experienced the end of day-care as an enormous loss and rejection and complained bitterly that she had just come to trust us and we had thrown her out. More than that, she missed the occupational therapist. She also struggled to attend all the different appointments. Her bingeing and vomiting started to spiral out of control and she returned to cutting and burning. I went on leave for a fortnight; we had scheduled a Care Programme Approach (CPA) for the day I returned. However, while I was away, she was admitted to a secure unit under section.

Sarah's case, while perhaps extreme, outlines some of the challenges we face in treating this client group:

- a fear of attachment or a reluctance to attach;
- the familiarity of self-damaging behaviours and the reluctance to replace them with new coping mechanisms – particularly those that involve trust in or communication with others;
- unavailability of professionals and other sources of support in the evening, at weekends and when treatment becomes less intensive or ends. This, combined with external stressors, fuels feelings of rejection, loss and abandonment.

THE NEED FOR CONSISTENT SUPPORT

Holmes (1996: 117–121) observes that support 'may be compared with invisible foundations upon which all buildings rest, and the external buttresses that some, especially those in poor conditions require. . . . Support often makes its presence known by its subsequent absence'. This was clear in my work with Debbie. An increase from two to three sessions a week (and less opportunity for her to decompensate between our meetings) enabled her to bring some of her behaviours under control. However, this improvement was precarious and easily overturned by breaks or times of extreme stress. Debbie herself acknowledged that if (in her head) everything was going wrong, she would (to use her words) 'put my f**k-it head on' and slide into an orgy of bingeing, vomiting, laxatives, cutting and burning. The worst episode had resulted in a second admission, which made her vow never to let things get so far out of control again.

Clearly, three sessions a week failed to provide adequate support. I could not offer her additional sessions; in any case, Debbie's determination to remain at work meant that four (or five) sessions were impossible. Before her admission, I had encouraged her to call if she felt at risk from herself; she was reluctant to do so, usually preferring to binge and vomit rather than disturb or – perhaps more accurately – find me angry or unresponsive. After her discharge, I emphasised that this was essential if we were to work together to avoid another period in hospital. Gradually, Debbie allowed herself to trust me and called when she felt she was going to harm herself. She knew that she could leave a message on my voicemail and I would return her call as quickly as possible. She was also aware that it was unlikely that I could speak for more than ten minutes and that – on occasions – I might not be available at all. My belief was that I would be available enough to strengthen her confidence in me. If I were unavailable, she would come to realise that it did not mean that I had rejected her. She would develop an ability to hold an internal image of 'us' in her internal world.

Debbie has never abused this arrangement; in truth, she is anxious about 'overstepping the mark' – with others as well as me. For example, one afternoon, I picked up a message from her. She sounded in distress and explained that she had bought a bagful of binge food and sharps. In a moment of clarity, she had left it in the kitchen and gone upstairs to the spare room, from where she was phoning. She said that she would stay there until I returned her call. When I did, we discussed a fairly detailed strategy for getting rid of her dangerous purchases. The conversation lasted less than five minutes.

The next day, she was jubilant but kept checking that it was alright to contact me in this way. We continued to explore her emotions, reactions and experiences and also looked at practical alternatives to harming herself. Sometimes, when extremely stressed, Debbie still resorts to the 'you're taking away my safety net' line of attack. However, with occasional telephone calls, she has managed to stop virtually everything except bingeing and vomiting. She is now bringing these slowly under control – admittedly with great difficulty. Telephone calls are infrequent. She may even leave a garbled message that ends: 'I'm alright now. You don't need to call me back. See you tomorrow'. Similarly, when she is away (on a business trip or on holiday somewhere she finds stressful – usually because of unfamiliar food), she keeps her appointments by telephone – even if she has time for no more than a brief check-in.

INCORPORATING NEW APPROACHES

While Debbie is a private client (and was originally treated in a private hospital) and functions far better than someone like Sarah, I believe there are ideas that we could consider in the treatment we provide in an NHS setting.

Our clients experience enormous difficulty in trusting us and may take months (or even years) to form an attachment to the professionals who treat them. Yet we hope that a move to a less-intensive form of treatment will not precipitate a serious relapse and often expect them to turn to strangers in their most difficult moments. This struggle to attach has implications for transfers to a different team. With limited resources (and time), the client may experience the most carefully considered ending or transition as shockingly abrupt: what we may think is an adequate time to end with one set of professionals and embark on the next stage of treatment with a new group could, in truth, be unintentionally inadequate.

We cannot be available 24 hours a day, seven days a week but can technology help address some of the problems? For example, some clients – like Debbie – may reach a point where they can call, feel reassured by a recording of a familiar and trusted voice and leave a message that requires no response. My colleagues at the Clinic for Dissociative Studies have described to me their clients' use of text or email that – like Debbie – require no response. (One young woman sends her psychotherapist texts containing sad or angry emoticons, which they discuss at the next session.) Similarly, even when I do call back, the client may not pick up but I can leave a message that provides some support until the next scheduled session – or, admittedly, sometimes the next voicemail. On occasions, clients want a response from us (and I include professionals in the NHS, the private sector and private practice). Can our schedules be flexible enough to allow a ten-minute telephone call?

We struggle to provide the best possible care with increasingly limited funding. Many fear that this 'feeds' the 'revolving-door' syndrome, which means that treatment often extends to a point at which the client can cope better than she did rather than to the point where she has progressed as far as she can. (At St George's, we have adopted a process of 'stepped' care, which allows clients with deeply entrenched difficulties a 12-week programme to progress as far as they can with a planned return to continue when they feel ready.) There is a need for mechanisms by which separate treatment teams within a trust are better able to work together to ensure that – as far as possible – clients continue to progress, albeit often gradually. Above all, we must pay serious attention to attachment difficulties and ensure that breaks and endings in treatment do not become a trigger for self-damaging behaviour that ultimately serves only to increase the risk of the client sabotaging what she has achieved.

REFERENCES

Ainsworth, M.D.S., Blehar, M.C., Waters, E. and Wall, S. (1978) *Patterns of Attachment: A Psychological Study of the Strange Situation*, Hilldale, NJ: Lawrence Erlbaum Associates, Inc.

Cockell, S.J., Zaitsoff, S.L. and Geller, J. (2004) 'Maintaining change following eating disorder treatment', *Professional Psychology: Research and Practice*, 35: 527–534.

Holmes, J. (1996) *Attachment, Intimacy, Autonomy: Using Attachment Theory in Adults Psychotherapy*, Northvale, NJ: Jason Aronson.

Klein, M. (1946) 'Notes on some schizoid mechanisms', in *Envy, Gratitude and Other Works 1946–1963*, London: Virago Press, 1988.

Lacey, J.H. and Evans, C.D.H. (1986) 'The impulsivist: a multi-impulsive personality disorder', *British Journal of Addiction*, 81: 641–649.

Lacey, J.H. (1993) 'Self-damaging and addictive behaviour in bulimia nervosa: a catchment area study', *British Journal of Psychiatry*, 163: 190–194.

Mahler, M.S., Pine, F. and Bergman, A. (1975) *The Psychological Birth of the Human Infant*, New York: Basic Books.

Main, M. and Solomon, J. (1986) 'Discovery of a new, insecure-disorganized/disoriented attachment pattern', in T.B. Brazelton and M.W. Yogman (eds) *Affective Development in Infancy* (pp. 95–124), Norwood, NJ: Ablex.

Prochaska, J.O., DiClemente, C.C. and Norcross, J.C. (1992) 'In search of how people change', *American Psychologist*, 47: 1102–1114.

Winnicott, D.W. (1951) 'Transitional objects and transitional phenomena', in *Through Paediatrics to Psychoanalysis*, London: Tavistock Publications, 1958.

Winnicott, D.W. (1962) 'Ego integration in child development', in *The Maturational Process and the Facilitating Environment*, London: Hogarth Press, 1965.

Winnicott, D.W. (1963) 'Dependence in infant care, in child-care, and in the psycho-analytic setting', in *The Maturational Process and the Facilitating Environment*, London: Hogarth Press, 1965.

Chapter 8

Self-harm in women's secure services

Reflections and strategies for treatment design

Rebecca Lawday

INTRODUCTION

I was asked to contribute to this text due to my recent experience of helping to develop and implement a model of care for a new medium secure and enhanced medium secure service for women at Arnold Lodge, a regional secure hospital. My task within the forensic psychology service was to pay attention to the need for gender sensitivity and to recommend and implement a long-term psychological treatment strategy that acknowledges the risks, needs and 'responsivity' of an often marginalised patient group. These include the need for these women to receive adequate care and understanding in relation to their behaviour, including self-harm.

This chapter will provide some background to the development of specialist services for women in secure healthcare. It will consider what we mean by 'enhanced' medium secure care, and present the overarching 'treatment stage' model that we are in the early stages of applying in our service. It will present considerations as to specific treatment needs, multiprofessional working and integrating approaches as well as discuss responsivity factors such as engagement, the importance of therapeutic relationships and the process of change, especially in relation to self injury. Self-injury is a common problem for women in this service and was in our minds when we designed it. While not focusing on it exclusively, the treatment programme is intended to address the underlying difficulties that give rise to self-harming behaviour and feelings.

My thanks go to Wendy Ifill, who is currently receiving care in our service. Wendy has contributed two sections to this chapter, giving us her perspective on the development of services for women and her own insights into self-injury within such services. She has asked to be credited in full.

WOMEN IN SECURE SERVICES

Women who access secure mental health services have been the subject of increased interest and funding following many years of campaigning by organisations such as WISH (Women in Secure Hospitals). Following recommendations in the Tilt report (Tilt *et al.*, 2000)[1] and the publication of documents such as *Making a Difference* (DH, 2000), *Into the Mainstream* (DH, 2002, 2003a) and the NIMHE briefing paper on women's mental health services (NIMHE and DH, 2003), guidance has been provided on modernising our mental health services. This includes the importance of accommodating gender-specific needs, and papers outline factors considered most important in the design of such services. Understanding and managing self-injury has become central to the design of services; in the physical design of new services and in the development of treatment strategies, policies and care pathways.

WENDY'S PERSPECTIVE: CONNECTING WITH OTHERS AND MANAGING CHANGE

Women in mental health services: weighing up the balance

The aim of this piece is to provide a service user's perspective on the place of women in mental health services, to consider whether this has needed improving and to discuss/provide opinion on potential improvements.

1 This report made a number of recommendations relevant to the physical and procedural security needs in high security care, as well as recommending a further review of medium secure provision. An objective was for patients to be cared for in conditions/environments commensurate with their level of risk and need. Specifically, recommendations supported the accelerated discharge of women patients not thought to require high secure care.

Lack of services

It has been my experience that women are still sent away from their own local areas to units away from home due to a lack of services. I have witnessed women with families who are not being able to access them. There are not enough women's units and quite often women who really need these services are sent to prison.

It is well recognised that men and women have different needs. Women's backgrounds are often linked in with care services, meaning that their children may have been removed from their care, or they have limited access. For women who do have access to their children, while in hospital children's visits are not financially supported, and for families travelling long distances there is more often than not [no] facilities for them to stay over.

Learning and progressing within services

As more women's services are opened, the needs of women in hospital are beginning to be addressed. I feel that there has been progression, albeit slow, within women's services. It has been recognised that women's needs differ from that of their male counterparts.

Gender-sensitive services for women

I personally prefer to be in a female-only environment where I am not overshadowed by male patients. I feel that most mixed services I have been in so far have been male-orientated. Women on mixed wards are often left out, with men getting much of the say on what goes on. I feel that women-only services is a positive way forward.

I feel that women's needs are complex and that often they end up in mental health services as a direct consequence of traumatic life experiences. Mixing with men who have been the perpetrators of crimes against women is hard for them, and they need to be in places where they feel secure. To be able to develop appropriate relationships in secure services is limited, and women often find themselves forming unhealthy relationships with men while on mixed wards. Women are, more often than not, vulnerable in these circumstances.

I do feel, however, that males working on female wards can act as positive male role models for women who have had negative experiences of men in their lives. Also, I'm not averse to mixing with men – after all, they are part of society and I can't avoid this! I have had some very positive experiences in mixed groups and also out of mental health services I have made some very good male friendships. However, there are things I prefer to do in women-only groups, like going to the gym without feeling I need to compete, or join in other groups where I don't feel overshadowed by men.

I would like to see more women-only groups such as yoga, dance, aromatherapy, aerobics etc.; not only because of men overpowering women, but also because of women's physical needs. Women miss out on non-sexual and sexual physical contact. For example, where do you get a cuddle from? Women are restricted from having sexual relationships but nothing is offered as an alternative. Touch is an essential for everyone, so perhaps alternatives in these services could include such things as aromatherapy, reflexology (hand and foot) and dance – appropriate ways of gaining physical contact with others.

Conclusion

For a long time now, women's needs have gone unnoticed. With a lack of women's services, women have had to play second-fiddle to men on mixed wards. Some women prefer to be on mixed wards. However, personally I prefer to be in women-only services. As more and more women-only units and wards open, it means that hopefully women can remain nearer to their home towns, and to family and friends. I feel women-only services are the way forward and that their needs can be met better than on mixed wards.

Wendy Ifill

While the overall prevalence of mental disorder in men and women is not thought to differ significantly, differences in the presentation of mental disorder, social and offending profiles between women and men in secure care have been observed. The difficulties particularly relevant to women who present to mental health services or who are detained in prison in the UK are anxiety, depression, eating disorders, borderline personality disorder and symptoms of post-traumatic stress disorder (PTSD) as well as post-natal depression and psychosis. Behaviours that cause concern include fire-setting and criminal damage as well as parasuicidal behaviours. In prison, women are relatively more likely than men to have a history of self-harm. Estimates of a history of childhood abuse and self-harm are reported as 70 per cent and 90 per cent respectively for women in high secure hospitals (Coid *et al.*, 2000).

Self-injury has complex functions, but is reported by patients to be utilised as a means of managing problematic relationships, strong emotions and difficult memories. When detained in secure services the likelihood is that both strong emotions and difficult memories will be triggered, and relationships can be a source of tension. 'Re-traumatisation' can occur within organisational and therapeutic processes that are viewed by the individual to be oppressive. Survivors of complex trauma can be reminded of and continue to interact in ways reminiscent of previous abusive experiences. The reciprocity of interpersonal dynamics on the ward can lead to confirmatory statements and actions by others that serve to support trauma-related beliefs. Examples of some institutional practices that some patients have identified as having the potential to re-confirm traumatic experiences are organisational processes (e.g. restraint procedures and the use of seclusion and observations), therapeutic processes (e.g. enforced medication, physical examination, 'interrogative' interviewing) and systemic processes (lack of choice, control and power). The tension created by understanding and putting limits on extreme responses to such (e.g. self-injury) remains a task for developing and established services.

Importantly, concern has been expressed that women in secure services often experience longer lengths of stay and transfers between facilities resulting from the risk they are deemed to pose to themselves as well as incidents of assaults against members of staff and fellow patients. One of my own clinical observations has been that the risks associated with an individual's potential for harm towards others in such services often appear inflated by an 'urge' to self-harm. This is especially the case when the act itself is not an easily achievable option (planning is required), when accompanied by intrusive experiences (hallucinations, images, thoughts) and when there is (as yet) a lack of well-rehearsed alternatives to coping with distress. An 'expressive' assault on another then becomes part of a 're-victimisation' pattern that ultimately leads to the individual being punished, contained or transferred, with increased levels of security. Or else the act is followed by self-punishment, often through self-injury, and so the cycle continues.

WOMEN'S ENHANCED MEDIUM SECURE CARE

The current objective to reduce the numbers of women inappropriately detained in high secure hospitals has led to the development of a number of women-only services in both the public and the private sector. The service in which I work, Arnold Lodge, is a medium secure facility that has over the last year provided a gender-sensitive service for women in standard medium secure and enhanced medium secure care.

Arnold Lodge women's service provides one of the three current National Health Service (NHS) pilot Women's Enhanced Medium Secure Services (WEMSSs), designed for women who require enhanced levels of care and treatment within a medium secure setting. The national programme has identified a group of women who do not require Category B, high secure care, but nor are they considered to be effectively managed in conditions of standard medium secure care. Recommendations were for services to provide an enhanced level of 'procedural' and 'relational' security beyond that available in standard medium secure care.

The physical design of the service at Arnold Lodge considered the need to minimise the risks associated with self-injury (i.e. likelihood, frequency, intensity and lethality) as the distinction between self-injury with and without suicidal intent is a complex one, for both patients and staff. Following on from advice regarding the physical design of units and the enhancement of relational security, the unit has been built being mindful to a preference for open spaces, separate/separable Intensive Care Unit areas, quiet areas, family visiting areas and limited beds (ten in each ward).

'Procedural security' important to the development of WEMSSs refers to organisational policies and processes for maintaining safety, preventing absconsion, preventing entry/possession of contraband and managing access to articles used to harm selves or others.

'Relational security', an organic process based on attachment theory, is defined as the nature and quality of therapeutic relationships, reflected in patient:staff ratios, interaction processes, training and interventions provided by staff. In the case of WEMSSs, patients talk not just about the need for additional staff but about the hope they have that staff will convey an understanding of self-injury above and beyond that experienced previously in other services.

The General Principles identified in section 8 of the *Into the Mainstream* document (DH, 2003a) highlights the need for a workforce to utilise therapeutic relationships to create security. Skills such as listening, being non-judgemental, empathic and respectful, understanding and managing complex problems, consistency and continuity of care, and staff as role models are encouraged. This desire is reflected in Wendy's perspective on service development: '. . . to be able to develop appropriate relationships in secure services is limited'. 'Males working on female wards can act as positive male role models for women who have had negative experiences of men in their lives.'

DEVELOPING A MODEL OF CARE AND TREATMENT

A review of the literature (Lart *et al.*, 1999) has suggested a lack of systematic information on current service models and therapeutic interventions in women's services, with published research being descriptive. Specific examples of positive practice were highlighted by the Department of Health at Northgate Hospital, Newton Lodge and St Andrews Hospital. The lack of published research comparing different models of care may have been a reflection of the requirements of academic journals for control groups that cannot always be achieved in smaller forensic services, which tend to adopt a more 'eclectic' approach. Individualised packages of treatment are recommended and provided using a variety of professional approaches. Where this is the case (as in Arnold Lodge), describing overarching treatment models of care becomes apparently complicated. In addition to this, an approach needs to consider the application of the 'what works' core principles of risk, need and responsivity (see Andrews and Bonta, 2003) and to ensure that the responsivity principle is gender informed.

A service that can provide a number of therapeutic opportunities, from a range of theoretical backgrounds, combined with a patient group presenting a complex array of psychological, interpersonal and biological needs, is not likely to fit neatly into a treatment model restricted to a single approach. There are a number of key issues to consider:

- the need to pay attention to the literature on the validity and utility of *specific approaches* to treating personality disorder;
- the need to prepare for specific *criminogenic needs* associated with women in secure services;
- the need to consider issues of treatment integrity with the above;
- the need to acknowledge the significant role of *trauma*;
- the need to accept *complex presentations* (PTSD, psychoses and personality disorder);
- the need to value the contribution of *different professionals* and patients, working towards a common goal using an integrative approach (reflective of 'new ways of working');
- the need to build in a process that supports a philosophy of *empowerment*, values the role of the *therapeutic relationship*, provides containment through consistency and promotes sustainable *change*.

Specific approaches

When planning the design of psychological input to a WEMSS, considering the empirical support for specific interventions that have used episodes of self-injury as outcomes is a reasonable first step. Hawton *et al.*'s (1998) systematic review of randomised contolled trials highlighted problem solving therapy and dialectical behavior therapy as having support for helping reduce incidents of self-injury. Given what we know about the patient population, services should also employ psychosocial interventions aimed at reducing the impact of stress, and should make attempts to address specific areas of need such as arson and substance misuse.

Complex trauma – the need for consistent therapeutic relationships

A characteristic that is often referred to in the interface between patients and staff in secure services is the potential for 'splitting'.

Although sometimes now used as a pejorative term, when working closely with individuals for whom relationships can be dangerous, and their own identity and self-esteem is fragile, one needs to manage expectations. It is difficult for some patients with complex type-II traumatic experiences to manage their relationships with those in the role of care-provider/authority. From an analytical perspective, in multidisciplinary teams, co-workers can become 'split' into those who represent to the patient the punitive figure who the patient/'inner child' is angry at, those who represent the abusive carer who the patient feels vulnerable around and those who represent the longing for connection, acceptance, nurturing and something different.

Jeff Young (2005) describes how individuals with borderline personality disorder are observed to flip between these modes/self states so rapidly that it can feel like different team members are talking about different people. In applying this thinking to self-injury in secure settings, the motive of the patient in deciding to injure herself might immediately appear different to different people. In the case of the punitive figure, he/she may think that the patient acted to express the intense anger he/she experienced in their interaction, or to punish herself; in the case of the abusive figure, he/she may consider the act to be one done to alert attention to her vulnerabilities; in the case of the idealised figure, he/she might consider the act to be a pattern of coping that we have come to understand, but that the patient has difficulty replacing with something less damaging. Ensuring adequate time and systems for communication and team reflection on such processes is recommended, alongside developing a shared narrative and accepted use of language.

Multidisciplinary teams

With the risk of 'splits' in the team, the complexity of psychological disturbance in this patient group, and the different professional/theoretical backgrounds and experiences from which a multidisciplinary team originate, it should not be assumed that there will automatically be a consistent approach to the care of each patient. Procedures for the management of decisions, discussion of approaches and interactions and the shared understanding of treatment stages should reflect this. Procedures for effective communication and reflection on the WEMSS at Arnold Lodge currently include computerised clinical notes accessed from around the hospital, a simplified access/observation procedure, nursing handover by a nurse-in-charge, feedback by visiting professionals, ward communications books, daily management meetings, daily patient ward/business meetings, weekly multidisciplinary team business meetings, fortnightly ward rounds, CPA process and monthly extended women's service meetings as well as individual professional and group staff supervision arrangements. There are many opportunities for communication and integration, but such systems each require careful implementation and review.

'Integrative eclecticism'

'It is generally accepted that psychotherapy has a single goal – the facilitation of change . . . most people see a therapist to achieve a positive outcome such as the removal of an unwanted symptom, the fulfillment of a goal, or the reaching of a life objective' (Seiser and Wastell, 2002: 116). Seiser and Wastell acknowledge the differing approaches and modes to such an objective (i.e. individual vs group), and that 'different therapeutic approaches measure change through insight, behavior, integration, actualization, cognitions, or balanced systems' (2002: 120). However, their text *Interventions and Techniques* concludes by suggesting an integration of techniques: 'the effective use of interventions that are working in harmony to advance the client's goals' (2002: 131). The benefit, it is posited, is derived from not just the approaches or techniques themselves, but also the sequence in which they are designed and planned in line with what we understand about the process of therapy.

Empowerment

The development of a transparent treatment model highlighting needs and expectations emerged from an understanding of women's needs being linked to the issue of disempowerment as reflected in historical economic, social, political and cultural attributes and opportunities (i.e. access to resources, opportunities and decision making). In forensic settings, it is difficult not to replicate such experiences given the lack of control patients often have over decision making in their care. Patients are observed to make attempts to empower themselves, sometimes in 'dangerous' ways such as interpersonal conflicts as well as self-injury.

According to WISH (Stafford, 1999), women surveyed in high secure hospitals were mostly from large working-class families, had experienced early abandonment or loss of a carer, had problematic attachment to foster families and over one-third were looked after in children's homes. In terms of attainment, 23 per cent were sent to special schools, 75 per cent had no educational qualifications and over one-quarter were never employed. As an adult, 76 per cent were solely dependent on social security payments prior to admission, over 80 per cent had not experienced a stable partnership as an adult and 40 per cent had children – mostly as lone parents.

It is also the case that women in secure care may have regularly received messages that they are not to talk, not to share – to keep secrets. Anna Motz (2004: 125) writes: 'women use their bodies to articulate what cannot be spoken or thought about . . . their bodies become quite literally the sites of battles and modes of communication'. Guidance from the *Into the Mainstream* document (DH, 2003b: 26) is that: 'Psychological therapies adhere to the principles of empowerment, partnership and giving women a sense of control over the pace and movement of the therapeutic process'. Overcoming such protection becomes a *readiness* consideration.

Readiness for treatment

In their recent overview of Australasian work on treatment readiness, Andrew Day and colleagues (2007) sought to articulate and further develop the construct. They describe how whereas the term '*responsivity*' has been concerned with adjusting treatment delivery in a way that maximizes learning, '*treatment readiness*' is an overarching term that encompasses both the internal components of responsivity (e.g. offender motivation, problem awareness, emotional capacity to engage with psychological treatment, goals and personal identity), and external components that may be specific to the custodial environment in which treatment is commonly offered (e.g. availability of programmes, institutional social climates, legal pressure to attend; see Ward *et al.*, 2004). When developing a new service, it is not only the patients who are asked to commit to a treatment model; the service and staff also have needs in respect of commitment, training and coordination to enhance the readiness of the establishment to provide effective treatment. This will continue to develop after a service opens its doors to patients, no matter how long the preparation period.

Jeffcote and Travers (2004: 27) highlighted the need to consider carefully issues of engagement in designing psychological services for women in secure settings: 'Apparent engagement may be misleading, reflecting the woman's expertise at being 'a good girl' and leading the professional into collusion. Lack of engagement can be misconstrued as a lack of motivation rather than reflecting a deep sense of worthlessness or fear of being known by another . . . Women often experience a strong pressure to "prove" they always fail'.

Issues of treatment readiness have historically meant that patients with complex presentations that include personality disorder have found themselves excluded from services, or have themselves had difficulty engaging with or remaining in treatment. Patterns of behaviour, coping and interrelating are entrenched and have become self-fulfilling, leading very often to an assumption that the path to change is a hopeless one. Particularly in medium security there is a sense of hope (and combined fear in some cases) that the next step could be living more independently. Without the pace and process towards this objective being carefully staged, the anxieties associated with rejection can become overwhelming; without the building of therapeutic relationships, the establishment of safety, and further therapeutic stages/phases, the likelihood of therapeutic success is lessened.

The question of change

Reflecting the issue of change in our treatment models is essential. Services designed to provide enhanced relational security should understand that positive change is often very slow, with many setbacks. When facing crises it is common for professionals to consider patients to have lost all of the progress they have made – this has sometimes been termed 'sabotage'. Feelings of hopelessness, betrayal, disappointment and anger in staff are common given the cyclical nature of patient pathology. For patients themselves, fear and anxiety prevents personal development, growth and exploration, and for many women this fear and anxiety is associated with the therapeutic relationships they are asked to make in forensic settings.

Being explicit about the language of change can help to manage expectations and alleviate anxieties around what should be provided from the inception of new services. As mentioned, readiness is a measure of the service as well as of the patient. One approach that has been utilised for understanding the sequence through which behaviour changes is Prochaska *et al.*'s (1992, 2003) naturalistic descriptions of changes in addictive behaviours. The six-stage process that they describe (pre-contemplation, contemplation, preparation, action, maintenance and termination) is combined by John Livesley (2003: 91) to reflect four core stages:

- *problem recognition*, which involves recognising and accepting problems and developing a commitment to change;
- *exploration*, whereby a collaborative description is used to develop an understanding of a given problem and its associated feelings and thoughts;
- *acquisition of alternatives*, which suggests new ways of responding to situations and handling feelings and impulses – a problem-solving stage that seeks to find new solutions to old problems;
- *consolidation and generalisation*, where steps are taken to ensure that new learning is strengthened and applied to everyday situations.

Such an approach is used to organise the management of specific problems, ranging from self-harming behaviour to maladaptive interpersonal patterns, and although it is described by Livesley in relation to individual therapy, can be applied to an overarching model of treatment approach. He writes: 'evidence suggests that the non-specific component makes the greatest contribution to change; an approach based on generic mechanisms promises to provide the most effective way to manage and treat core pathology' (Livesley, 2003: 115). Therapeutic strategies are suggested by Livesley that compliment the approach supported by Marsha Linehan and colleagues in the application of dialectical behavior therapy (see Table 8.1). These can be amalgamated as such:

- the importance of building and maintaining a therapeutic relationship;
- establishing and maintaining a consistent treatment process (adhering to the treatment frame);
- utilising validation ('communicating to the patient that her responses make sense and are understandable within her current life context or situation'; Linehan, 1993: 223);
- building and maintaining motivation.

Table 8.1 Therapeutic stages

Therapeutic stage	*Structured day (on ward) and therapy services*	*Individual work focus*	*Group work focus*
Change management	Daily business/ feedback meetings Social, recreational and leisure activities – stabilising structure Physical health promotion and exercise	Multidisciplinary assessments Timelines and formulation Therapeutic, collaborative relationship building	
Safety Pre-treatment – orientation and commitment	Daily business/ feedback meetings Social, recreational and leisure activities Physical health promotion and exercise and motor skills Motivational work Pattern of occupation Use of Intensive Care Unit in crisis periods	Timelines and formulation continued Pharmacology and concordance Review of physical health Psycho education and dialectical treatment orientation Coping strategy enhancement Grounding/ mindfulness Named Nurse session	Psycho education groups: mental health awareness Pre-therapy groups: lifestyles programme
Containment Stage 1 – Attaining basic capacities	Daily business/ feedback meetings Vocational placement exploration	Individual social problem solving session DBT individual therapy Named Nurse session	DBT skills groups – mindfulness

continued

Table 8.1 (continued)

Therapeutic stage	*Structured day (on ward) and therapy services*	*Individual work focus*	*Group work focus*
Control and regulation Stage 2 – Reducing post-traumatic stress	Daily business/ feedback meetings Soothing and expressive activities (e.g. gardening group; creative opportunities – art, music and drama) Staged leave opportunities	Cognitive behavioral strategy introduction – trauma-focused CBT – CBT for psychosis – schema/mode work Individual social problem solving session DBT individual therapy Named Nurse session	Social problem solving DBT skills groups (Cognitive Analytic Music Therapy Pilot)
Exploration and change Stage 3 – Increasing self-respect	Daily business/ feedback meetings Education and daily living skills Further leave opportunities	Individual session (CBT approaches continued) DBT individual therapy Named Nurse session	DBT skills groups Social skills/ communication/ interpersonal skills Substance misuse programme Arson treatment programme
Integration and synthesis Stage 4 – Achieving individual goals	Daily business/ feedback meetings Daily living skills continued Family work and parenting skills	DBT individual therapy Named Nurse session (on leave where appropriate)	Daily business/ feedback meetings Systemic approaches (e.g. family work) Pre-discharge group

Notes: CBT = cognitive behavioural therapy; DBT = dialectical behavioural therapy.

The application of validation to the treatment of self-injury is through:

- recognising and accepting behaviour and experience;
- acknowledging areas of competence;
- facilitating a search for meaning;
- managing validation ruptures;
- avoiding invalidating interventions;
- counteracting self-invalidation and reducing self-derogation.

Evidence from behavioural literature indicates that in order to change a behaviour one needs to be exposed to a different, novel experience and to both suppress the desire to act in one way and learn to associate another behaviour with the experience. This can only be achieved through learning (reinforcement processes). This needs time and patience. Those who have come to utilise any model of staged change will understand that a new experience will require consideration, action and maintenance. Our treatment stages model acknowledges the same phenomena, and therefore allows for and understands occasional 'lapses' into old ways of relating/acting – this includes self-injury. It is understood by all parts of the multidisciplinary team that the women will harm themselves, but it is clearly expressed that this is something that we (and they in the most part) would like to be different.

TREATMENT STAGE MODEL: APPLICATION

Treatment stages: overview

The overarching psychological 'treatment stages' model for the women's services at Arnold Lodge is based on recognition of the need to provide opportunities for meaningful change, at a pace that is individualised, but which tends to follow a predictable sequence. This sequence gives an overall structure to treatment and provides a framework for integrating different kinds of specific, change-focused interventions.

Treatments are offered across professional groups and support each other through recognition of treatment stages. These stages were proposed by Livesley (2003) and broadly are described by the terms change management; safety and containment; control and regulation; exploration and change; and integration and synthesis. The multimodal approaches within these stages are summarised in Table 8.1. The opportunity for change is provided through therapeutic relationships, increased self-knowledge, the provision of new experiences and the acquisition of new behaviours.

The provision of a ward-based daily programme provides support to all of the treatment stages by creating a holding and facilitating environment, initially by promoting engagement and familiarity essential to safety and containment, by offering new experiences to support exploration and change, and by allowing the opportunity for structured interpersonal activities, enabling learning to be applied and integrated into daily life.

Treatment stages: communication

The stages of treatment are communicated to staff and ultimately to patients as follows:

Coping with change

Moving from one placement to another new and unknown place can be daunting and it takes time to feel comfortable enough to start using the help that is on offer. For some this means that on moving to Arnold Lodge the focus of their care will be trying to make this change as stress free as possible – perhaps by having some visits by members of staff before the move and discussing issues to do with moving on/change, by coming to see the ward before they are moved there, and by transferring care plans from previous places.

Safety and containment

For many women in secure services, previous life experiences and mental health problems mean that they often report feeling unsafe in their environment. After coping with change, the next stage is for patients, staff and the wider care team to work together to understand and to gradually test out what feels safe for them. Over time, patients can start to access more opportunities and therefore reduce the external containment placed on them as they take responsibility for their own safety.

Exploration and change

Once patients have managed the change of moving to Arnold Lodge women's service and are feeling safe in a range of settings then the focus of treatment becomes characterised by interventions designed to reduce the impact of previous traumatic experiences and help with long-term treatment needs such as ongoing self-injury, aggression, violence, fire-setting, problems with relationships and problematic drug use.

During this stage the patient's safety and containment needs may continue to be tested out in time-bound settings of lesser security such as when accessing other areas of the hospital or when on escorted leave outside of the hospital. Risk assessment is ongoing.

Integration and synthesis

Once patients have demonstrated to themselves and their care team (and for some to the Ministry of Justice) that their health and risk are manageable within settings of lesser security or at placements in the community then the plan is to integrate what they have learned and practised at Arnold Lodge in other settings through leave opportunities. In addition to this, the focus will be on building feasible plans for the future. Relapse prevention work will then include planning for exposure to potential destabilisers and periods of increased stress, establishing professional and personal support networks and working to enhance future engagement with services and manage the change of moving on.

In the extract below, Wendy talks about her own self-injury and reflects on the importance of safety:

Self-harm

The aim of this piece is to give a mental health service user's perspective on self-harm and to help people to think more about self-harm.

A personal perspective

More often than not, self-harm for me is a cry for help. The intent is not suicide, but rather a desire to tell others that I'm struggling. Most often my method of self-harm is to ligate but I have cut in the past. I first started self-harming in prison where it was rife. I'd never seen or heard of anyone self-harming up until that point, so it was something that I learned while I was in prison.

When I ligate, my breathing becomes very shallow and I sometimes fall into a state of semi-consciousness, leading into a sense of relaxation and calm and my problems momentarily disappear. Obviously this is quite dangerous and I know of a few people who have died doing this, whether intentional or not. Even though I know potentially my actions could be fatal, it doesn't stop me doing it. It's a bit like being told you could die if you don't stop smoking, and yet you still continue. It can sometimes be addictive, and hard to stop.

A general perspective

The reasons why people self-harm differ, as do their methods of self-harm. Many women who self-harm come from abusive backgrounds, whether that be sexual, mental or physical, and there is a link between people's past histories and self-harm. This may be in as much as women who self-harm do so as a means of hurting themselves because it's what they feel they deserve.

It is important to remember that people who self-harm are exactly that, people, and they need to be seen as such, and not as someone who self-harms.

It is important to adopt an holistic approach to deal with the person as a whole, so that all of their needs are seen to [not just self-harm]. This includes a safe, secure environment, warmth, food, education, a sense of purpose, comfortable finances as well as physical, emotional and spiritual needs being seen to. Making sure someone has a secure, sound base is important in everyone's lives, and for a person who self-harms, and indeed has mental health problems, this is no exception.

Prevention of self-harm

It is important to recognise the signs before a person self-harms, as often when it gets to this point it is too late to prevent. Asking a person what they can do at this point is no good, as it's often hard for them to explain or do.

If signs can be recognised and plans put into action before the event then this is more beneficial. This could be things like helping me apply other coping mechanisms – going through techniques with staff to help when I dissociate, or asking me if I want to listen to my music, may be ways of preventing me from self-harming.

Indeed for myself, for people to offer me help at the onset of my drop in mood can prevent me from going down completely. I know my own coping mechanisms, but I can't always implement them by myself so for others to help me is useful.

Next steps

Sometimes after I have self-harmed, asking me what I want to do next may be a bit overwhelming for me. It's been hard to decide what to do beforehand, so making decisions at this point is very hard to do. At this point maybe all that can be done is to help me feel safe. If I am able to contribute to this decision by suggesting ways to help me feel safe then this is ideal. However, if not it may come to the point where staff (or someone else) may need to step in and intervene for my well-being.

Coping mechanisms

The majority of the time I don't self-harm and usually self-harm is the last resort. If I can apply other coping mechanisms then I will. These include:

- listening to music;
- watching television;
- writing (including) poetry, plays, projects;
- cooking (I find this relaxes me);
- talking to friends on the telephone;
- exercise;
- seeking staff support.

All of the above have different benefits; that is, exercise gets my adrenaline going, whereas music distracts me, making me concentrate on something else, and at the same time relaxing me.

Conclusion

Self-harm is a very individual thing, and people self-harm for many different reasons, use many different methods and for different outcomes. Any consequences to self-harm should be to benefit the person (i.e. to aid them to feel safe), and should not be punitive. For me, the reason for self-harming is to draw people's attention to the fact that I am struggling and that I may be unsafe. Self-harm in itself can be seen as one of my coping mechanisms as much as those above, and it's something I'm not sure I'll ever overcome.

Wendy Ifill

SUMMARY

There has been some support for the use of a stages of change/ 'treatment stages' model across services designed for treating individuals with complex needs. The Transtheoretical Model of Change (Prochaska and DiClemente, 1984) has been influential in considering motivation, engagement and readiness in forensic settings and is integral to some programmes currently delivered in Dangerous and Severe Personality Disorder sites in the UK for men as well as other women's enhanced services. For the women's service at Arnold Lodge, the treatment model/process described here allows for the coordination of a number of complementary approaches through a series of treatment phases and through balancing the principles of validation and change. This has promise in terms of simplicity, integrity, transparency and alliance with existing approaches. Individual treatment evaluation will inform the overall picture of effectiveness but so too will a description of the process of the stages themselves, alongside an anticipated reduction in problematic behaviours or symptoms.

REFERENCES

Andrews, D.A. and Bonta, J. (2003) *The Psychology of Criminal Conduct* (third edition), Cincinnati, OH: Anderson.

Coid, J., Kanton, N., Gault, S. and Jarman, B. (2000) 'Women admitted to secure forensic services: comparison of women and men', *Journal of Forensic Psychiatry*, 11: 275–295. Cited in Department of Health (2002) *Women's Mental Health: Into the Mainstream: Strategic Development of Mental Healthcare for Women*, London: DH.

Day, A., Howells, K., Casey, S., Ward, T. and Birgden, A. (2007) 'Treatment readiness: an overview of Australasian work', *Issues in Forensic Psychology*, 7: 21–25.

DH (Department of Health) (2000) *Secure Futures for Women: Making a Difference*, London: DH.

DH (2002) *Women's Mental Health: Into the Mainstream: Strategic Development of Mental Healthcare for Women*, London: DH.

DH (2003a) *Into the Mainstream: Analysis of Responses to the Consultation Document*, London: DH.

DH (2003b) *Mainstreaming Gender and Women's Mental Health: Implementation Guidance*, London: DH.

Hawton, K., Avensman, E., Townsend, E., Bremner, S. *et al.* (1998) 'Deliberate self-harm: systematic review of efficacy of psychosocial and pharmacological treatments in presenting repetition', *British Medical Journal*, 317: 441–447. Cited in Department of Health (2002) *Women's Mental Health: Into the Mainstream: Strategic Development of Mental Healthcare for Women*, London: DH.

Jeffcote, N. and Travers, R. (2004) 'Thinking about the needs of women in secure settings', in N. Jeffcote and T. Watson (eds) *Working Therapeutically with Women in Secure Mental Health Settings*, London and Philadelphia, PA: Jessica Kingsley Publishers.

Lart, R., Payne, S., Beaumont, B., Macdonald, G. and Mistry, T. (1999) *Women and Secure Psychiatric Services: A Literature Review*, Bristol: Bristol University. Cited in Department of Health (2002) *Women's Mental Health: Into the Mainstream: Strategic Development of Mental Healthcare for Women*, London: DH.

Linehan, M.M. (1993) *Cognitive Behavioral Treatment of Borderline Personality Disorder*, London and New York: Guilford Press.

Livesley, W.J. (2003) *Practical Management of Personality Disorder*, London and New York: Guilford Press.

Motz, A. (2004) 'Hiding and being lost: the experience of female patients and staff on a mixed sex ward', in N. Jeffcote and T. Watson (eds) *Working Therapeutically with Women in Secure Mental Health Settings*, London and Philadelphia, PA: Jessica Kingsley Publishers.

NIMHE (National Institute for Mental Health in England) and DH (Department of Health) (2003) *Women only and Women-Sensitive Mental Health Services*, London: NIMHE and DH.

Prochaska, J.O. and DiClemente, C.C. (1984) *The Transtheoretical*

Approach: Crossing Traditional Boundaries of Therapy, Homewood, IL: Dow Jones-Irwin.
Prochaska, J.O., DiClemente, C..C. and Norcross, J.C. (2003) 'In search of how people change', *American Psychologist*, 47: 1102–1114. Cited in Livesley, W.J. (2003) *Practical Management of Personality Disorder*, London and New York: Guilford Press.
Seiser, L. and Wastell, C. (2002) *Interventions and Techniques*, Buckingham and Philadelphia, PA: Open University Press.
Stafford, P. (1999) *Defining Gender Issues: Redefining Women's Services*, London: WISH. Cited in N. Jeffcote and T. Watson (eds) *Working Therapeutically with Women in Secure Mental Health Settings*, London and Philadelphia, PA: Jessica Kingsley Publishers.
Tilt, R., Perry, B., Martin, C., Maguire, M. and Preston, M. (2000) *Report of the Review of Security at the High Security Hospitals*, London: DH.
Ward, T., Day, A., Howells, K. and Birgden, A. (2004) 'The multifactor offender readiness model', *Aggression and Violent Behaviour*, 9: 645–673.
Young, J. (2005) Schema Therapy workshops, Cambridge, 2008.

Chapter 9

Self-harm cessation in secure settings

Elizabeth Grocutt

INTRODUCTION

> 'I self-harmed for different reasons, sometimes I needed to punish myself because my stepmother used to do the punishing so there were times when I self-harmed because in my head I deserved to be punished. Other times I deliberately disfigured myself in certain ways to make myself ugly so that it was easier for people to not like me or have relationships with me. Stopping is a very big achievement because self-harm has been such a huge part of my life, the self-punishment, self-loathing, despising myself as a person physically and mentally. I wake up in the morning now and I feel that I've moved on, I feel that I've got a life ahead of me and I don't need to hurt myself anymore, the people who hurt me have gone.'
>
> (Faye)

This chapter originated from a qualitative research project that sought to understand the personal journeys of women in secure settings who had chosen to no longer self-harm. The subtle yet important distinction between being engaged in self-harming and achieving and maintaining cessation was based on individuals' personal perceptions of their behaviours, allowing a service-user-led definition of change to be used. The aim of the research was to provide insight into what supported, facilitated and maintained this process.

The impact of living within a restricted institutional setting can increase the likelihood of individuals asserting control over their remaining spheres of influence through self-inflicted violence. As the above quote demonstrates, although self-harm has often played a substantive and complex role for this clinical population, significant changes can be achieved.

In this chapter, an overview of the self-harm literature in secure settings is presented, and the process of undertaking this research project and the subsequent findings are presented and discussed.

The prevalence of self-harm

In this chapter, self-harm is understood in the context of self-inflicted attacks to the body and is seen as distinct from conscious suicidal behaviour. Self-harm has been conceptualised as behaviour in which 'the body is going to be deliberately, and usually habitually, harmed rather than destroyed or killed, and that is harming the self' (Gardner, 2001: 3). Self-harm is recognised as a major mental health problem (Hawton *et al.*, 1997; NICE, 2004) and its impact on resources and services within the NHS is significant (Yeo, 1993; Drummond *et al.*, 1997). The UK has one of the highest incidence rates of self-harm in Europe (Horrocks, 2002) and its prevalence has continued to rise since the 1970s (NICE, 2004). Despite this documented growing trend, effective psychological treatments for self-harm are limited (Hawton *et al.*, 1998) and the processes involved in self-harm cessation remain to be fully understood. There remains an identified need for further qualitative research to understand clients' experiences of mental health services and treatments (NICE, 2004), in order to facilitate service-user led changes in the management of self-harm.

Self-harm in secure settings

Compared to other population groups, incidence rates of self-harm are highest in psychiatric and prison services (NICE, 2004); and women are disproportionately more likely than men to display self-harming behaviours within these settings (Burrow, 1992; Liebling, Chipchase and Velhangi, 1997).

Men and women in secure settings have distinct mental health needs, personal histories and pathways to hospital (Bartlett, 2004). It is acknowledged that women frequently exhibit complex mental health problems alongside their self-harming behaviours (Haw *et al.*, 2001). Women are more likely to use their bodies, through self-harm, to communicate distress that is too painful to verbalise (Motz, 2001), report histories of sexual abuse and to have suffered trauma as a result of this (Van der Kolk *et al.*, 1991; Low *et al.*, 2000).

The complex histories of women in secure settings illustrates how co-morbid psychological difficulties and institutional factors may contribute to the likelihood of self-harming behaviours, making it hard to determine the precise causes and maintaining factors of violent self-destructive acts. The question of how women are able to change violent and frequently entrenched behaviours, needs to be further understood.

Self-harm research in secure settings

Research studies have sought to understand the functions and purpose of self-harm within institutional settings from the individual's perspective while acknowledging the powerful systemic impact of self-harm on staff groups. This has focused on two main areas: first, studies exploring women's accounts of their self-harming behaviour; second, research studies that have evaluated self-harm psychological interventions in secure settings.

The reasons women give for self-harming in secure settings are well documented by Liebling and Chipchase (1995, 1996) and Liebling *et al.* (1997) who provide a rich and detailed account of the support needs and experiences of this client group. This qualitative research enabled the women's voices to be heard and highlighted the powerful dynamics operating within hospitals and the impact this had on their self-harm. For many women, self-harm provided a sense of personal control and served as a coping mechanism in surviving the challenges of living in a secure hospital.

The second area of research with women in secure services has evaluated psychological self-harm treatments. Low *et al.* (2001) reported a reduction in self-harm rates over the course of a year-long dialectical behaviour therapy (DBT; Linehan, 1993) treatment programme and six-month follow-up, in a high secure service. There is evidence to support the application of DBT skills in treating the emotional difficulties of this diverse clinical population. However, the central question of how and why women were able to stop self-harming remains to be fully understood.

Despite the magnitude of self-harm in secure settings, research findings that have informed self-harm treatments and clinical practice remain limited (Borrill *et al.*, 2003).

Self-harm cessation research

Self-harm research findings have illustrated how this behaviour can be maintained and perpetuated by interpersonal and emotional factors that are diverse and complex (Low *et al.*, 2000). In secure settings the ongoing ethical dilemmas of working collaboratively with the client, establishing trusting therapeutic relationships while managing self-harm effectively is constantly challenged (Gough and Hawkins, 2000). The boundaries of the therapeutic relationship are often tested and affected by the professionals' duty to prevent further self-harm and maintain a safe therapeutic setting (Liebling and Chipchase, 1996; Babiker and Arnold, 1997; Harrison, 1998). However, denying clients access to self-harming methods and removing this expression and control away from the individual, can increase episodes and severity of self-harm (Harrison, 1998).

Despite the many complex factors operating within women's lives, some women in secure settings reported adapting to less self-destructive coping mechanisms (Liebling *et al.*, 1997) through personal choice. Whether these changes to less violent forms of self-expression are influenced by the resolving of personal circumstances, therapeutic interventions or other factors remain to be fully understood. When an individual stops self-harming, alternative coping behaviours need to replace the function self-harm previously served (Motz, 2001); however, the process of recognising and adapting to these alternative coping mechanisms, from the individual's perspective is largely unknown.

AIMS OF THE RESEARCH

The reasons why women in secure settings self-harm are often complex and specific to the individual (Borrill *et al.*, 2003); and the processes involved in stopping self-harm, although unexplored, were likely to be as complex. It was anticipated that gaining an insight into the experiences of women involved in stopping self-harm could enhance understanding of the cessation process.

Additionally, unravelling the process of cessation from clients' perspectives could inform the future treatments needs of this vulnerable and diverse population.

A small-scale qualitative study[1] consisting of individual in-depth interviews were undertaken with women in secure mental health services. Seven women from three National Health Service (NHS) forensic mental health secure services across the UK who identified themselves as having begun cessation while in a secure setting were interviewed. These women were aged between 21 and 59. The length of their current hospital admission ranged from 1 to 22 years. The women were a homogenous sample, in the sense that they all identified themselves as having stopped self-harming. However, the complex role and impact that self-harm had played within their own lives was unique to the individual. The interviews were analysed using the methodological principles of Interpretative Phenomenological Analysis (IPA), as described by Smith (1996).[2]

All of the women identified themselves as in the process of stopping self-harm or having stopped self-harming. Enabling the individual to identify themselves as no longer self-harming facilitated a more service-user-led, as opposed to service-led definition of cessation. The criteria for defining self-harm included a range of behaviours that involved deliberately inflicting pain or injury to the body but without conscious suicidal intent.

THE INTERVIEW PROCESS

All of the women who participated in the study had severe and longstanding histories of self-harm. Many had begun self-harming in early adolescence and all were able to recall vividly when they began inflicting violence towards themselves. This violent act had

1 This study was undertaken as part of a doctorate in Clinical Psychology and was supervised by Ms A. Motz and Dr J. Timms.

2 IPA is a methodology that uses a small homogeneous sample of respondents to explore individuals' personal understanding of a phenomenon and the meaning they assign to their experiences (Smith and Osborn, 2003). IPA has been successfully applied to explore the personal impact of a range of life events and processes (Smith, 1999), including individuals' narratives of self-harm cessation in a community setting (Sinclair and Green, 2005).

played a destructive yet consistent role within these women's unpredictable and chaotic lives. Self-harm represented an integral component of their physical and emotional identity from an early age. At times during the interviews some women appeared to be experiencing a form of mourning for the loss of self-harm, in that it had previously provided an effective way of managing distress in their lives.

The women in this study had performed sustained and extreme self-inflicted attacks to their bodies, which had left many with disfigurements, severe physical disabilities and ongoing health complications. Although many women no longer self-harmed, their physical scars appeared to serve as a symbolic reminder of their past behaviours and identity.

All of the women throughout the interview, referred back to their self-harm narratives and the story of their escalating relationship with harming themselves. It was felt that in order for cessation to be explored, an acknowledgement about the purpose and context of their self-harm needed to be voiced. During the interviews many women revealed the physical scars and burns from their self-inflicted violence. This form of exposure could be interpreted as a need to communicate the level of extreme distress and chaos they experienced, or to initiate a response or reaction. Alternatively, revealing their scars appeared to provide a visible context for their cessation narrative and may have served as a symbol of the 'old self' in distinction to what they had since achieved.

SELF-HARM CESSATION FINDINGS

Three dominant themes emerged from the analysis that reflected salient factors attributed to self-harm cessation. They were: 'She was my rock', 'A big incentive' and 'It's about taking control of your life'. These themes, drawn from the women's experiences of cessation, will be explored in turn.

She was my rock

The first dominant theme, 'She was my rock', represented the role that women's relationships played in their ability to sustain cessation. Some women spoke about the long-term emotional gains from seeking out particular members of staff in times of distress as opposed to the immediate release provided by self-harm. For these women, therapeutic relationships were based on available, positive, boundaried and supportive interactions. Therapeutic relationships provided a sense of security, containment and care that, for some, was experienced as parental. Many women acknowledged the value of therapeutic relationships, which were experienced as collaborative, emotionally containing and supporting self-efficacy. These relationships appeared to provide a form of person-centred stable care previously absent in these women's lives. Many women spoke about their therapeutic care providing a sense of acknowledgement, respect and validation. The following quotes reflect the powerful relational dynamics between the women and their care-providers and highlight the significance and importance of these relationships for a clinical population who have frequently experienced abusive, inconsistent forms of care.

> 'Just to have someone there when I'm feeling down, to be able to tell someone if I want to do something and to have someone there saying, "No, you don't need to do it, you can get through this phase". It just got me through.'
>
> (Kate)

> 'I'm treated like a human being. It's really hard to explain . . . you can't understand how or why you can be so happy because someone has given me the time, someone has gone out of their way and given me time.'
>
> (Fiona)

> 'This nurse, she would treat me like a mother, she would . . . she would put me right whenever I was messing about or misbehaving, she would always be there, she would always be there. I took a lot of notice of her.'
>
> (Charlotte)

Within the ward environment the emotional support provided by fellow service users facilitated a sense of understanding and a feeling that they were not alone during their cessation journey. Therefore, these relationships provided a shared experience and support network to dissipate the uncertainty and challenges of being in an inpatient setting.

> 'They'll sit with me and give me their time. Sometimes I just talk to them, sometimes I just hug them, sometimes we just sit there and have a laugh.'
>
> (Faye)

Some women recalled past significant relationships with their mothers, children and partners that had provided emotional security and containment that dissipated the need to self-harm in times of distress. The women's identities as recipients and providers of care remained a powerful and positive influence in their lives. The hope of re-establishing relationships outside the hospital setting motivated and maintained cessation for these women. Furthermore, cessation was an outward visible sign, to professionals, family and service users, that these women were addressing and engaging in working towards change that would directly impact on their existing relationships.

> 'My really wanting to stop, was to have a relationship with my kids again, so although I've done it in a way for them it's more for me than it is for them.'
>
> (Claire)

A big incentive

From the second dominant theme, 'A big incentive', three sub-themes emerged: (a) events triggering cessation, (b) personal reasons to support cessation and (c) prior cessation episodes. This theme was reflective of women's varied experiences that served to initiate and sustain self-harm cessation. Furthermore, this theme demonstrated the processes involved in choosing to change an established behaviour that had served a significant function within these women's lives.

Events triggering cessation

The first sub-theme, 'events triggering cessation', reflected how some women experienced an incident that served as a catalyst to stopping self-harm. Two women recalled a particular self-harming episode when they no longer felt in control. These incidents represented a time when the women exceeded their own parameters of 'acceptable' self-harm; the subsequent shock and realisation of the severity of their violent actions served to promote change. Self-harm to these women now symbolised a loss of control and subsequently no longer fulfilled its previous purpose.

> 'I believed that each scar represented the face of each patient on my ward. That scared me to even think that I thought that, so that just stopped me self-harming.'
>
> (Faye)

> 'Since the time I slit my throat that's really when my whole life changed, from that day onwards I realised I wanted to live.'
>
> (Fiona)

Personal reasons to support cessation

The second sub-theme, 'personal reasons to support cessation', represented the process of identifying incentives to sustain stopping self-harming and changing longstanding behaviours. For many of these women, cessation was associated with the chance to re-establish contact with family members. Stopping self-harm held direct consequences in the women's personal lives and their relationships with others, as demonstrated in the following quotes:

> 'I felt I had to show I was making an effort in sorting my life out and that was a big incentive.'
>
> (Claire)

> 'Knowing the more I self-harmed the more I wouldn't see my nephews.'
>
> (Kate)

Some women commented on the absence of personal incentives to sustain cessation in the long term. These women spoke of experiencing minimal control over their lives and believed that their aspirations were out of their sphere of control. A sense of helplessness and inevitability was present within these women's narratives.

> 'If I could have a skin graft I'd stop self-harming. I'd have a reason. I'd have new arms. I'd be able to walk around without people staring.'
>
> (Joanna)

Prior cessation episodes

The third sub-theme, 'prior cessation episodes', represented women's narratives of past episodes of stopping self-harm. Previous cessation episodes represented a time of stability, when women were engaged in meaningful roles as care-providers or living independently. For some women, their social and emotional responsibilities within their family environments were linked to sustaining cessation. However, for other women, prior episodes of cessation were attributed to alternative forms of abuse happening that had replaced the functions and need to self-harm. Harm was directed towards the self in the context of alcohol misuse and violent relationships. This form of action can be understood as a salient memory of a different way of being, prior to hospital. Therefore, self-inflicted violence in hospital sustained what had already begun whereby the individual and the body were identified targets of abuse.

> 'I was working full time and I had to support my family. Mum and dad were still there as well, I had responsibilities for other people and I had to keep going for all of them.'
>
> (Tess)

> 'Throughout the six years after I had my son I didn't self-harm. I didn't need to self-harm because I had a husband who used to kick the shit out of me, so I suppose I was being damaged in other ways.'
>
> (Joanna)

It's about taking control of your life

The third dominant theme, 'It's about taking control of your life', encompassed the personal and difficult journey towards self-harm cessation. This theme encompassed two sub-themes: (a) 'you're still battling with it' and (b) pride and achievement.

You're still battling with it

The sub-theme 'You're still battling with it' reflected how, for many women, stopping self-harming was a difficult, long-term process. Ultimately it involved an altered relationship with their self-harm whereby it was perceived as more detrimental than positive to continue. Some women spoke of feeling coerced into stopping in the past when they did not feel able or willing to achieve this, which led to an ongoing battle between the woman and her care team. The decision to stop self-harming was an active choice that occurred when these women felt able to consider and engage with change. All of the women described a sense of ownership over their decision to stop self-harming. It literally meant taking control of their lives, as expressed in the following quotes.

> 'You're not letting it beat you, you're beating it. It's challenging yourself, it's like sitting there with a razor blade and saying, do you really want to be doing this?'
>
> (Tess)

> 'I go up and down and get a bit upset; sometimes I've been very close to doing it, sometimes it's been a real struggle but then I think about my kids.'
>
> (Joanna)

> 'I had to do it on my own when I felt ready; no one could do it for me.'
>
> (Charlotte)

Some women spoke about recent minor episodes of self-harm as reverting back to old behaviours but still continued to identify themselves as being in the process of changing their behaviour. These women no longer perceived themselves as self-harmers.

> 'I'm trying to look at it as a blip and not see it as something coming back as a permanent answer.'
>
> (Joanna)

Many women spoke of the challenges of the ward environment and other women's self-harm having a potential destabilising impact on their own battles to stop self-harming. An emotionally uncontained and chaotic environment contributed to the likelihood of self-harming.

> 'I get so angry when they come into the communal area with blood on them or something tied around their neck, it's really hard for me to see it, it makes me want to do it.'
>
> (Fiona)

Many women described the process of cessation as an ongoing personal battle of survival that fundamentally involved seeking alternative outlets to channel their self-inflicted violence. Some women spoke of therapeutic interventions supporting them through their cessation journey. For others, a range of coping methods was cited including taking medication, artistic and recreational activities, leaving the ward environment for short periods of time, self-nurturing exercises and seeking support from staff and residents. All of the women spoke about the exploratory path of finding an alternative, less destructive, coping method that worked for them. As reflected in the quotes, these women made an active decision to take control of their self-harm and find alternative ways of expressing their distress.

> 'little things like watching television, listening to music, going for walks, taking a bath, the smallest of the smallest things that were actually big things. Things that meant a great deal as you had very little of anything in the hospital I was in, so you just had to make the best of it and you had to survive.'
>
> (Charlotte)

> 'Once you've written a poem and read it back you've got more understanding of yourself and how you are feeling and sometimes it takes away the need to cut.'
>
> (Joanna)

> 'Just try and do something different like have a fag. But then you've got to be careful as it's quite hard to say "No, I'll just smoke it and not burn myself".'
>
> (Fiona)

All of the women spoke about how the temptation to self-harm remained with them and that it required considerable willpower to override these feelings. Self-harm had provided a powerful and effective coping method for these women over a number of years. Most of the women described their self-harm as a well-rehearsed ritual whereby the anticipation and planning for an opportunity to act were as powerful as the immediate emotional release after self-harming. Several women explained how self-harm provided them with an immediate adrenaline rush and sense of relief and resolve that was difficult to replace.

Pride and achievement

The second sub-theme, 'pride and achievement', represented women's altered self-perceptions that emerged from engaging in the process of stopping self-harm. The women appeared to have altered their relationship with themselves and their bodies whereby they no longer held themselves solely responsible for their pasts or felt a need to inflict further violence. This change was demonstrated in the women's narratives of enhanced self-control, self-efficacy and confidence. For the majority, managing to resist the urge to self-harm enhanced their self-esteem and belief that they were able to initiate changes within their lives.

For women who had experienced multiple losses and disempowerment, tackling their self-harm was a significant step in altering their self-perception as a 'self-harmer' and, fundamentally, their lives. These women's narratives were also reflective of having acknowledged their past emotional difficulties that underpinned their self-harm, and from this difficult process, developed a sense of empowerment and control.

> 'I used to blame myself for everything that went wrong in my past but I don't anymore.'
>
> (Joanna)

> 'Yes, I was really proud when I stopped self-harming and my family were proud because they said I couldn't do it and the nurses were proud.'
>
> (Faye)

> 'I think I'm a more worthwhile person now, I don't have to hurt myself. The people who hurt me are gone.'
>
> (Tess)

> 'I've got aims now. I've got a reason to carry on. I've got a reason to wake up in the morning.'
>
> (Claire)

DISCUSSION

This study aimed to explore women's personal experiences of self-harm cessation within secure settings through detailed interviews. It was anticipated that these accounts would provide an insight into the psychological processes and personal challenges involved in changing a complex functional behaviour, along with informing the therapeutic needs of this vulnerable and diverse population.

Three dominant themes emerged from the women's narratives that reflected the importance of accessing support from valued relationships, regaining control over their lives and identifying personal incentives to influence and sustain cessation. The process towards achieving cessation and maintaining it was underpinned by complex interactions between the women and their caregivers in a therapeutic milieu, where change, recovery and hope were nurtured and supported.

The role of relationships in cessation

The theme 'She was my rock' represented the numerous ways in which relationships were associated with supporting the process of self-harm cessation. The significance of relationships in women's self-harm cessation journey was apparent, to different degrees, across the three dominant themes. In building therapeutic relationships with this vulnerable clinical population, the message needs to be conveyed to the women that their distress is acknowledged and understood; only then can the facilitation of a verbal dialogue begin, from what was previously communicated through self-harm (Motz, 2001). This study found evidence of the positive role of therapeutic relationships in sustaining self-harm cessation, demonstrated in women's narratives of enhanced self-efficacy, self-worth and empowerment. The results from this study support Aiyegbusi's (2004) findings that, despite this clinical population's traumatic histories, forming therapeutic relationships enabled women to develop self-soothing abilities and improve their self-esteem and psychosocial skills. Furthermore, this study demonstrated how women were able to use these relationships positively to support them through their difficulties and establish a sense of emotional containment within themselves, others and their environment.

Attachment theory acknowledges the importance of relationships throughout the lifespan (Bowlby, 1988). Attachment figures provide a multitude of emotional functions, one of which is to provide a 'safe base' in times of distress (Bowlby, 1988). Women in secure hospitals frequently display disturbed attachment styles and have difficulty forming relationships because of their insecure attachments in childhood (Agrawal *et al.*, 2004). As this clinical population frequently expresses their distress interpersonally, attachment theory can provide a valuable insight into understanding the complex presentations of clients' behaviour (Schuengel and Van Ijzendoorn, 2001) and how these difficulties can be enacted within relationships and the ward dynamics between staff and patients.

The development of a 'safe base' in secure settings is recognised as an important therapeutic concept in facilitating the individual to recognise, tolerate, regulate and express emotions without resorting to self-harm (Schuengel and Van Ijzendoorn, 2001). Furthermore, the concept of a 'safe base' can be applied to the ward environment in providing an emotionally containing and boundaried therapeutic space (Adshead, 2004). This study found evidence that therapeutic relationships that were experienced as caring, genuine and non-judgemental were an integral component to the women developing a sense of emotional and physical containment previously absent in their lives. The availabliity of emotionally containing support structures provided the women with the opportunity to find alternative resolutions to their distress without resorting to self-directed violent behaviour.

The therapeutic relationship between therapist and client can facilitate the exploration of alternative outlets of distress while providing the space in which unresolved issues, serving to maintain self-harm, can be addressed and understood (Levenkron, 1998; Gardner, 2001; Motz, 2001). This study found evidence that self-harm cessation was positively influenced by the development of trusting therapeutic relationships that facilitated the exploration and processing of past and current difficulties. Through the process of therapy the clinical psychologist can become the client's 'rock' and provide a 'safe base'; however, this study demonstrated that this role is not exclusive to the therapist. There was evidence of therapeutic relationships not only providing a trusting and safe milieu in which to support cessation, but also nurturing the growth of responsibility and self-efficacy within the individual. Women who were able to develop trust and tolerate the process of thinking about themselves and being thought of, were able to utilise the therapeutic relationship to build on their fragmented sense of self.

In addition, supportive relationships between fellow female service users appeared to contribute to an environment where self-harm recovery was perceived as achievable, and at times, represented a collectively shared goal. However, this sense of hope was fragile and susceptible to change. Ward settings oscillated between a settled and supportive atmosphere to a traumatising, unpredictable environment. Exposure to other women's self-harm appeared to have a negative impact on women's sense of safety and their perception of their own ability to sustain cessation.

Sustaining personal relationships outside the hospital setting provided a vital connection to women's former lives and identities. This study found evidence of the dual significance to women in accessing attachment figures and providing care to others. An aspect of self-harm recovery appeared to involve the capacity to shift between the roles of recipient and provider of care. These findings highlight the importance of not only nurturing and encouraging self-efficacy within this client group (Bartlett and Hassell, 2001) but also promoting and modelling 'healthy' attachment relationships within this damaged population (Adshead, 2004). In a clinical population who has limited or insufficient attachment experiences, those women who were able to use an attachment figure as a secure base utilised this to understand and work through interpersonal difficulties. Relational skills developed in these settings hold potential long-term implications in helping women manage their distress within and beyond the hospital setting and to re-establish and build relationships. Attachment theory can provide a framework in which to understand the development and presentation of self-harming behaviours and the re-enactment of relationship difficulties through self-directed violent actions.

The *National Service Frameworks for Mental Health* (DH, 1999) recommended that services move towards delivering a holistic-based recovery model of care, away from the predominant medical model framework, to reflect the psychological and social dimensions of clients' lives. The development of women's mental health services has been informed by attachment theory in secure settings (Adshead, 2004) and the recovery model of care (Coleman, 1999). The frameworks for providing specialist mental health services for women have been disseminated through women's mental health policy (DH, 2002) and reflected through services recognising women's specific mental health needs and emphasising relational and person-centred care (Jeffcote and Travers, 2004).

The results from the current study lend support to the application of the recovery model and attachment theory in informing therapeutic work with women who self-harm. However, providing and sustaining relational-based services requires the continued delivery of staff training, supervision and support, alongside acknowledging the significant challenges and levels of commitment required from teams and services (Jeffcote and Travers, 2004).

The role of personal incentives

The theme 'A big incentive' reflected how women's personal aspirations and goals influenced the self-harm cessation process. Stopping self-harm represented one achievement in working towards long-term life changes. It was also associated with facilitating the process of re-engaging with previously valued roles and relationships. Women's former care roles are often neglected by professionals in secure settings (Bartlett and Hassell, 2001). This study highlighted how women's care roles beyond the hospital setting remained an important dimension to their personal identities and facilitated a sense of hope for the future.

Some women described either an absence of incentives to stop self-harming or identified factors that were beyond their control. These findings highlight how this vulnerable clinical population is at a higher risk of experiencing services as disempowering and controlling (Bartlett and Hassell, 2001) and the women are likely to draw on their past, negative or inconsistent, experiences of care. The results demonstrated the importance of empowering women and working with the individual's goals towards a sense of recovery as defined by them. The client's definition of stopping self-harm may be incongruent with her care team's expectations of cessation, but must be acknowledged and worked with nevertheless. Mental health services that work with the woman to enhance a sense of ownership over her care and develop personal incentives are crucial in order to counterbalance the many restrictions that operate within a secure institutional setting (Bland, Mezey and Dolan, 1999).

The role of previous cessation experiences

Despite women's longstanding histories of self-harm, many recalled prior episodes in their lives when they were not self-harming and used these incidents as inspirations, motivating them to succeed again. This study supports previous research findings (Sinclair and Green, 2005) that stability and control within individuals' lives are positively associated with maintaining cessation. Furthermore, the themes from this study reflected how women's relationships appeared not only to maintain and support cessation, but when these deteriorated or changed unexpectedly, also acted as a trigger to relapse and re-engage in self-destructive behaviours. These findings demonstrate the importance of prioritising and understanding the complex nature of relationships within the client's life and incorporating these interpersonal issues within relapse prevention work to maintain cessation (Marlatt, 1995). There are also implications, from an attachment perspective, in services providing consistent short-term and long-term enhanced care provisions, with an emphasis on recognising the importance of nurturing therapeutic contacts across services for this vulnerable clinical population, to reduce the risk of relapse and re-enactment of past relationships through the activation of abandonment, rejection and loss of a supportive figure.

Taking control

The theme 'It's about taking control of your life' represented the ongoing personal battle of sustaining cessation, but from this process emerged a sense of pride and achievement. All of the women identified a period in their lives when self-harm no longer provided the emotional gains previously experienced. For many of the women, self-harm was associated with their identity and a representation of their life experiences and expression of their internal world. The findings demonstrated that women were able to communicate their distress, without attacking their bodies, through replacing old functions of coping with new behaviours (Motz, 2001).

CONCLUSIONS

The process of achieving cessation resulted in a sense of pride and self-control, which was evident in the room from women's determined tone of voice, altered posture and improved eye contact; they appeared comfortable within themselves and their abilities when discussing this personal battle that they had conquered. These positive actions and emotions contributed to the development of an altered self-perception and were reflected in women's accounts of enhanced self-efficacy and self-esteem. This study indicated that sustaining self-harm cessation facilitated a sense of hope, control and empowerment, previously absent in these women's lives.

This study raised a number of important issues regarding how secure services can support women working towards self-harm cessation. The findings provided further evidence for the application of attachment theory in secure services in providing a robust, containing and developmental framework to understand and inform the therapeutic needs of women who are in the process of stopping self-harm. The study also highlighted positive aspects of the recovery model expecially when working alongside women to achieve individualised and meaningful short- and long-term aspirations, which included self-harm cessation. It demonstrated that a therapeutic approach that is informed by attachment theory, the recovery model and relapse prevention work can begin to address the multiple, diverse and complex needs of this clinical population.

The challenges of sustaining these therapeutic principles within a climate of constant change, where staff turnover is high and staff can feel overwhelmed at the range of clients presenting with very different issues, needs to be acknowledged (Watson *et al.*, 2004). In maintaining such services, it is paramount to provide and receive ongoing training and supervision, as self-harm is often a difficult and divisive issue within staff teams (Motz, 2001).

This study highlighted the significance of relationships, recognising and working with personal incentives and taking control and responsibility, in sustaining women's journeys towards self-harm cessation and towards a less destructive relationship with themselves. Future research can build on these findings to understand the treatment needs of this small but complex clinical population. Understanding the long-term implications of maintaining self-harm cessation will provide an insight into the adjustment process beyond a secure environment. Furthermore, interviewing women at particular time intervals of cessation may identify specific support needs and types of therapeutic input required to assist their achievements. This research has provided a valuable insight into an often hidden world of women's personal experiences of stopping self-harm in secure settings and the challenges they overcame to succeed.

The themes discovered in this research study revealed the importance of individual processes in the cessation of self-harm. Therefore, it is not possible to suggest a formulaic intervention plan for clinical application. However, it does provide insights as to how services can help to facilitate and work alongside women towards this change. Self-harm cessation has been described as a slow and difficult process; requiring personal motivation, long-term input and a supportive therapeutic setting (Sansone *et al.*, 2004). The current study found evidence that supported Sansone *et al.*'s (2004) findings and identified what a 'supportive setting' represented from a small sample of women who no longer self-harmed. This study targeted the most vulnerable, complex clinical population likely to engage in self-harm; and identified critical factors that facilitated and sustained change.

Stopping self-harm represented a fundamental, symbolic and important change for the women in taking control of their lives. For many women, this was the first step to moving away from their identity as a self-harmer and to changing how they perceived themselves and others. Many women were willing to try and develop a trusting therapeutic relationship, despite their previous experiences of abusive, inconsistent and rejecting relationships. For many women, distancing themselves from their self-harm also involved moving away emotionally from their previous lives and experiences. Stopping self-harm not only altered their own perceptions of themselves but also influenced how they were perceived by others. From their accounts, the women's hopes and aspirations were recognised, acknowledged and incorporated into their care. This sense of being understood, acknowledged and respected was an integral step in supporting the process of self-harm cessation.

This research highlighted that women with complex self-harming histories were able to successfully change their violent and destructive relationship with themselves and their bodies. This process was made evident by the women's distinction between their old identity, associated with coping with their personal histories and self-harm, and their altered robust sense of self, which was hopeful, reflective and able to tolerate experiences without resorting to self-inflicted violence. The process of cessation was a difficult, challenging journey that required significant perseverance, as self-harm had often provided an important and reliable function within these women's lives.

Running through all of the women's narratives was a sense of hope and achievement and the belief that, despite what had occurred in the past, the future held positive possibilities that were accessible and worth living for.

> 'It's not been easy, I've caved in at times but when I didn't cut up or do anything the last time I thought, I can cope with life without self-harming which I didn't previously think I could say about myself. You have to want to stop doing it for you, you can't do it for anybody else, you've got to really want it. I don't know where that inner strength came from but I've cracked it and it's given me my pride back.'
>
> (Tess)

REFERENCES

Adshead, G. (2004) 'Three degrees of security: attachment and forensic institutions', in F. Pfafflin and G. Adshead (eds) *A Matter of Security: The Application of Attachment Theory to Forensic Psychiatry and Psychotherapy* (pp. 147–166), London: Jessica Kingsley Publishers.

Agrawal, H.R., Gunderson, J., Holmes, B.M. and Lyons-Ruth, K. (2004) 'Attachment studies with borderline participants: a review', *Harvard Review of Psychiatry*, 2: 94–104.

Aiyegbusi, A. (2004) 'Forensic mental health nursing: care with security in mind', in F. Pfafflin and G. Adshead (eds) *A Matter of Security: The Application of Attachment Theory to Forensic Psychiatry and Psychotherapy* (pp. 167–192), London: Jessica Kingsley Publishers.

Babiker, G. and Arnold, L. (1997) *The Language of Injury: Comprehending Self-Mutilation*, Leicester: British Psychological Society.

Bartlett, A. (2004) 'The care of women in forensic mental health services', *Forensic Psychiatry*, 11: 25–28.

Bartlett, A. and Hassell, Y. (2001) 'Do women need special secure services?', *Advances in Psychiatric Treatment*, 7: 302–309.

Bland, J., Mezey, G. and Dolan, B. (1999) 'Special women, special needs: a descriptive study of female special hospital patients', *Journal of Forensic Psychiatry*, 10: 34–35.

Borrill, J., Burnett, R., Atkins, R., Miller, S., Briggs, D., Weaver, T. and Maden, A. (2003) 'Patterns of deliberate self-harm and attempted suicide among white and black/mixed race female prisoners', *Criminal Behaviour and Mental Health*, 13: 229–240.

Bowlby, J. (1988) *A Secure Base: Clinical Applications of Attachment Theory*, London: Routledge.

Burrow, S. (1992) 'The deliberate self-harming behaviour of patients within a British special hospital', *Journal of Advanced Nursing*, 17: 138–148.

Coleman, R. (1999) *Recovery: An Alien Concept*, Gloucester: Handsell Publishing.

DH (Department of Health) (1999) *National Service Framework for Mental Health: Modern Standards and Service Models for Mental Health*, London: DH.

DH (2002) *Women's Mental Health: Into the Mainstream: Strategic Development of Mental Health Care for Women*, London: DH.

Drummond, M.F., O'Brien, B., Stoddart, G.L. and Torrance, G.W. (1997) *Methods for the Economic Evaluation of Health Care Programmes*, Oxford: Oxford University Press.

Gardner, F. (2001) *Self-Harm: A Psychotherapeutic Approach*, Hove: Brunner-Routledge.

Gough, K. and Hawkins, A. (2000) 'Staff attitudes to self-harm and its management in a forensic psychiatric service', *British Journal of Forensic Practice*, 2: 22–28.

Harrison, A. (1998) 'Self-harm: a harmful procedure', *Nursing Times*, 94: 37–38.

Haw, C., Hawton, K., Houston, K. and Townsend, E. (2001) 'Psychiatric and personality disorders in deliberate self-harm patients', *British Journal of Psychiatry*, 178: 48–54.

Hawton, K., Fagg, J., Simkin, S., Bale, E. and Bond, A. (1997) 'Trends in deliberate self-harm in Oxford, 1985–1995, and their implications for clinical services and the prevention of suicide', *British Journal of Psychiatry*, 171: 556–560.

Hawton, K., Arensman, E., Townsend, E., Bremmer, S., Feldman, E., Goldney, R., Gunnell, D., Hazell, P., van Heeringen, K., House, A., Owens, D., Sakinofsky, I. and Traskman-Bendz, L. (1998) 'Deliberate self-harm: systematic review of efficacy of psychological and pharmacological treatments in preventing repetition', *British Medical Journal*, 317: 441–447.

Horrocks, J. (2002) 'Self-poisoning and self-injury in adults', *Clinical Medicine*, 2: 509–512.

Jeffcote, N. and Travers, R. (2004) 'Thinking about the needs of women in secure settings', in N. Jeffcote and T. Watson (eds) *Working Therapeutically with Women in Secure Mental Health Settings* (pp. 19–30), London: Jessica Kingsley Publishers.

Levenkron, S. (1998) *Cutting: Understanding and Overcoming Self-Mutilation*, London: W.W. Norton.

Liebling, H. and Chipchase, H. (1995) 'Research with women who self-harm and training needs of staff who work with them', *Special Hospital Research Bulletin*, 4: 14–17.

Liebling, H. and Chipchase, H. (1996) 'Feminist group therapy for women who self-harm: an initial evaluation', *Feminism & Psychology*, 2: 24–29.

Liebling, H., Chipchase, H. and Velhangi, R. (1997) 'Why do women harm themselves? Surviving special hospitals', *Feminism & Psychology*, 7: 427–437.

Linehan, M. (1993) *Cognitive-Behavioural Treatment of Borderline Personality Disorder*, New York: Guilford Press.

Low, G., Jones, D., MacLeod, A., Power, M. and Duggan, C. (2000) 'Childhood trauma, dissociation and self-harming behaviour: a pilot study', *British Journal of Medical Psychology*, 73: 269–278.

Low, G., Jones, D., Duggan, C., Power, M. and MacLeod, A. (2001) 'The treatment of deliberate self-harm in borderline personality disorder using dialectical behaviour therapy: a pilot study in a high secure hospital', *Behavioural and Cognitive Psychotherapy*, 29: 85–92.

Marlatt, G.A. (1995) 'Relapse prevention: theoretical rationale and overview of the model', in G.A. Marlatt and J.R. Morgan (eds) *Relapse Prevention: Maintenance Strategies in the Treatment of Addictive Behaviors* (pp. 3–67), New York: Guilford Press.

Motz, A. (2001) *The Psychology of Female Violence: Crimes Against the Body*, Hove: Brunner-Routledge.

NICE (National Institute for Clinical Excellence) (2004) *Self-Harm: The Short-Term Physical and Psychological Management and Secondary Prevention of Self-Harm in Primary and Secondary Care*, London: NICE.

Sansone, R.A., Levitt, J. L. and Sansone, L.A. (2004) 'An overview of psychotherapy strategies for the management of self-harm behavior', in J.L. Levitt, R.A. Sansone and L. Cohn (eds) *Self-Harm Behavior and Eating Disorders. Dynamics, Assessment, and Treatment* (pp. 121–134), New York: Brunner-Routledge.

Schuengel, C. and Van Ijzendoorn, M.H. (2001) 'Attachment in mental health institutions: a critical review of assumptions, clinical implications, and research strategies', *Attachment & Human Development*, 3: 304–323.

Sinclair, J. and Green, J. (2005) 'Understanding resolution of deliberate self-harm: qualitative interview study of patients' experiences', *British Medical Journal*, 10: 1136–1141.

Smith, J.A. (1996) 'Beyond the divide between cognition and discourse: using interpretative phenomenological analysis in health psychology', *Psychology and Health*, 11: 261–271.

Smith, J.A. (1999) 'Towards a relational self: social engagement during pregnancy and psychological preparation for motherhood', *British Journal of Social Psychology*, 38: 409–426.

Smith, J.A. and Osborn, M. (2003) 'Interpretative phenomenological analysis', in J.A. Smith (ed.) *Qualitative Psychology: A Practical Guide to Methods* (pp. 51–80), London: Sage Publications.

Van der Kolk, B.A., Perry, J.C. and Herman, J.L. (1991) 'Childhood origins of self-destructive behaviour', *American Journal of Psychiatry*, 148: 1665–1671.

Watson, T., Bragg, A. and Jeffcote, N. (2004) 'Working together: integrated multi-disciplinary practice with women', in N. Jeffcote and T.

Watson (eds) *Working Therapeutically with Women in Secure Mental Health Settings* (pp. 91–107), London: Jessica Kingsley Publishers.
Yeo, H.M. (1993) 'The cost of treatment of deliberate self-harm', *Archives of Emergency Medicine*, 10: 8–14.

Conclusion: 'If you prick us do we not bleed?'

Anna Motz

Throughout this book the nature of self-harm has been captured in clinical vignettes, illustrating how the act itself engages others in what can at times seem a compelling and dangerous dance. In this final chapter I will consider the sense in which self-harm has meaning as a way of affirming the humanity of people who feel they are 'other', and have been treated as such, as in the quotation in the title of this chapter, from Shylock, the Jew, in the *Merchant of Venice*. Shylock goes on to ask further questions, which could also be asked by people who self-harm: 'If you tickle us do we not laugh? If you poison us do we not die? And if you wrong us shall we not revenge?' (Shakespeare, *The Merchant of Venice* Act III, Scene 1). In other words, are we human? And is it not human to respond to cruelty with revenge, to kindness with pleasure and to tickling with laughter? This raises one of the central questions of this book: how the treatment of those who self-harm can perpetuate the behaviour, the 'cure' exacerbating the symptom.

Whether in prisons, mental health secure units, residential care settings, eating disorders wards or in the community, the responses to the self-harming individual can mirror their fear and desperation. Professionals who respond in a shocked or angry way to self-harmers are often manifesting deep anxiety about the potential for self-harm to be fatal, or to cause non-fatal but irreparable damage. The anger can also be a reaction to the hostile intentions of those who self-harm and as such reveals an unconscious communication: the self-harmer has successfully projected their anger into the 'carer', who can quickly become a persecutor. Examples of this kind of response are often found in A&E departments, as Scanlon and Adlam allude to in this volume. People who self-harm are sometimes considered unworthy of medical treatment as they have 'brought this on themselves'; this punitive attitude mirrors the aggression in the act of self-harm itself. Even in mental healthcare settings, the violence of the act of self-harm can force a kind of unwanted physical intimacy, in which the nurses and medical staff come into close contact with bodily injuries, as well as distraught mental states; unsurprisingly, this can evoke feelings of disgust and anger, as well as empathy.

I will discuss the existence of unmanageable self-harm later in this concluding chapter, because it is clear that sometimes self-harm does culminate in the ultimate self-harm – suicide – even if this was not the intended outcome, and that at other times it has political, cultural or religious meanings and functions that defy management. To deny this type of self-harm, or to write as if all self-harm could be 'managed' and transformed into less damaging activity, would be to misrepresent a powerful and, at times, deadly, behaviour. Self-harm can be a risk factor for suicide, although I argue that it also serves a powerful self-preservative role. It needs to be considered carefully as an urgent communication and understood with reference to the particular individual, the nature of the self-injury, the particular responses it evokes and the imagined outcome present in the mind of the self-injurer. This is clearly a highly complex and urgent task.

THE MEANING OF SELF-HARM

This book explores the notion of self-harm as a fundamentally relational activity throughout. The apparently paradoxical nature of self-harm and its compulsive quality create a powerful challenge for clinicians working in the area, and for family members and friends. It may be, however, that any attempt to find one meaning, a unitary and convincing explanation for self-harm, misses the point:

> When there are so many possible causes, when so many factors are or may be at work or compete to be the dominant thesis of the aetiology of the behaviour, the result is that the act becomes shrouded in disagreement and elusiveness and this elusiveness may be part of the power of the act. It remains outside our understanding and therefore symbolically outside our control. It confounds us, and confronts us with difficult feelings generated by confusion and impotence.

> Indeed, this may be how it is for those who self-harm too – who feel in its compulsive grip for reasons that they too find hard to fathom. A part of the mind wants to stop and another part feels it cannot and worries about itself.
>
> (Norris and Maher, this volume: 91)

The meaning of self-harm can be ambiguous, as it can have different significance for the same person at different times, but the notion of the divided mind alluded to above is central to self-harm. It is this splitting that characterises self-harm, and contributes to its apparent mystery. How can a destructive act be seen as one that actually serves to protect the person from pain? How can anyone wilfully inflict damage onto themselves? How can the pain be a kind of healing? I answer these questions by referring to the divided self, and a form of dialectical relationship between the various moments of self-harming, in which the person plays different roles in relation to distinct aspects of themselves. Cutting is an act of violence but also, and fundamentally, an activity with splitting, dividing and separating at its core.

THE VIOLENCE OF SELF-HARM

The desire to eliminate impure feelings is one of the unconscious fantasies that can motivate self-harm, and the relief found in the act of making tangible psychic pain – transforming it into concrete, visceral sensation – is another. Sylvia Plath (1962) describes the experience of cutting her thumb, instead of the onion she was chopping, drawing neat and graphic allusions to the look of her bandaged thumb and the sinister hoods of the Ku Klux Klansmen – men who tried to annihilate those they thought embodied Otherness. She also uses the central motifs of the kamikaze pilot, and saboteur, clearly making links to the suicidal self within the apparently contented cook, immersed in daily activity.

It is undeniable that self-harm is an act of potent aggression, even if this is not always consciously accessible to the mind of the self-harmer. Behind the assault against the self there is another, hidden aggressor, whose skin is symbolically being pierced. In Chapter 3 of this volume, Scanlon and Adlam argue that self-harm is the response to a violent state of mind that has been pushed into the person who then expels it through self-harm. This is similar to the 'trap' of mutual suspicion and fear that Norris and Maher describe in Chapter 4, but in my view self-harm is not simply an unthinking response to violence or trauma. It is not the stance of victimhood or passivity; it is a self-created genre, and a rebellious, sometimes desperate gesture. The behaviour is consciously chosen, even if the unconscious motivations are not, and may remain largely unknown.

FORENSIC PSYCHOTHERAPY: MANAGING THE IMPACT OF SELF-HARM

The premise of forensic psychotherapy, namely that victim and perpetrator co-exist in the same person, is also seen clearly in self-harm, in which the divided self is writ large, against itself. This splitting of the self is a process that is mirrored in the polarised responses it evokes. Throughout this book we can see this dichotomy at work and also gain a clear sense of how, through projective identification, other people, systems and organisations behave like parts of the mind of the self-harmer, alternating between caring and punitive responses.

Psychotherapeutic approaches to understanding the violence of self-harm enable staff to manage both punitive and rescuing countertransference feelings and to preserve clear and consistent boundaries with self-harmers. An important aspect of self-harm is its immediacy, the urgency of the response it demands, which can make thinking difficult. For those who rely on violence, whether directed against the self or against others, difficult psychic states are habitually converted into action. The professionals who work with them need to be able to help them think about and manage their feelings without acting on them. Forensic psychotherapy can help staff to become aware of the intensity of the projected thoughts and feelings of the patients and not simply retaliate or be seduced by the patients, literally or metaphorically.

Like the carers who get caught in the trapped roles described by Norris and Maher, the nursing teams and therapists who work with those who repeatedly self-harm can also get caught in unhelpful and polarised roles in relation to self-harmers. One hypothesis is that carers, and those who come into contact with self-harmers, also have unwanted violent impulses and rages, their own unacceptable and frightening feelings, which they successfully project into those they nurse. The function of the patients for staff teams of all disciplines is therefore not a straightforward one and at times these 'difficult' or 'personality-disordered' individuals can serve as metaphorical 'poison containers', repositories for the unwanted, destructive and savage aspects of those who choose to work with them; this is the traditional role of a scapegoat.[1] It is one of the dynamics that may be operational in the encounters that Scanlon and Adlam describe as forms of 'reciprocal violence'. Such forces, I suggest, operate on an unconscious level, and it is equally the case that nursing and other therapeutic staff also project their own vulnerability, helplessness and need for care into these patients. They can then feel envious of those who receive their care.

Once again the seminal work of Menzies Lyth (1959) resonates with the experience of those who work with people who self-harm. Following her radical thesis that tasks can serve as defences against psychic pain, it could be suggested that just as the self-harmer feels relief from converting inchoate emotional pain into concrete, tangible, manageable physical wounds, so too can carers actually feel relieved when presented with a relatively simple, albeit distressing, task of dressing a wound, or cutting a ligature rather than facing the deathly inactivity of depression. There is an action to be performed, with a beginning, middle and end. Such acts focus the mind, and allocate roles that help create meaning in what could otherwise be a myriad of painful attempts at relating through the haze of trauma and misunderstanding.

Just as it is relatively easy to get drawn into responding to the self-harmer as simply a victim of unmanageable distress, and to nurse the wounds, it is also possible to be drawn into a punishing and controlling stance, as described earlier. The far more difficult stance for professionals and carers is to contain one's own emotional responses, reflect on them and and finally use them to understand what is being communicated, through these projective identifications. Aiyegbusi (2004: 119) eloquently describes this in relation to nursing women who severely self-harm, and who attack the staff who care for them: 'The only means patients have of communicating their distress is to make the nurses who care for them suffer emotionally. However, if nurses can learn to contain

1 The phrase 'poison containers' was coined by Lloyd deMause in his historical and analytic exploration of child abuse.

the patients' projections, therapeutically meaningful work can take place'. The countertransference feelings towards those who self-harm are powerful and it is essential that supervision is provided in which the clinician can address this. The urge to protect self-harmers and, alternatively, to have punitive feelings towards them, are to be expected in undertaking treatment with this client group.

THE CURE PERPETUATES THE PROBLEM: RECIPROCAL VIOLENCE?

In a ward setting, the impact of patient self-injury on nursing staff can be profound. A central question for any staff team is how to deal with and appropriately manage self-injury. The patient places great importance on the relationship with healthcare professionals and desperately craves the ideal care and protection, of which she was so often deprived in early life, and is almost invariably disappointed. The carer is idealised and then denigrated, particularly if she responds to the patient's vulnerability by colluding with and maintaining a 'special' relationship in which boundaries are overstepped (Adshead, 1997). When this dynamic is allowed to intensify unchecked there is real risk of destructive enactments. The patient can feel themselves to be so needy, and also so powerful, that a slight hurt or misunderstanding can escalate quickly into justification for a self-harm attempt, either as retaliation or to elicit the sought for help.

Staff working with people who self-harm can feel helpless, anxious and incompetent as a result of the projections they receive. Those members of the nursing staff who have to stitch a patient's wounds, or find her in a nearly strangled state, will inevitably be affected by the experience; to some extent the staff can become victims of the self-harm attempt; they can be assaulted with the horror and pain that patients who self-harm are not able to contain and so project on those around them.

Throughout this book the authors have shown how self-harmers can unconsciously create situations in which they will themselves be treated sadistically, often because of strong feelings that self-harm creates in those around them. The unconscious hostility of self-harm, the sense in which it is also an assault on others, is communicated. When the self-harmer is then turned on in anger she becomes a victim of her own and others' sadistic impulses and re-creates the situation of the original trauma. This can be understood as the compulsion to repeat, demonstrating that an underlying conflict has not yet been resolved, or, more benignly, as an attempt to master the trauma through re-creating the original situation but this time hoping for some resolution of the conflict. Therapists and all members of the multidisciplinary team need to resist the force of these projections in order to understand them, and help the person to understand herself, and manage her self-destructive impulses.

REFLECTIVE PRACTICE AND SUPERVISION GROUPS FOR STAFF TEAMS

It is essential that all carers and professional staff who work with people who self-harm have adequate time to reflect on their experience. This way the impact of the work can be recognised and made sense of, rather than simply discharged in unthinking activity, or translated into mute fury at those who evoke these responses. The need for supported time for training, supervision and reflective practice is evident in all the settings described in this book: In Chapter 4, Norris and Maher poignantly discuss the force of identifications between residential staff groups and the looked-after children with whom they work; such identification and the unconscious re-awakening of trauma can be deeply unsettling for the workers and cause profound disturbances in thinking about and working with the young people. As Tim Kent, Team Manager for Looked After Children in Tower Hamlets and psychoanalytic psychotherapist in training, describes:

> [O]ften the boundary between role of 'parent/carer' and the staff's own experience is so confusing for them – confirming what Norris and Maher say about the essential application of adequately resourced trained therapeutic groups/consultation . . . but for this to happen one also really needs senior management to sign up to the plan, ideally across the National Health Service and Social Services Departments so that commissioners recognize the ways trauma/projection/parallel processes impact on and in the organization.
>
> (Kent, 2008)

Kleinot, Grocutt, Lawday, Maher, Norris and Motz all argue for the need for close supervision, reflective spaces and real containment for all therapeutic staff who work with self-harming individuals. The model of such groups varies across settings but I would strongly recommend a psychodynamic focus that takes into account the unconscious processes that self-harm involves, and its impact on the emotional and rational functioning of the therapeutic team. In Chapter 3, Scanlon and Adlam indicate that such groups can serve as mirrors for what happens on the ward, or in the clinical setting, and that group analysts can use the information gained from observing and commenting on the workings of the group to help understand what happens with the clients, whose treatment they also recommend should take place within a group:

> [A] central task for these groups is to create a reflective space within which the reflective group serves as a hall of mirrors, or a resonant echo chamber, where the dynamic issues may be amplified and condensed (Foulkes, 1948, 1964). As the supervisees become better able to *reflect-in-action* in the supervision group, so they will be able to use this experience as a bridge to transferring this enhanced reflective functioning back into the here and now of the therapeutic space itself.
>
> (Scanlon and Adlam, this volume: 74)

IMPACT ON CULTURE: AESTHETICS, PROTEST AND SELF-HARM

The meaning of self-harm varies tremendously, depending on context and its manifestation. Like Greenwood in Chapter 7, I locate eating disorders firmly within the realm of self-harming behaviour and view this as particularly significant for young women who are often attacking not only their own bodies but also their mothers, who are symbolically located in their bodies, and also the social expectation that to look upon young women is to gaze at beauty. Femininity, sexual attractiveness and the soft, smooth skin of youth is highly idealised and there is a pressure on young women to give those who gaze at them some satisfaction. For women, and men, who have been sexually abused or otherwise traumatised, the look of the other, and the desire that can be awakened is terrifying. Marking the skin, defacing beauty, can be seen as a way of warding off overtures. Likewise, embracing an eating disorder can be a way of warding off contact with others, escaping into a world that others cannot enter or control.

There is a profound sense in which eating-disordered women and girls form their own, outsider, society in which they wage war on their own appetites and on the expectations imposed on them. The websites that have been established fairly recently testify to this battle, and to the creation of a virtual community in which illness is embraced and romanticised, though some with eating disorders remain completely isolated from others who share their condition. I discuss pro-anorexia and bulimia websites in more detail elsewhere (Motz, 2008) in the context of exploring female eating disorders as an expression of self-directed violence and describe the seductive pull of these websites:

> These sites often have angel, dragonfly and butterfly motifs, evoking an image of an idealised state of prepubescent innocence and an otherworldly quality. One site chillingly has an image of a spider's web with the slogan 'Tell me it's not worth dying for'. The romantic ideal of absolute thinness seems a denial of the corporeal and establishes the drive against hunger and weight gain as a form of spiritual quest. The recurring image of wings evokes angels, moths, butterflies and birds: fragile airborne creatures with very little substance.
> (Motz, 2008: 212)

The link between self-harm and the written or artistic symbol is an essential one, in that the act creates a tangible mark on the skin, or inside the body, that expresses something meaningful in a concrete way. It can be used as a signifier to others, to be read, reacted to and noticed or serve as a private 'talisman' as Heather Jones terms it in Chapter 2. But through self-harming a language is being used and, when this is made public, the results are arresting, powerful and often disturbing. The affective communication through the physical display of this self-injury is highly powerful. The pain of self-harming is not often felt at the moment of impact when the body tends to anaesthetise itself and release endorphins, but as the scars form the wounds become more painful and uncomfortable. The role of the scars, and their signification to others, is part of the symbolism of self-harm. The angel motif again appears repeatedly in relation to self-harm websites and there is a clear idealisation of darkness, blood-letting and withdrawal from mainstream society.

Because the physical expression of trauma is such an essential aspect of self-harm, and words are not always enough to convey the depths of feelings, arts therapies are, in my view, uniquely helpful. As Garland (2004: 38) describes, trauma impacts on symbolic functioning such that the painful event cannot be thought about, but is concretely identified with: 'To whatever extent there is an inability to think about a painful event, there is almost always a resort to identification'. In a sense, self-harm could be seen as a form of identification with a violent persecutor, who inflicts pain on the body. The arts therapies can offer a different form of symbolisation for those who have undergone trauma. They can enable the self-harmer to symbolise and in doing so to transform inexpressible thoughts and feelings into something else. Whether through dance, drama, art or music, the arts therapies can reach the person who self-harms at an imaginative level and engage them in the pursuit of self-expression and communication.

In the case of Crystal, in Chapter 1, who became mute during part of the therapy with me, it was clear that she needed to recoil from language, and this led to a period of breakdown in expressive contact; she seemed to retreat and enter a preverbal state, evoking infancy. Although the therapy survived this and she was able to think with me about this withdrawal, there was a prolonged period when it threatened to overwhelm her engagement. I considered it highly significant that although she retreated from this verbal therapy, she was able to sustain a highly creative level of functioning in her art therapy in the women-only unit to which she was later transferred. It seemed that in the art therapy she was not only able to communicate outside of spoken language, but also could engage in physical activity, making marks outside of herself and symbolising her mental states in a way that could be held up and seen. This process of externalising her feelings and making something symbolic to represent them was essential to her, perhaps also performing the same function of self-harm by making her private pain public. In her sensitive analysis of the 'violent creation' involved in self-harm, Milia (2000) describes how art therapy can be effective as a treatment for people who self-harm.

MEMENTO MORI

In a recent (2008) documentary film by Morgan Matthews on the bereaved families of servicemen and women who were killed in Iraq and Afghanistan – *The Fallen* – parents of the dead are seen having their backs and arms tattooed with the names and images of their lost relatives. As part of their grieving they seek to remember, and to inscribe on their own flesh the memories of their sons, daughters, brothers and sisters, so that they will have them with them, and on them, indelibly imprinted on their skin. The pain of having the tattoo made seems to be part of the sacrifice, willingly made by these family members. This aspect of remembrance reveals the fantasy that through loving connection and physical inscription the dead will somehow be brought back to life, or at least, not forgotten about, literally incorporated into the bodies of the living. It also points to the need for a physical signifier of what has been lost. An image in the mind is not enough: 'Set me as a seal upon thine heart, as a seal upon thine arm: for love is strong as death' (Song of Songs, *King James Bible*, Chapter 8).

In a similar fashion, self-harm can be an insignia of pain and trauma, inscribed in order that it should not be forgotten; the traumatic event is preserved in concrete form on the flesh. People who self-harm, like the bereaved who mourn their dead are immersed in the rituals of remembering unspeakable acts or unbearable secrets. It is only human to feel that the past, no matter how traumatic, is important and needs to be enshrined. The relatives of people killed in service of the British Army loved their dead, and cannot bear to separate from them, to lose them into oblivion, or for those who have religious faith, to wait to see them again in the Afterlife. They want their images and names all around them, carved into their skin.

A parallel exists here too for self-harmers, who may feel fiercely loyal to their past, and who often retain loving feelings towards those who have abused them. The rituals of self-harming, like the rituals involved in grieving, can serve as comforting containers for painful emotions and traumatic memories; the scars are, at one level, memento mori for past lives.

UNMANAGEABLE SELF-HARM

Not all self-harm is manageable. Some is lethal, even when this was not the intended outcome. Repeated self-injury increases the risk of permanent damage and there is always a danger that even without suicidal intention, self-harm can result in death. Inserting or swallowing objects, tying ligatures and making deeper cuts in the same place are all risky and can lead to serious harm, against conscious wishes to die. Political protest can also be unmanageable in a therapeutic sense; the person who chooses to harm themselves and face almost certain death in a political statement, like a self-immolation or hunger strike, is not engaging in self-harm that requires management; in fact, it is defiant protest beyond intervention.

As Robin Anderson describes when discussing suicide and self-harm in adolescents, there is often an unconscious hope not to die, but there is a real possibility that miscalculations can be fatal:

> The danger here is that young people may be unaware of the dangers of what they are doing and so put themselves at grave risk even when they do not wish to die . . . This is a kind of Russian Roulette which has an element of a desperate and dangerous game of playing with one's life, and this is of course, a game that can be lost.
>
> (Anderson, 2008: 63)

It is a tragic fact that sometimes death is the result of 'misadventure', the lethal consequence of self-harm attempts that went wrong or, because of a series of coincidences, were fatally mis-timed. The possibility of fatal harm is often present in a self-harm attempt and, in some cases, this risk simply cannot be managed, and a series of events conspire that make death the outcome of what was an attempt at staying alive. People who work or live with those who self-harm are trying to contain the anxiety of this awareness while remaining as vigilant as possible to the risks inherent in self-harm activities. In those tragic cases when self-harm causes death, even when this was not the intention, the impact on carers and therapists is devastating. The death can feel like an attack on all hope and a mockery of the treatment and thus leaves both staff teams and individuals feeling guilty, angry and despairing, as if they have become murderers rather than carers. The death, often sudden and violent, has the effect of killing off hope in professional staff, who are left feeling that any possibility of change and recovery in others has been lost, and that they themselves have failed. The fantasy of rescue, which has unconsciously driven many carers, is irrevocably shattered. For those who discover the bodies of those who have died, the traumatic impact can be enormous, and the shock difficult to bear. The violent impact on carers of acts of self-harm, whether or not they are fatal, can, at times, be experienced viscerally, as intense physical sensations.

MANAGING SELF-HARM IN THE COMMUNITY

There is a vast literature available to those who self-harm, some of which can be found on the web. I have listed other books that are particularly relevant and well written in the appendix entitled 'Further reading'. While many of the self-harm websites are aimed at recovery and information, some are used in an underground way to support and maintain a secret society that encourages the use of self-harm as a weapon against other people.

The information available from various mental health agencies is highly relevant for individuals who self-harm as well as for families and carers who are affected by it. One of the best websites is run by MIND (www.mind.org.uk), which asks and answers the following question, addressing the self-preservative function of self-harm, while acknowledging the deep distress and despair of many self-harmers.

> Is self-harm an attempt to commit suicide?
>
> Self-harm is about trying to stay alive, despite the pain people are in. Although, there is a relationship between self-harm and suicide, many more people self-harm than kill themselves, and most people don't hurt themselves so badly as to risk their lives. Of those who do, suicide may not have been their intention; it's the feelings they want to wipe out . . . whether someone wants to live or die may seem to be a straightforward choice. But some people are suspended in a grey state of survival, where choices and decisions are kept on hold. This is where self-harm happens.

The colour, texture and experience of self-harm can be preferable to the 'grey state of survival' alluded to on the MIND website. The vitality of blood is chosen over the suffocation of the grey haze of depression and unarticulated rage.

SELF HARM AS REACHING OUT

Rather than viewing self-harm as a form of suicide, I have attempted throughout this book to show how it is an expression of hope and a means of reaching out to others. It is meaningful communication whose understanding and management requires persistence, courage and patience, both in people who self-harm, and in those who care for them.

Self-harm is essentially an attempt to relate to others, expressing the need for containment, understanding and holding. It can also express the terror of intimacy, and an immersion in the self, creating a barrier of damaged skin that distorts contact. It can be seen as an act of displaced aggression onto the self, revealing the desire to hurt and punish others. In self-harm both destructive and life preservative drives are powerful and in conflict. Self-harm clearly reveals a struggle between life and death wishes but the resounding message from this book is that the dominant motivations are the life instincts, the desire to love and the urgent need to communicate one's states of mind to another, in the hope that they will respond with care and understanding.

REFERENCES

Adshead, G. (1997) 'Written on the body: deliberate self-harm and violence', in E.V. Welldon and C. van Velson (eds) *A Practical Guide to Forensic Psychotherapy*, London: Jessica Kingsley Publishers.

Aiyegbusi, A. (2004) 'Thinking under fire: the challenge for forensic mental health nurses working with women in secure care', in N. Jeffcote and T. Watson (eds) *Working Therapeutically with Women in Secure Mental Health Settings*, London: Jessica Kingsley Publishers.

Anderson, R. (2008) 'A psychoanalytical approach to suicide in adolescents', in S. Briggs, A. Lemma and W. Crouch (eds) *Relating to Self-Harm and Suicide: Psychoanalytic Perspectives on Practice, Theory and Prevention*, Hove: Routledge.

deMause, L. (1990) 'The history of child assault', *The Journal of Psychohistory*, 18(1): 1–29.

Foulkes, S.H. (1948) *Introduction to Group-Analytic Psychotherapy: Studies in the Social Integration of Individuals and Groups*, London: Heinemann.

Foulkes, S.H. (1964) *Therapeutic Group Analysis*, London: Allen & Unwin.

Garland, C. (2004) 'Traumatic events and their impact on symbolic functioning', in S. Levy and A. Lemma (eds) *The Perversion of Loss: Psychoanalytic Perspectives on Trauma*, London: Whurr Publishers.

Kent, T. (2008) Personal communication.

Menzies Lyth, I. (1959) 'The functioning of social systems as a defence

against anxiety', in I. Menzies Lyth (ed.) *Containing Anxiety in Institutions*, London: Free Association Books.
Milia, D. (2000) *Self Mutilation and Art Therapy: Violent Creation*, London: Jessica Kingsley Publishers.
Motz, A. (2008) *The Psychology of Female Violence: Crimes Against the Body* (second edition), Hove: Routledge.
Plath, S. (1962) *Collected Poems*, Faber: London, 2002.
Shakespeare, W. *The Merchant of Venice*, Act III, Scene I.
Song of Songs, *King James Bible*, Chapter 8.

Further reading

MEMOIRS

Hornbacher, M. (1998) *Wasted: Coming Back from an Addiction to Starvation*, London: Flamingo.
Kaysen, S. (2000) *Girl, Interrupted*, London: Virago Press.
Kettlewell, C. (2000) *Skin Game: A Memoir*, New York: St Martin's Griffin.
Leatham, V. (2006) *Bloodletting: A True Story of Secrets, Self-harm and Survival*, London: Alison and Busby.
Plath, S. (1963) *The Bell Jar*, London: Faber and Faber.
Smith, C. (2005) *Cutting it Out: A Journey Through Psychotherapy and Self Harm*, London: Jessica Kingsley Publishers.

PSYCHOLOGICAL GUIDES TO TREATMENT AND UNDERSTANDING

Alderman, T. (1997) *The Scarred Soul: Understanding and Ending Self-Mutilation.*
Babika, G. and Arnold, L. (1997) *The Language of Self Injury: Comprehending Self Mutilation*, Leicester: BPS Books.
Bateman, A. and Fonagy, P. (2004) A *Psychotherapy for Borderline Personality Disorder: Mentalisation Based Treatment*, Oxford: Oxford University Press.
Briggs, S., Lemma, A. and Crouch, W. (eds) (2008) *Relating to Self-Harm and Suicide: Psychoanalytic Perspectives on Practice, Theory and Prevention*, Hove: Routledge.
Favazza, A. (1996) *Bodies Under Siege: Self-Mutilation and Body Modification in Psychiatry and Culture* (second edition), Maryland, MD: John Hopkins University Press.

Gardner, F. (2001) *Self-Harm: A Psychotherapeutic Approach*, Hove: Brunner-Routledge.

Hawton, K. Rodham, K. and Evans, E. (2006) *By Their Own Young Hand: Deliberate Self Harm and Suicidal Ideas in Adolescents*, London: Jessica Kingsley Publishers.

Levenkron, S. (1999) *Cuting: Understanding and Overcoming Self Mutilation*, London: W.W. Norton.

Linehan, M.M. (1993) *Cognitive Behavioural Treatment of Borderline Personality Disorder*, New York: Guilford Press.

Ougrin, D., Ng, A. and Zundel, T. (Eds) (2009) *Self-harm in Young People: A Therapeutic Assessment Manual*, London: Hodder Arnold.

Milia, D. (2000) *Self-Mutilation and Art Therapy: Violent Creation*, London: Jessica Kingsley Publishers.

Index

Note: page numbers in **bold** refer to diagrams and information contained within tables.